*Liberating the
Will of Australia*

Liberating the Will of Australia

Towards the Flourishing of the
Land and All Its Peoples

Geoffrey Burn

WIPF & STOCK · Eugene, Oregon

LIBERATING THE WILL OF AUSTRALIA
Towards the Flourishing of the Land and All Its Peoples

Copyright © 2020 Geoffrey Burn. All rights reserved. Except for brief quotations in critical publications or reviews, no part of this book may be reproduced in any manner without prior written permission from the publisher. Write: Permissions, Wipf and Stock Publishers, 199 W. 8th Ave., Suite 3, Eugene, OR 97401.

Wipf & Stock
An Imprint of Wipf and Stock Publishers
199 W. 8th Ave., Suite 3
Eugene, OR 97401

www.wipfandstock.com

PAPERBACK ISBN: 978-1-7252-6382-6
HARDCOVER ISBN: 978-1-7252-6383-3
EBOOK ISBN: 978-1-7252-6384-0

Manufactured in the U.S.A. 07/15/20

Biblical quotations, unless noted otherwise, are from the New Revised Standard Version Bible, copyright © 1989, Division of Christian Education of the National Council of the Churches of Christ in the United States of America. Used by permission. All rights reserved.

Warning

This book contains the names of deceased Aboriginal and Torres Strait Islander people.

Contents

Preface | ix
Acknowledgements | xiii
Abbreviations | xvii

OVERTURE | 1

FIRST MOVEMENT: BINDING | 15
    I. Bound Willing and True Freedom | 20
    II. Bound Willing in Ezekiel | 33
    III. Being Stuck in the Past in Australia | 40

INTERMEZZO: THE LAND AND LAW | 53
    I. Land in Indigenous Cultures in Australia | 58
    II. An Outline Narrative of Land in Recent Decades | 64
    III. A Narrative About Land in Half a Century of Australian Legislation and Law | 67
    IV. Theological Reflection: Binding and Loosing | 94

SECOND MOVEMENT: LOOSING | 101
    I. Forgiveness and Repentance | 107
    II. Reconciliation and Changing the Social and Economic Structures in Corinth | 126
    III. The Risk of the Future in Australia | 150

FINALE | 155

Endnotes | 165
Bibliography | 209

Preface

I BEGAN MY WORKING life as a research scientist. After about ten years of working in that field, I answered what was a strong calling into the ordained ministry in the Anglican Church. During my theological preparation for ordination, I came across theological ideas that were both challenging and exciting, as I began to explore how theology could help us to understand political issues on a large scale, and direct us towards actions that could lead to human flourishing in the very complicated and intricately connected ecosystem and universe in which we live.

In around 2002 I embarked on study and reflection which has eventually led to this book being written. Initially, I had intended to try to write about how international politics is based on the myth of redemptive violence: that we overcome aggression by being more powerful than those who seek to do us harm. It was my PhD supervisor, Tim Gorringe, who suggested that I make a study of land in Australia. I was surprised by what I found. I am ashamed to say that, born in 1960, I had managed to grow up in Australia and study to degree level without really engaging with what was happening for the First Peoples in Australia. It took me seven years to complete my PhD as I read widely in history, anthropology and law, as well as theology, keeping up with developments through reading the media and making an extended visit to Australia to listen to whomever would talk with me. Writing my thesis was my first act of repentance: listening and then developing something from the Christian theological tradition that I felt brought some deep insights into why there was still such dis-ease amongst the First Peoples in Australia, and also why so many people, who had worked so hard, were disappointed that their actions had not produced as much good as they had hoped.

Such a work is of little use if it is hidden in a PhD thesis, a piece of academic work which is inaccessible to most of the people who might find it of value. After completion of the thesis, I determined to write a more accessible account of its key insights, with the hope that it might be of some value to everyone in Australia. This process, however, has taken me over nine years to bring to completion. There were several reasons for this.

The first, and most important, reason for the length of time that it has taken to write this book is that I became aware that what I had written in my thesis seemed to have deeply upset some people who have worked in the legal profession for the welfare of the First Peoples, people whose work I had greatly admired, and who were very generous to me during my research and the writing of my thesis. It was clear that I had got the tone of what I had written wrong and, in pursuing what I believed was an important insight, I had not given a properly nuanced account of what had happened. In particular, in my concern to present how the failure to recognize the humanity of the First Peoples and their relationship to the land had worked its way through the whole of Australian history, I failed to properly discuss how there were several ways that some of the legal judgements and acts of parliament were attempting to redress part of this failure. So, writing this book is a second act of repentance, seeking to give a truer reading of the situation in Australia. It has taken me a long time to find a more acceptable tone of voice. I had several false starts and this is the best that I can do for the moment. I hope that others will be able to take what I have written and develop any insights in this work in ways that are more helpful than I can currently see.

The second reason why it has taken so long to write this book is that I was unsure of how to write it for a wider audience. In particular, the work is inherently theological in that the theological ideas are not reducible to some other system of discourse; it is not possible to understand the situation in Australia without reference to God and the rich and generous ways of God in the world. Moreover, I am reading the Bible in ways that might be unfamiliar to many in the Church, and so it requires considerable work to validate reading the Bible in this way. The result, I hope, is that the eyes of the reader are opened to see how the Bible and Christian theology can be a much deeper resource for reflection on real political issues. The consequence of this is that this book is a work of practical Christian theology. I hope that there is enough in this book for those who are not from the Christian faith to be able to see something of value in it.

The final reason for my tardiness in writing is personal: I have been working in some situations of deep conflict, first within the church, and then as a chaplain in a team of chaplains of different faiths in a prison, taking on responsibility for managing the team and being part of the senior management team of the prison soon after starting work in prison. This has taken a lot of energy and in itself has been a focus of theological reflection.

As the time since I finished the initial research got longer and longer, I wondered if the moment of opportunity had passed, so that what I had to say was no longer of any value. Most of the time the work sat shelved at the back of my mind. But whenever I had the opportunity to speak about my ideas, and as I heard and read about the push for the reception of the Uluru Statement from the Heart, I was always in touch with a passion deep within me that the fundamental ideas contained in my thesis are still of value and need to be made more available, especially if responding to the Statement is to be a process which gets to the heart of Australia's wounded spirit. It was on an eight-day individually guided prayer retreat at St Beuno's in October 2018 that this work surfaced so powerfully in me that I could no longer refrain from writing the book, and the framework for the book emerged during my prayer. Others have kindly allowed me to draw back from my commitments outside my paid employment for a period so that I can work on this in the evenings and on my rest days from my work in the prison.

It is always a risk to offer one's ideas for the consideration of others. I offer this book, in all its awkwardness of style and its shortcomings in vision, for I am part of the problem that it is seeking to address, in the humble hope that some will find it of value, and will be able to use some of the ideas it contains in order to bring good for all the peoples in Australia.

Acknowledgements

MANY HAVE HELPED TO make this work possible.
 I began this research whilst in St Austell, and Tim Gorringe of Exeter University agreed to supervise it. I came to Tim with a desire to work on a political theology of reconciliation in conversation with a real problem, and I am grateful to him for suggesting that I focus on land in Australia. When we moved to Kent, so that Helen could work full-time in the Eythorne Benefice and in theological training in the Diocese of Canterbury, Gareth Jones kindly agreed to take over supervision of my research and he arranged for my fees to be waived by Canterbury Christ Church University College. The college's interlibrary loan facility made doing this research possible. Besides Gareth, Stephen Barton and Robin Gill, members of my PhD panel there, gave valuable help. Ralph Norman, at Canterbury Christ Church University College, read through my disparate pieces of work and helped me see what I was trying to say. When we moved west again with work, Tim Gorringe took me back on again as a student. I am grateful for the way that he has steered the initial project of producing a PhD thesis to completion. David Horrell kindly read and advised me on the New Testament material, more than once. Stephen Barton pointed me towards some particularly crucial articles and books throughout my research. At critical points, Walter Moberly was a helpful dialogue partner on some of the biblical material, particularly my reading of the Old Testament, and more generally on "biblical theology."
 An important part of my research was the trip I made to Australia in 2005. John and Norma Brown helped me organize my trip, suggesting people to visit and making some contacts for me, and provided generous hospitality when I was in Canberra. John has had many leading roles that have arisen out of his work in the Uniting Church, including co-chair of the National Sorry Day Committee, co-chair of the Myall Creek

Memorial Committee, and Uniting Church of Australia covenanting officer. In Darwin, Pat McIntyre, barrister, a leading player in establishing mediation in Australia, and part of the Mawul Rom Project, was a generous host, giving me the use of his chambers, telling me whom to see, and making many introductions for me. I greatly enjoyed our numerous conversations late into the night. I am grateful to all those who gave their time to speak me on the trip, including: Greg Anderson; Howard Amery (Aboriginal Resources and Development Services, Uniting Church of Australia); John Bond (secretary for the National Day of Healing); Pru Phillips-Brown (deputy director, Department of the Chief Minister, Office of Indigenous Policy in the Northern Territory Government); George Browning (Anglican bishop of Canberra and Goulburn); Mark Byrne (project and advocacy officer, Uniya Jesuit Social Justice Centre, Sydney); Barry Clarke (media officer of the Northern Land Council); Fred Chaney (deputy director of the Native Title Tribunal and former Federal Government minister); Gillian Cowlishaw (anthropologist); Mick Dodson (professor of law at the Australian National University, key Aboriginal leader, on many national bodies); Sue Duncombe and Alan Ogg (leading players in establishing mediation in Australia, and part of the Mawul Rom Project); Charmaine Foley (Queensland coordinator for Reconciliation project from 1996 to 2000); Philip Freirer (Anglican bishop of the Northern Territory); Norman Habel (theologian); Jackie Huggins (leading Aboriginal activist working for reconciliation, academic, and on many national bodies); Kimberly Hunter (chair of the Australian and Torres Strait Islander Commission in Darwin); Jack Lewis (barrister); Mike Lynskey (director of Reconciliation Australia); Malcolm McClintock (part of a reconciliation group in Sydney); Michael O'Donnell (barrister); Ian O'Reilly (chair of the Northern Territory reconciliation group); Deborah Bird Rose (anthropologist); John and Elaine Telford (New South Wales coordinators for the Reconciliation Project, and Elaine is also a key member of the Women's Reconciliation Network); Graeme Vines (dean of Anglican students at Nungalinya College); Jessica Weir (formerly with Australian Institute of Aboriginal and Torres Strait Islander Studies and then a postgraduate student of Deborah Bird Rose); Neil Westbury (executive officer of the Department of the Chief Minister, Office of Indigenous Policy, Northern Territory Government, secretary of the Council for Aboriginal Reconciliation and advisor in the Prime Minister's Department [1996–1999], and first CEO of Reconciliation Australia). Henry Reynolds took time out of his

European tour to speak with me in London. Thank you to my parents, Jim and Joan Burn, who looked after Anna and Catherine at their home in Sydney while I travelled backwards and forwards, and also for looking after me when I was in Sydney. I am grateful to my uncle, David Burn, who provided a car for me to use while I was in Australia.

The list of people who saw me when I was in Australia is testimony to the generosity and openness of Australian people to entertain and speak with someone whom they had never met before. I hope that this piece of work is worthy of their generosity.

Early on in my research, Corneliu Constantineanu kindly gave me a copy of his literature review on reconciliation. The following people have kindly and helpfully engaged with me either in conversation, or by correspondence, or by sending me copies of their work: Anthony Bash, Dianne Bell, Cilliers Breytenbach, Douglas Campbell, Warren Carter, Rosemary Crumlin, Frederick Danker, Stephen Dawes, Barbara Hill, John Inge, Paul Joyce, Andrew Louth, Ian McIntosh, Margaret Mitchell, Roger Mitchell, Walter Moberly, Rachel Muers, Peter Oakes, Stanley Porter, John Ramsland, Murray Ray, Deborah Bird Rose, Robert Schreiter, Anthony Thiselton, Miroslav Volf, Bernd Wannenwetsch and Haddon Wilmer. Martin Graham put me in contact with Roger Mitchell, who in turn pointed me to the work of Brian Mills. I am grateful for the kind assistance given to me by the Sisters of the Love of God in Oxford.

My PhD studies were begun while I was in my final year as associate minister in the Parish of St Austell. The bishop and parish kindly gave me two days a week in that final year to begin this work. Since then, many people and organizations have helpfully contributed towards the cost of doing this research, including the Appleton Trust, the Tim Burke Memorial Fund, Ecclesiastical Insurance, the Diocese of Gloucester, the J C Green Charitable Trust, the Newby Trust Ltd., the Philpotts and Boyd Educational Foundation, the Bishop of St Germans, and the Henry Smith Charitable Trust. Graham Smith rekindled my connections with computer science, and kindly brought me up to speed with work on websites, employing me to do some work for him, and I was able to do some sessional teaching for the computer science department of the University of Kent.

John Brown and Pat McIntyre kindly read my thesis when it was approaching its final form, and I greatly value the extensive conversations that I had with Pat about my thesis as a whole, and the legal material in particular. I am also very grateful to Joe McIntyre for reading the legal material, and for helping me to understand more clearly the working of the non-indigenous legal system in Australia, and so helping me to untangle the argument that I was trying to make. Without Pat and Joe, my thesis and this book would have been considerably weaker than it is. Of course, any remaining errors are mine, but I hope that they will not obscure the force of my argument.

I am grateful to David Horrell and Nigel Biggar, who pointed out flaws in my argument when examining my PhD thesis. I hope that this rethinking of the material addresses the problems that they raised with me.

Thanks to Annemarie Paulin-Campbell, who sensitively led me on my individually guided retreat in October 2018, allowing the need to write this book to surface.

I thank Bob Mayo for reading an early draft of this book. I am grateful to Anna Burn for her incisive and deep engagement with the final draft of this book, helping me to see more clearly what I was trying to say.

I am grateful to Fr Rory (Gregory) Geoghegan SJ for allowing me to include my photograph of one of his sculptures that appears on page 156.

I am grateful to the Society of Biblical Literature for their Hebrew, Greek and transliteration fonts, which have been used in this book.

Abbreviations

ALR Act	*Aboriginal Land Rights (Northern Territory) Act 1976* (Cth)
Mabo (2)	*Mabo and Others v State of Queensland (No 2)* (1992) 175 CLR 1
Milirrpum	*Milirrpum and Others v Nabalco Pty. Ltd. and the Commonwealth of Australia* (1971) 17 FLR 141
NNTT	National Native Title Tribunal
NT Act	*Native Title Act 1993* (Cth)
RD Act	*Racial Discrimination Act 1975* (Cth)
Ward	*Western Australia v Ward* (2002) 213 CLR 1
Wik	*The Wik Peoples v Queensland and Others; The Thayorre People v Queensland and Others* (1996) 187 CLR 1
Yorta Yorta	*Members of the Yorta Yorta Aboriginal Community v Victoria and Others* (2002) 214 CLR 422

Overture

This photograph was taken by myself in Canberra on the National Day of Healing in May 2005. The paving in front of the billboard formed the stage on which Aboriginal artists performed: dancing, playing music, and singing.[1] The billboard for the Australian Ballet performance is attached to wooden fencing around a construction site. The title of the ballet is White, and its strap line is "Escape into a timeless white world of elegance, style and gorgeous music."[2] On the top of this poster is a smaller one, partially covering the poster about the wonders of whiteness, but not removing it, nor hiding it from view, declaring the National Day of Healing. How can a nation that is very conscious of constructing itself deal with its past and go into the future in a way that is more than just placing a sticking plaster over the deep-seated myth of normality of whiteness portrayed by the dominant culture, where the First Peoples are more than just an interesting spectacle to be watched by a mixed crowd? How can the welfare of all the peoples be assured in this great land?

> With the rise of instantaneous, "as it happened" news coverage, events get fragmented into pieces that the audience then impressionistically reassembles to fit their pre-judgments. But time is precisely what you need to think of things that are new—things that exceed the conventional wisdom.[3]

> ... increasingly we become constitutionally ill-disposed to that slow work of listening, reflecting, deliberating ...[4]

I AM INVITING YOU to take time to think new things, things that exceed conventional wisdom, for conventional wisdom has failed. Most people in Australia would not want to cause harm to the First Peoples in Australia but welfare metrics show that harm continues to be done. There have been many developments in recent decades in the relationships between the First Peoples in Australia and those who came after, but Indigenous women and men, who have been at the forefront of the struggle for decades, despair that they have grown old and tired, and they feel that little has been achieved. Jackie Huggins writes:

> We older leaders were young and energetic once, but we have grown weary from repeated defeats. The tiredness sets into our bones. Our hearts ache to think of our elders who lived through small wins only to see even greater losses. What we gain we do not grasp for long. For Indigenous people, powerlessness and impermanence go hand in hand.[5]

Reflecting on his decades of work for the welfare of First Peoples, Galarrwuy Yunupingu wrote a powerful lament in an article in 2008. I urge you to read the entire article, where wave after wave of prose reflect the waves of power that he has experienced crashing over him and his people. Here is a small extract that captures some of the feeling of his article:

I am seeing now that too much of the past is for nothing. I have walked the corridors of power; I have negotiated and cajoled and praised and begged prime ministers and ministers, travelled the world and been feted; I have opened the doors to men of power and prestige; I have had a place at the table of the best and the brightest in the Australian nation—and at times success has seemed so close, yet it always slips away. And behind me, in the world of my father, the Yolngu world is always under threat, being swallowed up by whitefellas.

This is a weight that is bearing down on me; it is a pressure that I feel now every moment of my life—it frustrates me and drives me crazy; at night it is like a splinter in my mind. The solutions to the future, simple though I thought they were, have become harder and harder to grasp. I have learnt from experience that nothing is ever what it seems.[6]

The purpose of this book is to understand why it is that many First Peoples in Australia find themselves in the position so eloquently expressed by Jackie Huggins and Galarrwuy Yunupingu, and also to ask whether anything can be done about it. In particular, it is answering two questions:

- Why does harm continue to be done to the First Peoples in Australia, even when good is intended?
- Is there a way into the future which does not continue to perpetuate this harmful dynamic?

A consultation process with the Indigenous Peoples in Australia, an unprecedented act of listening in Australian history, resulted in a report from the Referendum Council, which contains the Uluru Statement from the Heart.[7] This is a statement of what the First Peoples feel they need in order to be safe in Australia. The consultation process resulted in proposals for three reforms: voice, treaty and truth.[8] The Voice is about Indigenous Peoples having some control over policies that affect them. Treaty is about the unfinished business of the occupation of The Land without making any agreements with those who were already there. Truth is about telling the multiple histories and making peace after what has happened. Politicians have been rushing to do nothing with it. The Uluru Statement of the Heart was not only addressed to politicians, but to all the peoples in Australia. What are we to do with it? The report raises an important subsidiary question that will also be addressed by this book:

- If the changes requested in the report from the Referendum Council and the Uluru Statement from the Heart are implemented, will it deliver security and space for the First Peoples to thrive?

The answers to these questions are easy to state, but it will take the whole book to explore and comprehend them, because they require a different sort of thinking, seeing things in a different way. The answers to the questions, challenging, incomprehensible and unimaginable as they may be at this point, are as follows:

- Harm continues to be done to the First Peoples in Australia because the failure to negotiate a just way of living with those who were already in the land, when the first British incomers arrived, has become bound up in the essential nature of Australia.
- The only way to stop harming the First Peoples in Australia is for Australia to repent of the way that is was founded, where repentance is more than an apology, but requires the willingness to renegotiate the very foundations of the nation.
- Without this repentance, implementing the Uluru Statement of the Heart will not be safe for the First Peoples in Australia.

The argument that is being made in this book will be summarized in the following paragraph. This will then be expanded in the rest of the Overture, introducing the structure and argument of the whole book.

In summary, the argument of the book is as follows. What has become known as the nation of Australia was founded on the failure to negotiate a way of living with those who were already in the land. The nation was bound at its birth to a way of living that denied the truth of what was found. For reasons that will become apparent later, this will be called the Root Sin. In particular, the nation and its law were founded on the legal fiction—in this case, also a falsehood—that the land was unoccupied. This remains true whether this concept, *terra nullius*, was worked out at the time or only as a later legal explanation and justification of the situation that ensued. A key theological concept, *bound willing*, will be introduced. Bound willing explains how actions that flow from such binding result in the further binding of the will, which is so drastic that often, even when people want to choose that which is good, harm is done, because those thus bound are unable to see what good is. This is critical for understanding why harm often continues to be done to the

First Peoples in Australia, even when good is intended. This situation will continue in perpetuity unless there is deep *repentance* by Australia. Repentance is more than an apology; repentance must undo the Root Sin. But repentance is only part of the process; the other part is *forgiveness*. Forgiveness is not simply accepting an apology: forgiveness names the wrongdoing and makes demands about what must be done in order to put things right. Repentance makes the space for those who have been harmed to be able to explore the full depths of the harm that has been done and so be clear about what must be done in order to move into the future in freedom. Forgiveness cannot be given until there has been an acceptable repentance. This means that repentance and forgiveness are intertwined processes, negotiations about what must be done to right the wrongs of the past, a process where the end cannot be known from the beginning. Whilst the book will discuss both repentance and forgiveness, the focus will be on the moral imperative for the nation of Australia to repent of the Root Sin. The process of repentance and forgiveness is a deeply hopeful process because it is working in harmony with the way that God is working in the world. More than that, the generosity of God is generative, meaning that creative things will emerge during such a process which could not have been imagined at the beginning, as gifts of God. At the end of the process, all who have been involved will recognize that justice has been established, a deeper justice than could have been imagined at the beginning. Whatever has managed to be addressed by this process will no longer cause damage in the future.

There are two distinct audiences who are being addressed by this book. I am hoping, firstly, that what is written will enable First Peoples to understand why their problems have proved so difficult to resolve, that it will be a moment of revelation and of seeing, an "Aha" moment. Further, I hope that it will embolden them to continue to demand repentance from Australia, being forthright in naming everything that must be done before forgiveness can be given. The refusal to stop speaking takes a lot of courage and resource and I hope that they will be encouraged and strengthened to keep stating what must be done. In some ways, I hope that this book will clarify and focus their demands. Secondly, I am also hoping that reading this book will also be a moment of revelation and of seeing for the rest of the peoples in Australia, that it will clarify their confusion about why harm continues to be done, even when good is intended. For this second group of people, there is also a moral imperative: there must be repentance in order to stop the perpetuation of harm into the future. Only repentance will make a safe space for the First Peoples to be able to express and to be given all that is needed in order for them flourish as peoples, to remove Galarrwuy Yunipingu's splinter, to enable Jackie Huggins and all her people to stand refreshed and able to exercise rightful power towards their futures.

It is very early in the book to have to define terms, but the message of this book is quite subtle and care needs to be taken with the terminology that is used, so that what is being said can be clear. For example, the name Australia is commonly used to refer both to a land mass and also a nation whose establishment began at least as early as the landing of the First Fleet. People speak of "Australians," a term which includes all citizens that the nation of Australia claims as its own, without acknowledging that some of these people, not least many First Peoples, have at least a difficult, if not an ambivalent, relationship with, or a downright denial of, the nation of Australia as it is currently constructed. It is important to use words in such a way that what is said can be as precise as possible, whilst not making accidental assimilative assertions by how language is used, and also not using language in a way that offends those who are being written about. Therefore, the following terminology will be used in the rest of this book:

- *The Land* will be used when writing of the whole ecosystem of the land mass that is commonly called Australia and its waters, independent of any claims of relationship to it by any people who live there. It is important that this should not be called Australia, for this confuses The Land with the nation that has established itself on The Land, with particular laws and relationships to The Land, and relationships with others who also live in The Land, who have different relationships to The Land.

- *Australia* will refer to the nation-state that is commonly called by this name and the states and territories of Australia and any other bodies constituted by legal systems arising from British settlements in The Land.

- *Australian law* will refer to the legal system, founded in British law, which has developed since the original colonization of The Land by the first British incomers, and which is the legal system of Australia. It also refers to all the legal systems of the states and territories of Australia and any other tiers of government which can pass laws that are based on the same foundations.

- *First Peoples* means those who are descended from those who were present in The Land when the first British people started to live there and who have chosen to identify as such. Such peoples "define themselves according to their lineages and cultures that tie them to places and ways of life that existed long before colonisation."[9] Sometimes they are also called the "Indigenous Peoples of Australia" or "Indigenous Australians," but that risks assimilating them into the Australian national project, eliding their multiple layers of identity and overlooking the way that Australia was founded. Instead, I will use "Indigenous Peoples in Australia," allowing them to state their own relationship to the nation of Australia.

- *Aboriginal* and *Torres Strait Islander* will be used when it is important to distinguish between things pertaining to these two different First Peoples. The terms "First Peoples," "Aboriginal," and "Torres Strait Islanders" have become the acceptable way of referring to peoples in these groups.

- *Subsequent Peoples* means anyone who does not trace her primary descent as coming from the First Peoples. This includes all those descended from the first British settlers, or from those who have come subsequently, who see themselves primarily as citizens of Australia, choosing to submit themselves to Australian law. It includes those incomers who are not yet citizens. Sometimes I will speak of "we." When I do this, I am primarily acknowledging that I too am part of the Subsequent Peoples and that this book is also being addressed to myself.

Clearly, any encounters between peoples change all of those who are involved and so these categories overlap. In particular, many First Peoples have multiple layers of identity and have varying commitments to the different parts of their heritage. Some sit easily with this but for others it is deeply traumatic.[10] Whilst this is important, this fuzziness in naming has no impact on the central argument of this book, which is about how the foundational denial of the identity of the inhabitants of The Land has insinuated itself into the very fabric of the Australian nation and its legal system, and, therefore, what must be done in order to rescue not only the First Peoples, but all the peoples in Australia, from its devastating effects.

There is much emotive language used in describing the history following the arrival of the first Europeans who established themselves in The Land. This is partly because of the perspective from which the story is told but it is also because there are multiple stories to tell and no one wants their story to be lost or to be treated as secondary to the overarching narrative of someone else. What is indisputable, however, is that no treaty was made between those who were already living in The Land and those who came two and a half centuries ago. From this has grown a nation, called Australia, which is founded on a failure to recognize the full humanity of those already living in The Land. It did not recognize any of: their identities as peoples, their territorial lands, their languages, and their culture.[11] This failure, right at the beginning, continues to work its way out today, and will continue to do so in the future, unless it is properly addressed. It is the reason why the First Peoples in Australia always feel as if they are under siege and why interventions, well-intentioned or otherwise, continue to fail to deliver all that is hoped of them.

Recently, it has become popular in Australia to talk about three parts of the "Australian story." Even the final report from the Referendum Council indulges in this process of myth creation.[12] The first phase was the settlement by the First Peoples; the second was the coming of the First Fleet; and the third is the arrival of generations of migrants from all parts of the world. There is a fundamental flaw in this myth, namely that, ontologically, there are only two phases: the history before the arrival of the First Fleet, and the history afterwards. The reason for this is that the arrival of the First Fleet saw the beginnings of Australian law, and all those who acknowledge this law, whether they were been born in the country or have arrived since, are essentially the same in that they live in a system founded on the Root Sin. No one who is born into the country, or who comes to the country from elsewhere, can say that they are not part of the problem, for, in accepting the notion of the nation of Australia and its legal system, they are part of continuing the problem. Further, it simply is not true when the report from the Referendum Council states that "there is no doubt our constitutional system, our system of government, the rule of law, and our public institutions inherited from Britain are the heritage of the Australian people and enure for the benefit of all of us, including the First Peoples":[13] it is exactly these institutions which continue to have a detrimental effect on the First Peoples in Australia because they are founded on the nonexistence of these peoples.

The culture in Australia is changing, with a greater willingness to acknowledge the past and a greater commitment to agreement-making and seeking to put things right. This is hard work and its value is not to be underestimated. Nevertheless, the Root Sin has not been addressed. If all the harm done to the First Peoples in Australia is like a tree that has grown from the Root Sin, then what has been happening is that some of the branches of have been lopped off, but the Root Sin is still firmly in the ground and continues to put forth more branches, whilst providing life to those branches which have not yet been removed, consequently continuing to damage the First Peoples in Australia. That is, what is happening is not enough and the roots need to be dug out. This issue is the primary focus of this book.

It will be argued that Christian theology has the power to both give a deep enough explanation of the problem as well as help us to know what must be done to resolve it. I am aware that the church and its theology have often been part of the problem for the First Peoples in Australia. The church has participated in programs that have led to people being alienated from their land and losing some or all of those systems which supported their existence in The Land, indeed their very existence; theology became a weapon. This is something that I deeply regret. Nonetheless, it is in returning to find deeper meanings of various theological concepts that hope for the future can be found—a real hope, not a just pious desire. Theology is needed because the problem is a spiritual one. It is hoped that the theology that is developed here is restorative, that it can be a healing lens through which to see what has been happening and what needs to happen in order to put it right.

The outline of the book is as follows.

The First Movement, Binding, lays out the theological foundations for understanding how the Root Sin continues to work its way out today. It begins by introducing the concept of bound willing. I will be drawing heavily on the work of Alistair McFadyen in order to explain the dynamics of bound willing.[14] In his book, he uses two case studies—child sexual abuse and the Nazi holocaust—to explain, develop, and test the doctrine of bound willing and the nature of salvation, the liberating work of God to release people from all that binds them. These case studies of traumatic and incomprehensible events show how theology gives both a deeper understanding of the dynamics of complex problems and also how release from these problems can come about. It is important to understand that I am not suggesting that the situation in Australia is like either of these case studies. Rather, understanding the underlying dynamics of these examples gives a new way of looking at what has happened in Australia since the coming of the first Europeans, which is key to understanding why harm continues to be done to the First Peoples in

Australia, even when good is intended, as well as showing the way out of this continuing problem. The second case study is important because it helps to shift the perspective from individualism to see the dynamics of how whole nations can become gripped and driven by forces of which they are not fully aware, and where the individual is caught up in systems from which there seems to be no escape. These theological concepts are then used to interpret the biblical book of Ezekiel in a way that may be unfamiliar to many readers, but a way which is truer to the theological worldview of its writer. It will be seen that the original people addressed by Ezekiel believed that they were being adversely affected by the sins of their forebears, things for which they themselves were not responsible. They wanted to draw a line under the past and say that they were not the same as their ancestors. Ezekiel, however, says that the actions of his hearers are in continuity with those of their forebears and that they are responsible for the outworking of the past in the present. He calls on the present generation to repent, to turn away from these actions, to turn to God. The message of Ezekiel to his nation, that it continues to sin in the ways of its ancestors, is applicable to Australia today; it is not possible to draw a line under the past because Australia is bound up in continuing to damage the First Peoples in ways that are firmly rooted in its past. Both the theological foundational material and the study of Ezekiel raise the possibility of change through repentance. A final section in the First Movement begins to show how bound willing helps us to understand what has been happening in Australia, especially where policies that were meant to be good have caused harm.

I have chosen the term "movement" rather than the more common "part" because it captures the idea that the situation is not static. The First Movement is entitled "Binding" because the direction of travel is towards being more deeply trapped in the results of the Root Sin, whilst the Second Movement is called "Loosing" because it is about what must be done in order to free all the peoples in Australia from the effect of the binding.

Having started with a musical metaphor, the part of the book that follows the First Movement has been called the Intermezzo, for it rehearses some of the themes of the First and Second Movements. It is a study of the history of land through the courts and legislature over a period of half a century. This is a critical topic because Aboriginal identity is bound up in The Land and so it is a good barometer of how Australia treats its relationships with its First Peoples. More than that, it provides an extended example of whether the theological idea of bound willing gives us any insights into the dynamics of the situation. It will be concluded that there were some significant acts of repentance, namely various Lands Acts, but even these introduced new ways of damaging the First Peoples because of the ways that they were set up and in the way that claims had to be made. Other actions, such as Native Title Acts, have proved much less stable and are the ones which most obviously show both unintentional and intentional destructive behavior by politicians and judges in managing them, behavior which is in continuity with the Root Sin. Most of all, all of this work was inherently limited, for it was only asking whether the claims in the laws of the First Peoples could also be recognized in Australian law and only for land for which there was no stronger title claim. This is logical, of course, for Australian law could not step outside itself to renegotiate its foundation in negotiation with the laws of the First Peoples. But this is just another way of saying that the process was not strong enough to address the Root Sin in the foundation of Australia.

The Second Movement, Loosing, is about what needs to be done in order to liberate Australia from the Root Sin. The first section introduces the theological concepts of repentance and forgiveness. Critically, it will be seen that repentance is more than a confession or an apology, but also involves putting right the harm that was done. Apologizing accepts the instability of an unknown future, where things must change. Repentance creates a space for the victims to be able to express *everything* (absolutely everything, not just what they think is politically possible) that they *need* (not just desires, but what is really needed) in order to regain their life. Likewise, forgiveness does not overlook what has been done and can only be given when there has been true repentance. Neither forgiveness nor repentance can stand alone, but they are intertwined in a process, the result of which is the establishment of justice. The second section is a case study of the church in Corinth in the middle of the first century CE. The reason for making this study is to show that repentance for the church in Corinth had to involve the total reordering of all of their social and economic relationships; nothing short of a complete change in the foundations of their life would be a repentance of the problems in their community. A byproduct of this study is that the word "reconciliation" is given a fuller and deeper meaning. People have rightly become very wary of using this term in Australia because it has never been properly defined and its misuse has caused much grief. Strictly speaking, the process of reconciliation describes the process of parties negotiating repentance and forgiveness, and the parties will have become reconciled when this has been achieved. The point at which reconciliation is reached is also the point at which it will be noticed that justice has been established, a deeper justice that could not have been imagined at the beginning of the process, a justice that comes as a gift of God. The final section of the Second Movement returns to the situation in Australia and to the Uluru Statement from the Heart. The whole of the book has been moving towards the point of asking what must be done in Australia in order to stop harm being done to the First Peoples in Australia. The answer is that the nation of Australia must repent of the Root Sin. Necessarily, there are multiple local elements to this because of all of the actions that have followed on from the Root Sin, but the national repentance of the Root Sin is essential. The question that must be asked about any process involving the nation of Australia and the First Peoples is whether the actions of the nation of Australia are a true and real repentance of the Root Sin. There is an important question as to whether the Uluru Statement from the Heart is asking enough of Australia before forgiveness is given. A reconciliatory process has to begin somewhere and the generous offer made by in the Uluru Statement from the Heart is a move of the First Peoples towards forgiveness. I remain, however, deeply concerned by this offer, for it seems to be both premature and it also does not seem to be asking for enough. Whilst it has been informed by what seems politically possible, if it is not met by a genuine repentance by the Australian nation, then its acceptance by the Australian nation will only entangle it in the power of the Root Sin, completely disabling it, and it will not be able to achieve what is hoped for by the First Peoples in Australia.

The book will be brought together in the Finale, which includes a personal story of my own, where I was addressed by a very different land, when I first understood the nature of the new beginning that could come out the mess of the past.

This book is not about blame. Blame puts the focus in the wrong place, trying to find people at fault and then punishing them in some way because of their fault. Blame takes the focus away from looking carefully at the problem and what needs to be done to fix it. Blame also assumes that the problem is in the past, rather than being continually reproduced in the present. Instead, we need to allow ourselves to be challenged by the reality of the situation and then act courageously to do what needs to be done to put it right. There is a will in Australia to do good for the First Peoples in Australia. This book is about liberating that will, so that all the peoples of The Land, and The Land itself, can flourish. I hope that you will find that this book is ultimately a message of hope, that there is a way out so that the all peoples who dwell in The Land can coexist for the welfare of all.

Before embarking on the First Movement, there are two final things that need to be said at this point, concerning the scope of this work and the level of this book.

Concerning the scope of this work, whilst it is focused on Australia, and all the examples are drawn from Australia, the theological development is applicable to all colonized peoples. I hope that the insights contained here will be developed by others to help them understand their own contexts.

Any book must have a particular audience in mind. I am hoping that this is accessible to all the peoples in Australia. I have tried to walk the narrow way between having an academically rigorous and theologically sound narrative whilst also keeping it accessible to all who may wish to read it. Sometimes this means that the book progresses by means of assertion rather than engagement with the views of others. Those who wish to also see the arguments behind some of my assertions are referred to my thesis,[15] but must be aware that my thinking has progressed in the ten years since I completed my thesis, and what is presented here is somewhat more nuanced. Moreover, my earlier work developed the theology of reconciliation and considered what the reconciliation might look like in Australia, where the purpose of this book is much narrower, focusing on the Root Sin and what must be done about it, for it still has not been addressed in Australia. With this in mind, I have made extensive use of endnotes. Some of the endnotes are simply an acknowledgement of my sources, but others are notes for further reflection by those who wish to take the ideas further. It should be possible to grasp the central ideas of this book without referring to the endnotes at all, but the endnotes are an important resource for deeper reflection on what is being raised in body of the book.

I hope that you will take the time to consider old things and new as they are presented in this book: time to listen, reflect, deliberate and act.

First Movement

Binding

The past is not dead and gone; it isn't even past.[16]

White man, hear me! History, as nearly no one seems to know, is not merely something to be read. And it does not refer merely, or even principally, to the past. On the contrary, the great force of history comes from the fact that we carry it within us, are unconsciously controlled by it in many ways, and history is literally *present* in all that we do. It could scarcely be otherwise, since it is to history that we owe our frames of reference, our identities, and our aspirations. And it is with great pain and terror that one begins to realize this. In great pain and terror one begins to assess the history which has placed one where one is, and formed one's point of view. In great pain and terror because, thereafter, one enters into battle with that historical creation, Oneself, and attempts to re-create oneself according to a principle more humane and more liberating: one begins the attempt to achieve a level of personal maturity and freedom which robs history of its tyrannical power, and also changes history.[17]

TODAY, WE RECOGNIZE THAT the ways in which our forebears treated the First Peoples was abhorrent, but we see ourselves as different. We see differently now and we think that we can draw a line under the past and proceed into the future with different practices that arise from our new understanding. It is certainly true that the culture is changing in Australia, but it is also true that policies and practices today continue to cause damage. Some problems are so complex that there seems to be no good option.[18] To think that we can just draw a line under the past is a fatal mistake, because the ways of the past continue to shape us in the present and we are not always able to see clearly nor to know what is good. The result is that sometimes harm is done even when good is intended.

This First Movement, Binding, will introduce the theological concept of *bound willing*, which shows how our wills are shaped by our history, so that we cannot always choose what is good, even when we wish to do it. The will is bound because it is limited in its ability to respond more fully to the love of God, who is the source of all that is good, and to act from that place. This is true not only of individuals, but also of groups, societies and nations. The Second Movement, Loosing, will look at concrete practices which enable us to receive the liberating love of God, so allowing our wills to be set free from those things which bind them.

This use of Christian theology brings both explanatory and hortatory power: it both helps the situation to be understood and also shows what needs to be done in order to put it right. More than that, it is deeply hopeful, because, in God, there is external help to redeem the situation. This book is therefore not about apportioning blame but about being able to acknowledge the full depth of the pathology in the presence of God, which is liberating because God is always moving to towards the world in order to bring life; the movement of God is not towards blame and punishment but towards restoration.

The first section of this movement will introduce the concept of bound willing. Alistair McFadyen gives the best contemporary exploration of bound willing that I have come across, and I recommend reading his book for those who wish to explore these concepts in more detail.[19] In his book, he uses two case studies—child sexual abuse and the Nazi holocaust—to explain, develop, and test the doctrine of bound willing and the nature of salvation, the liberating work of God to release us from all that binds us. These case studies, of traumatic and incomprehensible events, show both how theology gives both a deeper understanding of the dynamics of complex problems and also how release from these problems can come about. It is important to understand that I am not suggesting that the situation in Australia is like either of these case studies. Rather, understanding the underlying dynamics of these examples gives a new way of looking at what has happened in Australia since the coming of the first Europeans, which is key to understanding why harm continues to be done to the First Peoples in Australia, even when good is intended, as well as showing the way out of this continuing problem. The second case study is important because it helps us to shift our perspective from individualism to see the dynamics of how whole nations can become gripped and driven by forces of which they are not fully aware, where the individual is caught up in systems from which there seems to be no escape.

In the second section, these theological tools are used to read the biblical book of Ezekiel. It is a case study of how bound willing has been working itself out in a nation over many generations.

The final section in this movement will briefly look at the situation in Australia, giving further definition of what we have been calling the Root Sin, and also giving three simple case studies of how bound willing can help us to understand why things went wrong when good was intended.

The Intermezzo will give a much larger case study of the dynamics of bound willing, being an examination of The Land in court cases and legislation over a period of half a century.

I

Bound Willing and True Freedom

WE ARE USED TO thinking of society as a collection of individuals who have the free will to choose how they will act. When looking at a wrong action, moral reasoning traces back from the action to the thing that caused it. Moral judgment requires the relationship between the act and the individual to be personal, a person acting freely, and we escape responsibility if the act can be shown to be compelled, determined, or otherwise unavoidable. In this system, we cannot be morally praised or blamed for that which we have not freely chosen or could not avoid. Even if wrongdoing is done by freely willing agent, the person may still not be accounted guilty, because, for example, the wrong action may have been an unforeseen consequence of an action (or inaction).[20]

The theological concept of bound willing asserts that we are never truly free; we can only be free *from*. Human beings are shaped by what happens to them and how they respond to what has happened. This includes being shaped by our culture; we are parts of communities which have been shaped by their histories.[21] There is a tension between the passive and the active, between sin as a fundamental distortion received with one's humanity and the way that one actively enacts and personally joins oneself to it.

Bound willing further posits that there has been a total and universal moral collapse which makes avoidance of wrong actions problematic, and that we are accountable for this situation and for our individual acts of sin which this situation preconditions us to commit.[22] Moreover, people are guilty not of their own acts but they also inherit the guilt of others' actions; human beings do not enjoy the sort of freedom which enables personal action and moral accountability. Rather, they are bound to sin, not to freedom.

Now, I am aware that this could seem very negative, but it is only negative if we are thinking that there is a negative judgment associated with this, even that we might be punished for our wrongdoing. Rather, this is a liberating way of viewing the world, because we can acknowledge and understand the complexities of the situations in which we find ourselves, that we are part of something that is much bigger than individuals, and that we are at a loss to see how to put things right. It is the other half of the story of bound willing which reveals that we can be set free from our bound willing, for God is at work in the world to bring good. In turning to God, we see that our bound wills have blocked the overflowing love of God from bringing good, and in turning towards God we position ourselves so that good is able to come as our wills are freed from their bondage to sin. The concrete practices which can take hold of this liberation will be explored in the Second Movement.

In order to help understand the dynamics of these theological concepts, we turn to the work of Alistair McFadyen. Unlike McFadyen's rigor, we will be proceeding by example rather than by doctrinal development.

McFadyen has two major case studies in his book: the experience of children who have been sexually abused; and the Nazi holocaust of Jewish and Gypsy peoples, as well as other groups of people. He also spends considerable time considering the plight of women, who are often oppressed in our society. He has a deep concern that both popular and academic ways of talking about these issues do not have sufficient explanatory power to comprehend the full depths of these pathologies, nor are they able to offer any real way of resolving the problems. His presentation is subtle and full of compassion. Inevitably, any summary of this work is not going to be able to capture the full nuances of his argument and it risks being taken up with what seem like technical philosophical and theological issues, whilst appearing to abandon any compassion for the real damage and pain that is caused by the pathologies that he discusses. This is especially the case here, where the main purpose is to lay out his theological framework in order to cast light on a different situation, namely, understanding the plight of the First Peoples in Australia and the possibilities for life-giving transformation for all the peoples in The Land. There seems to be no way around this, and so I apologize in advance for those who have experienced the traumas that will be so quickly covered here, drawing out the theological insights rather than a full description of the pain that has been experienced. Please accept my apology for this and please take time to seek help concerning any personal issues that are opened up by these examples.

The first case study is of the sexual abuse of children, which he defines thus: "children are sexually abused when they are involved in sexual activity, are exposed to sexual stimuli or are used as sexual stimuli by anybody significantly older than they are."[23] The study is focused on the experience of those who are abused. It demonstrates that abuse can only happen through isolation and the construction of a false normality, a world where what is good and right and true has been radically distorted and redefined. It can lead to the internalization of the dynamics of the abuse, so that a person's direction in life is reoriented, disorienting a person's desire and will.

In more detail, the sexual abuse of children will include many of the following features.[24] Sexual abuse can only happen if a child is *isolated*, from the effective care, interference and concern of other adults, and from the codes, values and interpretive frameworks belonging to normal social relationships. Abuse can only happen to those who are already isolated or can be made to be so. There is a need to stop others knowing about it, usually by disenabling the child from telling others, so abuse can even happen in public spaces; *physical seclusion* is not necessarily needed. Abuse creates a *false normality*, making the wrong seem normal, such as it occurring during bathing. It can be unwittingly reinforced by others who misinterpret the child's complaint, for example, by thinking that the child is complaining about being bathed by her father, rather than what the father is doing during the bath. An abuser may create *illusions of consent*. If this has been done, then the child may internalize feelings of guilt, blame and responsibility, and she can become inextricably bound into the realities of the abusive relationship. In this situation, she is less likely to seek outside help. Often abusers make sure that they are the *most significant emotional relationship* for child, so that the child cannot get out because he does not want to lose that relationship, even if he senses that some of what happens is bad. The person being abused is *bound in silence*; no one is allowed to be told about the relationship. Various forms of *threat* may be used to force compliance. Common threats are: firstly, that the abuser is more powerful than any others who might try to help (now and at any time in the future); secondly, if the abused person tells someone and is believed, then she would be stigmatized, and so she will not be worthy of the care that others are allowed; and thirdly, being blamed for the consequences (e.g., the father goes to jail and family is broken up). *Secrecy* is essential. Secrecy encloses. It not only stops bringing information to public expression, but it also inhibits communication, and the processes of understanding, judging and evaluating the information represented by the abuse. Abuse is almost always confusing, sometimes traumatically so. Secrecy is itself confusing: if this is all right, how come I can't tell anyone? The child may *internalize* the abuse, coming to believe that it is something he has caused to be done. He has then taken the abuse as the unalterable baseline against which his identity must be worked out. Sex with a child is not only socially inappropriate, but developmentally premature, psychologically, emotionally, spiritually and physiologically; it *traumatizes* sexual relationships. Premature sexualization will become a central feature of their sexual development, and sex may become obsessional or something to be feared; it may have unrealistic emotional significance, or else it may become disconnected from the emotions. Sexual abuse may lead to fear and anxiety and to becoming a *powerless* victim in relationships, or becoming *like the abuser* in relationships.

McFadyen summarizes the findings of his study in the following way:

- The sexual abuse of children is fundamentally an abuse of trust and of power which exploits the age-related differentials between child and abuser, as well as enlisting, abusing, distorting and disorienting the child's needs for intimacy, affirmation, security, trust and guidance.
- Abuse is not adequately construed in terms of acts which might then have certain consequences; it is better thought of in terms of an expansive dynamic of disoriented relationality which may affect all of the child's relationships (including that to herself) and invade the relational ecology of other sets of relationships. (It is thus impossible clearly and cleanly to separate act from consequence.)
- Its core dynamic is that of entrapment and isolation, through which social and psychological transcendence may be blocked.
- That dynamic effects a form of traumatic confusion concerning the nature of reality in all its dimensions (social, moral, personal, material).[25]
- A particular source of confusion is the incorporation of the child's active agency in psychologically "accommodating" to the abuse and keeping it secret.

- As a consequence, abuse easily leads to a radical distortion of the very core of self-identity,
- which becomes the means of transmission of the consequences of the abuse into an entire ecology of relating and is capable of passing on the effects of abuse trans-generationally.[26]

It is particularly tragic that the distorted willing of the perpetrators affects the willing of their victims. In the case of the survivors[27] of childhood sexual abuse, where there are age-related disparities of power, status and knowledge, the child's willing cannot be an operative cause of the abuse, but the fact that survivor's basic patterns of intentionality (including willing) are distorted strongly suggests that the distortion of willing may be traceable back to the situation of the abuse itself. In abuse, the abuser confuses the victim's willing, for example, because the relationship with the abuser outweighs the abuse, or the use of rewards, inducements or other benefits, or because the initiation of abuse is seductively incremental. In the first two cases, the willing for the inducements may be confused with willing the abuse, especially so when desire for benefits leads to initiation of abuse, so eliminating the distinction between means and ends. "Childhood sexual abuse abuses the child's active willing and intentionality, and this is why it can have such long-term traumatic consequences."[28] For incremental abuse, the gradient is so shallow that it obfuscates not only when the relationship became abusive, but also the point at which willing became operative. What seems abusive does not seem to be so different from the step before so, looking back, the victim can be easily convinced that the abuse was willingly accepted from the beginning. Secrecy encloses the abuse as a total context for all the child's willing, and so no willing in relation to abuse can be free from it.[29]

Those who have survived sexual abuse as children or who have worked with people who have been sexually abused as children will recognize how the distortion of the will in survivors carries on into later life and affects the ways that people form relationships. This full description is needed in order to be able to see how to best restore the damage that has been done in such an abusive relationship, something that will be returned to below, after considering the second case study.

The first case study has shown the basic dynamics of bound willing. The second case study is the Nazi holocaust of Jewish, Gypsy and other peoples, and so explores the binding of the will of a whole nation. The focus is on the perpetrators rather than the victims. Alistair McFadyen draws heavily on the work of Zygmunt Bauman, who argues that modernity was the essential framework for enabling the holocausts to happen.[30] The genocide was not driven by ideas, but by pragmatic issues due to the failure of other attempted solutions to the "Jewish problem," and it was intricately tied up with the country being in a war, where the goal of the country was to fulfill what it saw as its historic destiny. This destiny was related to racist ideas and it built on previous historical developments, such as "the historical relationship between the churches and the Jews; the defeat of Germany in World War I and the conditions of the armistice; the perceived threat of Bolshevism; social Darwinism; the science of eugenics; [and] the rise of rationality and its fantasies of perfection."[31] That is, the Second World War and its eventual holocaust did not come out of a vacuum, but was a continuation and development of the distorted willing of the German nation that was already in place.

This holocaust can be seen as taking one of the ideas of modernity to its extreme end: the triumph of rationality in planning and action, which is threatened whenever irrationality intrudes into and interrupts efficient organization. German society was trying to create the perfect society without problems of emotions and irrationality.[32] Science and technology were dominant in all areas of life in order to do this. Anything that got in their way was a problem to be eliminated. Nazi policy towards Jewish and Gypsy peoples and others was designed to eliminate pathogens that they believed threatened a perfectly rational social order based on the purity of race.[33]

In the Nazi worldview, the Jewish and Gypsy peoples were a nation without a state, so they could not participate in the Darwinian struggle between the races by the normal means of diplomacy and war. Instead they were dispersed amongst the nations, and so they could be presented as peoples involved in international conspiratorial action to undermine and overtake the nations of the world. It was believed that intermarriage with these peoples would dilute the Arian bloodline. Jewishness could not be cultivated out of Jewish people, so it had to be removed by their exclusion. This turned Germans into participants or bystanders in a bureaucratic, administrative process which dealt with the commonly perceived "Jewish question" in a rational, and therefore apparently civilized and, above all, legal manner.[34]

Initially, the plan was to remove Jewish and Gypsy peoples and others from the German state. The invasion of other countries in the war introduced two further problems: greater numbers of such people were living in the areas controlled by Germany, and they needed to be taken further away. This situation gradually morphed into a further instance of the one of the most shameful things in history, where one group of people seeks to totally remove another group of people from the face of the earth.

McFadyen argues that this was only possible because of a triumph of reason over all other considerations, where all decisions and actions were subjected to the question of whether they were the best way of implementing the goal; the goal itself could not be discussed: "In the Nazi's Final Solution, we not only encounter the politics of a totalitarian ideology; we also find the totalitarian tendencies of technical-instrumental reason, of rational expertise in establishing and implementing means toward the end set by the political agenda."[35] Implementation therefore becomes "objective": once the goals are set, only the means of implementing them can be discussed, not the ends. Whether one liked or approved of what was being done was only allowing nonrational, personal and subjective things to intrude. There was thus a shift for evaluation from the moral and political to the instrumental, and the instrumental discourse became totalitarian, redefining ends without the competition of other rationalities; goodness was redefined as meeting the requirements of the efficient functioning of the system.[36] The bureaucracy needed to implement this reduced people from subjects to objects and so people disappear. Appeals could only be made as procedural questions concerning the proper application of the rules (e.g., to prove Aryan descent), but the rules could not be questioned.[37]

There is a question as to how people could be caught up in such a program. McFadyen argues that the logic of the situation was that the distastefulness of the task was seen as a sign not of its being evil but of its necessity in pursuit of the greater good: people would not be asked to do such things unless it was absolutely necessary. Individual wills had to be subjected to the great task. Sensitivity to what was being done was decreased by repeated action. Group loyalty and solidarity was key to the continuing action.[38]

The "Final Solution" was the act of a society, people continuing to do the tasks that they had done prior to their incorporation into genocide, such as making railway time tables, maintaining tracks and so on. It was hard for individuals to take responsibility because the task was broken down into separate actions which did not allow the workforce to piece it all together. This functional specialization separates the work of one group from other parts of the process and the end product. The meaning of one's actions is hidden because the meaning is in the interaction and total product of the actions; a single task has no intrinsic meaning, so moral evaluation and responsibility are somehow externalized. Even those directly killing could or would have experienced it in nonpersonal and nonmoral categories: they were just fulfilling orders, which were legally and procedurally correct. The principal moral virtues become loyalty, discipline, obedience, particularly in the face of conflict with one's own wishes or views: "*Bureaucracy's double feat is the moralization of technology, coupled with the denial of the moral significance of nontechnical issues.*"[39]

Perhaps the most insidious part of the whole process is the incorporation of the Jewish people themselves in the project of genocide. The Jewish people were included in the process, such as managing ghettos and selecting people for "transport," perhaps thinking they could help to alleviate the problem. Within ghettos, the authority of the Jewish council was total, but only within the parameters set by the state. Cooperation was rational. When it became clear that the policy was to kill all Jewish people, then resistance came, even in face of almost certain lethal and total retribution. The Nazis were always careful to give choice in order to give the illusion of some freedom, but whichever choice was taken would lead towards their desired ends. In camps, they went even further and aimed at destroying people's personhood, encouraging competition for survival.[40]

Does the concept of bound willing give us any further insight into the dynamics underlying the Nazi-led holocaust? Clearly, the holocaust could not have happened without the will and desire of the Nazi leaders. This, however, was not free willing, but it was shaped by the historical foundations of the German nation. As stated earlier, these included the historic relationship between the church and Jewish people, the nature of the ending of the First World War, social Darwinism, eugenics, and perceived threats from other powers at the time. Further, the willing was shaped by the changing circumstances of the war, leading to genocide being seen as the only feasible solution to what they perceived was a problem. Each successive measure further conditioned the will in an incremental way so that it became unclear at which point certain actions became willed; the final outcome was far from the initial intended action. People in Germany were compelled to submission of their wills to an objective reality which required the holocaust. Willing was not disabled, but displaced towards "objective" and "rational" ends which were beyond dispute. "Everything except open rebellion led to *practical* participation in constructing a racial order, which had the further effect of normalizing and radicalizing both the practices and the construction of reality required and engendered through racially ordering dynamics."[41] Many did rebel and suffered the consequences of doing so, as they were crushed by the dominating will of the nation. Participation, or the failure of resistance, resulted in further hardening of people's wills. Willing had become bound to choosing ways to implement an end rather than having a free choice between competing ends. For participants in the genocide, it may have felt that they were not personally accountable for their actions, that it was a passive acceptance of reality. This is not a true understanding, however, for participation was aligning one's energies with the dominant will of the nation and becoming part of what was happening. That willing was not able to discuss the meaning of things but only whether that which was required was being done in the most efficient way. McFadyen writes:

> What we observe here, then, is not the exclusion of either morality or willing, but their sequestration, colonisation and co-option, their total orientation towards fulfilling the allotted task, and do so well—beyond what is merely demanded. So willing, virtue and the moral are not functioning here as portents and agents of transcendence. They are entirely bent towards and thereby "redouble" the dynamics into which they are—even unwittingly—incorporated.[42]

The study of two concrete pathologies, the sexual abuse of children and the Nazi holocaust, has shown that complex situations cannot be simply described as resulting from the choices of the free wills of individuals. It should be clear that the range of possible choices that can be seen in any situation is radically circumscribed by the history of those involved. Willing is not just a personal dynamic but it is shaped by incorporation into pathological dynamics which are both within and also outside the person. In some cases, like that of being sexually abused or being caught up in the Nazi holocaust, the ability of the individual's will to make choices may be overcome by a superior force. "Here willing is not so much disempowered as 'bent' by a superior attractive force, pulled into the vortex of a pathological dynamic and oriented towards its service. The effect which this may have in restricting the number of possible objects of immediate choice is far less significant than its capacity to appropriate the means and criteria by and direction in which choices are made (by defining 'reality', 'normality', 'the good' or 'rationality') as all immediate objects of possible choosing are incorporated into the dynamic of this pathological orientation."[43]

The sexual abuse of children and the Nazi holocaust have been called pathologies, but that means that there must be some notion of good against which deviations from the good can be measured. It is critical to have a deep enough understanding of what the good is, otherwise we will not be able to comprehend the full depth of the pathology, nor will we be able to see the full possibilities for recovery. The discussion of bound willing reminds us that our idea of good is distorted and so there needs to be an external reference to help us comprehend and reach towards that which is good. Moreover, the pathologies have been shown to be dynamic and relational and so any definition of good must also be dynamic and relational.

Christians understand God as Trinity. This means that relationship is at the heart of the nature of God, and not just any relationship, but a dynamic of being for each other, of seeking the welfare of each other, of a continual process of filling and the overflowing of life. This love cannot be contained in itself, but overflows in creative plenitude. The whole of creation is invited to be caught up in this joyful dynamic movement towards fulfillment. Joy and faith in worship are the answering dynamic of the creation, as it is caught up in God's own being in and towards the whole of creation. McFadyen writes:

> This carries at least four immediate implications. First, the integral order of the world is dynamic and relational. Second, this relationality is an immediate consequence of the movement of God *in* and *through* the world as well as *towards* the world; which is to say, third, that the integrity of the world does not separate it from God. Rather, the world's very integrity as a dynamic system and order includes and is indeed founded on relation to and the presence of the *dynamics* of God. Finally, the relational and dynamic order of the world is directed and called towards its own perfection through this relationship with God.[44]

This is a dynamic image, so fullness is not a static condition to be attained, but a continual process of filling to overflowing as a result of the dynamic abundance of God. Sin, then, "is that which counters the dynamics of God in creation and salvation."[45] But sin is only known in the context of God's active countering of it: it is only in the perspective of this salvific orientation of God's movement towards us that we are aware of the depths and nature of sin. "We know sin only in the context of God's resistance to our resistance to God."[46]

A change in life comes when a person responds to God's overwhelming life and turns to God in faith, to receive change in her deepest being, gradually being released from the bondage of the will that blocks communion with God. Faith is the work of the Spirit of God in a person. In the words of McFadyen, faith

> excites willing into a new orientation upon God . . . In faith, one internalises the dynamics of a God who is radically and genuinely for us. The spirit of faith is the excited and redirected energy (desire) through which a person answers by orienting herself in an excess of joy, which repeats and redoubles as it internalises God's excessive movement *towards her*. In faith, one commits personal energy in consensual response to the dynamic in which God is for us, and finds oneself simultaneously filled with joy in God and oneself and others. Through the commitment of such personal energy, that dynamic is internalised and redoubled. In the dynamic joy of faith, letting "God be God" enables one to stretch towards being genuinely and fully oneself.[47]

Human beings are made for worship; all human beings give their lives in worship. To worship is to orient and order one's life around a reality as primary to and constitutive of what one considers to be of worth and to be true; it is what one gives personal energy to as the ground and criterion of active life-intentionality. Worship of God is the active and attentive response to the dynamic order of God, directing and stretching our energies towards God; worship intensifies being as communion. Bound willing, therefore, directs our worship towards things which are not God and which take our life away. Turning towards the overflowing love of God sets us free from the things which have bound our wills and the love of God enhances and energizes that choice.

Critically, the gift of God is not restoring what was lost, but bringing something new out the present reality. This is seen fundamentally in the death and resurrection of Jesus. The resurrection narratives show that the resurrection was awkward and confusing precisely because it did not deny or disregard what had happened. Moreover, something entirely new was present in the resurrected Jesus, whose bodily life was now different and who could no longer die. The implication is that nothing which has been done need be the final word, that God can bring good out of that which was damaging, but not by returning to some, possibly imagined, pristine past, but by working with what is there to bring something that cannot be imagined.[48]

It can be seen now how both child sexual abuse and the Nazi holocaust are truly pathologies: both block the dynamic flourishing that arises from being turned towards God by directing energy towards something that closes down the possibilities of life. In child sexual abuse, the abuser blocks the dynamic ecology of being in communion, focusing all energy on relating to the abuser; the child is inhibited from being able to relate to others, particularly God, who is the only one whose relationship is entirely free from damaging consequences. More than that, such abuse is sedimented in the structures of a person's identity and so limits his capacity for orientation towards the abundance of life that comes from being able to respond to God in worship. Abuse has blocked the possibility of transcendence. In the Nazi holocaust, the peculiarities of the Germanic peoples were absolutized by Nazi ideology. Whilst there is a right place for joy at the particularities of one's people, it is dangerous when these become absolutized, especially when the way of achieving this perceived purity is the extermination of the other. Raising particular characteristics to being the goal towards which a nation works—that is, directs its energy; that is, what it worships—is to set up something that is static and other than God as the object of worship, which results in the restriction of the life of any who are different in some way. The deliberate destruction of the Jewish people is bad enough in itself, but it has a deeper significance, for Israel's vocation was to worship God and so to draw all other peoples into the abundance of life that comes from this worship. Walter Wink writes that "Israel's vocation is to be a light to the nations: to teach them to worship Yahweh as the absolute, and not to worship the absolutized faculties of their own nations."[49] This is not to say that the practice of Jewishness at any point in history completely fulfilled this purpose, but it does say that the worship of national identity can only be pursued through the dismantling and destruction of everything that God intended the nation of Israel to be.

This section began with the desire to have a way of describing pathological situations which is powerful enough to give a deep description of the pathology, one which both explains the dynamics of the situation and is also hopeful because it shows us a way of working with it that gets beyond punishment following the determination of guilt. The theological concept of bound willing was introduced as a way of giving a thick description of situations and McFadyen demonstrated the usefulness of this concept with his case studies. This is a work of hope because we can understand the deeper dynamic of bound willing as being ways in which we are blocked from responding to the generative love of God. If "binding" is the word to describe what happens to the will in being born into and being shaped by sin, then "loosing" describes the process of being freed from this captivity by the overflowing love of God. Both of these are processes, or movements, hence the titles of the major sections of the book. The Second Movement will consider how to take hold of this liberating movement of God. Before we get to that, the next section will show how the concept of bound willing can help us to read the biblical book Ezekiel in a different and illuminating way, giving us more insight into how bound willing works in whole nations over a period of many generations. Then the final section will begin to look at how bound willing describes what has been happening in Australia. The Intermezzo is an extended study which shows how the dynamics of bound willing inherently limited the possible outcomes of the fight over land within the Australian legal system.

II

Bound Willing in Ezekiel

THE PREVIOUS SECTION INTRODUCED the theological concept of bound willing and the gift of God in releasing people from that binding. This will be an underlying theme throughout the whole book. In this section we will look at the book of Ezekiel from the Bible, which was written about a period in Israel's history in the sixth century BCE. Ezekiel sees Israel at the time as a nation that was continuing to sin in ways that are shaped by the past. It will be argued here that either they could not see this or they refused to acknowledge it. Through the prophet Ezekiel, God calls the nation to repent, which it does not do. Even so, the generosity of God overflows in the promise to restore the nation to the land of Israel in the future. Part of the reason for including this study is to help us shift from thinking about individuals and individual responsibility to being able to think in terms of the nation as an entity, which is more than just a collection of individuals, and also to begin to think about problems that have stretched over multiple generations.

Throughout the twentieth century, the dominant reading of Ezekiel was to see it as a crucial point along the trajectory from a "primitive" notion of corporate responsibility to a "modern" one of individual responsibility.[50] The key text for this interpretive move is Ezekiel 18, where Ezekiel uses an image from the laws for individuals as an analogy in order to be able to speak of the national situation in Israel at the time. This text will be discussed in more detail below, but first it is necessary to consider the ideological stance which underlies the misleading interpretation of Ezekiel.

Ezekiel 18 is not part of a trajectory towards individual responsibility. The prophet is speaking to a *community* in crisis. He is responding to a *community* complaining that their *fathers* (i.e., the previous generations) had sinned, and it is they (i.e., the present generation) who are being punished. That is, the purpose of Ezekiel 18 "is to demonstrate the collective responsibility of the contemporary house of Israel for the national disaster which she is suffering."[51] Paul Joyce argues convincingly that, "although a single man is considered in each of the three test-cases [Ezekiel 18:5–18], it is the cause of the nation's predicament which is being explored; the proverb blames the sins of *previous generations* for the sufferings of the *present*, and accordingly the individuals of the test-cases represent a *generation* . . . the possibility of Yahweh judging individuals in isolation from their contemporaries is not considered. This is because the question at issue is a different one, namely, 'Why is this inevitably communal national crisis happening?'"[52]

Joel Kaminsky rightly criticizes the way of thinking that sees Ezekiel on the trajectory from communal to individual conceptions of identity and responsibility, noting that this way of thinking reflects a modern bias towards privileging the individual over the communal, which has been adopted in biblical interpretation in the political project of wanting to construct a trajectory from what is construed as the messiness of the communal, law-based religion of Israel to the purity of the individual, grace-filled Christianity. Besides the problematic ideological position of such an argument, Kaminsky notes that the idea of communal responsibility is present in the books of the Old Testament that many scholars believe were written late, such as Daniel 6:25 and Esther 9:7–10, and so no such trajectory exists in the Old Testament.[53]

The centrality of the corporate as well as the individual continues to be present in the New Testament and so it was not something that was superseded with the coming of Jesus. For example, God addresses the "angel" of each of the seven churches in Revelation 2 and 3. Here God is speaking to the spirit of each church as a corporate body, not to individuals. As a second example, Paul also writes to churches, as well as speaking to particular individuals. His image of being incorporated into Christ, being "in Christ," is central to his way of thinking and he even talks of all having died in the death of Christ (2 Corinthians 5:14–15), something Westerners find it hard to understand. A third example is that whole households were baptized (e.g., Acts 10:33, 48; 16:15; 16:33). As a final example, Matthew sees the work of Jesus as being about the renewal of the community of Israel. Stephen Barton writes that the central preoccupation of Matthew is "the revelation of the divine presence (kingdom of heaven) in the coming of Jesus as messiah, in fulfillment of scripture, to call Israel to repentance and through a renewed Israel to bring God's blessings on the nations of the world."[54]

Thinking corporately is innate to many other cultures. For example: the identity of people as being part of a village is central to notions of justice in Bougainville;[55] Vincent Donovan gives the example of a whole tribe of Masai converting to Christianity, because it was impossible for the tribe to be split;[56] and there is an African saying, "I am because we are, and because we are therefore I am."[57] All of these point to the fact that it is possible to conceive of the world very differently. That is not to say that these worldviews are perfect, but they provide encouragement for reconsidering the nature of corporate entities.[58] In fact, biblically, corporate entities are part of the created order.[59]

Not only does the corporate remain important in the Bible, but so does corporate responsibility. For example: Jesus castigates the lawyers of his time as a group and holds them responsible for the sins of their forebears (Luke 11:45–54); Jesus laments over Jerusalem as a corporate entity (Matthew 23:37 ∥ Luke 11:34); and Jesus says that Jerusalem will be destroyed because it "did not recognize the time of your visitation from God" (Luke 19:41–44). Furthermore, the Second Movement will show how the church in Corinth could not see how they had been shaped by the past and so they, as a community, had not truly understood the gospel of Jesus Christ.

So, all through the Bible, we see the importance of thinking in terms of corporate entities, not just individuals, and understanding that such groups can be held responsible as a group for failures. Having seen this, we can return to the book of Ezekiel, confident that Ezekiel is indeed addressing communities of people and holding them corporately responsible for their sin, knowing that this is not some sort of ancient failure to understand the primacy of the individual, but part of the way that world is under God.

Ezekiel gives one of the most robust responses in the Bible to the claim by a group of people that they are guiltless: they say that their present problems are the result of the sins of people in the past and not themselves. Ezekiel is addressing the generation of people who were alive at the time of the defeat of Judah by the Babylonians.[60] Both Ezekiel and his readers regard the crisis as a punishment for sin. What is contested is who sinned.⁶¹ The people to whom Ezekiel is speaking quote the parable, "The fathers have eaten sour grapes, and the children's teeth are set on edge" (Ezekiel 18:2). That is, they claim that their present predicament is the result of the sins of their forebears, not their own sin; they prefer to think of themselves as being unjustly punished rather than admitting their guilt (18:19), even to the point of claiming that it is God who is unjust rather than them (18:25, 29).⁶² Ezekiel claims that they are being punished for their own sins.

In order to be able to understand how Ezekiel deals with the people's complaint in chapter 18, it is important to see that Ezekiel is consistent throughout the whole book in listing the sins of the present generation, that the way that they are sinning is the same as their forebears, and that it is the whole nation that is being addressed, although the leaders are also singled out for their culpability for the state of the nation. Right at the beginning of Ezekiel, God makes it clear that it is the present generation of people that are sinning, that they are sinning in the same ways as their ancestors, and that it is the nation as a whole which is being addressed:

> He said to me, Mortal, I am sending you to the people of Israel, to a nation of rebels who have rebelled against me; they and their ancestors have transgressed against me to this very day. The descendants are impudent and stubborn. I am sending you to them and you shall say to them, "Thus says the Lord God." (2:3–4)

They are described as a "rebellious house" (2:5, 6, 7, 8; cf. 3:7). At various places, Ezekiel lists catalogues of the sins of the present generation. For example, in 5:5–11, the people have rebelled against God's ordinances and statutes and defiled the temple "with all your detestable things and with all your abominations" (5:8). Jerusalem and the temple area are filled with the worship of things which are not God (ch. 8). The land is "full of bloodshed and the city full of perversity" (9:9). People "devise iniquity" and give "wicked counsel" (11:2; cf. 13:1–9) and "have killed many in this city, and filled its streets with the slain" (11:6). In 16:1–34, the people are pictured as having taken the gifts of God and used them to create idolatrous images and shrines and to give offerings to other gods, places of idolatrous worship have proliferated, they have killed their children and offered them to other gods, and they have consorted with other nations. In 22:1–16, there is a catalogue of wrongs: fathers and mothers are being treated with contempt, aliens face extortion, and the orphan and widow are wronged in law (22:7-8); there are lewd religious practices and distorted sexual relationships (22:8-11); the economic system is broken with bribes and extortion (22:12); and there is violence and death (22:13). The leaders are castigated for their part in perpetuating this culture (22:23-30; cf. ch. 34). It is clear that it is the present generation that is being judged for their sin (e.g., 7:3-4, 8, 9, 19). They are a "rebellious house, who have eyes to see but do not see, who have ears to hear but do not hear; for they are a rebellious house" (12:2-3). In chapter 20, Ezekiel argues that there has been a consistent pattern and history of rebellion in the people of Israel from the time it was brought out of Egypt, which is being continued by the people of the present day. He finishes by saying:

> Will you defile yourselves after the manner of your ancestors and go astray after their detestable things? When you offer your gifts and make your children pass through the fire, you defile yourselves with all your idols to this day. (20:30-31; cf. 22:2-4).

In chapter 18, Ezekiel addresses the people's claim that they are being punished for the sins of their ancestors. He asks:

> What do you mean by repeating this proverb concerning the land of Israel, "The parents have eaten sour grapes, and the children's teeth are set on edge?" (18:2)

Ezekiel claims that God is just because the proverb is not true: God only punishes the guilty party. Ezekiel makes his case by giving three examples (18:5-18), which seem to be reflecting on Deuteronomy 24:16.[63] It is important to note that Ezekiel is arguing by analogy: he is using legal language (i.e., for relationships between human beings) for the examples, and raising them to speak about relationships between human beings and God.[64] Ezekiel is speaking to the whole community, not just to individuals. Paul Joyce notes that the "sour grapes" proverb (18:2) is a complaint of the present *generation* and that he addresses the people collectively as the "House of Israel" (18:25, 29, 30, 31)[65] and there are other uses of the plural form of address in the same chapter (18:2, 3, 19, 32);[66] although the legal examples that Ezekiel uses are about individuals from different generations, Ezekiel is speaking to the community as a whole. That is, when Ezekiel uses the legal metaphor to speak of the relationship between God and people, the individuality is about generations, not about persons.

The people claim to be in the third category: their fathers have sinned, and they are innocent (18:14-18). Ezekiel, however, says that the present generation is sinful; they are suffering the punishment of God for their own sin, for God only punishes the guilty.[67] Of course, Ezekiel must show that the present generation really is guilty, which he does do, as was shown above. In a cheeky move, Ezekiel uses a generational parable back against the people when he says, "See, everyone who uses proverbs will use this proverb about you, 'Like mother, like daughter.' You are the daughter of your mother . . ." (16:44–45). That is, there is a generational proverb which is true of the people, and it is that they are continuing to behave like those who were before them.

In summary, in the initial encounter of Ezekiel with God, God pronounces the guilt of the present generation. Ezekiel consistently makes the important point that they are not only sinning, but also sinning *in the same way* as previous generations. God sees Israel as a corporate entity, with a continuity of existence through time that is more extensive than any particular generation, and which has a consistent history of sin; moreover, the present generation is continuing to sin in the same way as its forebears. That is, Ezekiel was prophesying to a nation whose actions showed that their will had been bound by their past and present actions.

Because the sins of the people are so obvious to the reader of Ezekiel, it is easy to assume that they were equally obvious to those living at the time. What if, however, the belief that they were being unfairly treated (18:25, 29) because of the sins of their ancestors (18:2) was genuine? That is, what if they could not see that the way that they were living was a deep anathema to God? What if they weren't just being obdurate but rather genuinely could not see that there were any problems (12:2–3)? If this is the case, then we see that the bound will of Israel has blinded it to being able to see what is good.

This reading of Ezekiel should make us wary about any assertions that a line can simply be drawn under the past, claiming that it was the previous generations who did wrong, for subsequent generations, it seems, may continue to sin in the same way as past generations. In fact, the statistics and stories of continuing disadvantage of the First Peoples in Australia would, I suggest, mean that Australia is in a similar position to the people who were being addressed by Ezekiel.

Ezekiel goes further than his interlocutors and speaks of the dynamics of God's relationship with people: it is possible both for righteous people to fall out of favor with God by their sin and also for sinful people to come back into favor through repentance (18:19–29). That is, there is no accounting, where the good is weighed against the bad, but it is the current relationship that matters. This heightens the sense of the responsibility of the present generation, because they could have repented and averted the present disaster, but they did not. However, this is also a passage of hope: the people could be fatally deflated because they are the generation which is being punished after a long period of God's forbearance (see ch. 20), but Ezekiel promises the possibility of redemption if the people do repent. God desires that the people repent (18:23, 32).[68] Ezekiel finishes his argument in chapter 18 with the call to corporate repentance: "the final words of the chapter (vv. 30b–32) focus on the challenge to repentance. 'Get yourselves a new heart and a new spirit! Why will you die, O house of Israel?' (v. 31); 'Turn and live' (v. 32). These words make explicit the challenge to repentance which is clearly implied in vv. 21–24 and 26–28."[69]

Note that "the call to repentance is addressed to the community *as a whole*, and it is the restoration of the whole people of God for which Ezekiel presses."[70] Even more than that, Ezekiel has a vision of the restoration of the nation (e.g., chs. 36 and 37); God's generosity goes beyond the dynamics of the responsibility of repentance.

Ezekiel says that the problems of the past that are continuing into the present can be addressed by the repentance of the nation. In doing so, the present generation can do more than repent of its own sins; it is breaking the pattern of bound willing that has been inherited from the past. The nature of repentance will be explored further in the Second Movement, Loosing. In particular, we will look at what must be done in Australia to repent of the present continuation of the sins of the past. But before we can do that, we need to understand the way in which Australia's will has become bound, which is the purpose of the next section.

III

Being Stuck in the Past in Australia

THIS BOOK IS BEING written to help all the peoples of The Land to understand, when there is a will to work with the First Peoples of The Land in order to bring good, and when so much passion and energy and resource has been put into it, often bringing much good, why it is that policies and programs are still causing damage, and why is there still considerable disease amongst the First Peoples in Australia. The moral imperative that will arise from this is addressed to the Subsequent Peoples.

The key theological tool that we will use at this point is the concept of bound willing, which was introduced in the section I above and which was demonstrated in section II in the life the people of Israel over two and a half millennia ago. This section will focus on understanding the spiritual dynamic of the pathology in Australia and the Second Movement of this book, Loosing, will consider the concrete practices that will enable liberation from those things binding Australia's will.

The situation in Australia is unusual amongst international conflicts in that there is a clear starting point: what became the nation of Australia came into being with the planting of a British flag in the soil of The Land.[71] Several things were bound up with this action: firstly, it did not recognize the relationship of the First Peoples to The Land, a relationship which was much more complex than the British concept of sovereignty and ownership; secondly, it was a unilateral declaration and the First Peoples did not cede their rights over The Land; thirdly, it did not recognize the systems of law of those inhabiting The Land; and fourthly, even in British law, ownership is a bundle of rights, and so it missed an opportunity to negotiate what a shared coexistence might look like. In summary, this action failed to engage with the full humanity of the First Peoples. These failures were in the very conception of what eventually became known as the nation of Australia.[72] Right from the beginning, the Subsequent Peoples could not see clearly about how to relate to the First Peoples because the will of Australia was born in bondage.

This act of Captain Arthur Phillip did not come out of nowhere: it was part of the expansion of European nations into other parts of the world, forming colonies and taking land and resources; it did not recognize the resistance it met from the First Peoples of The Land as war waged to protect the ownership of the land; it was part of a culture which did not regard people from different ethnic groupings as equals or even human; it was based in a particular understanding of ownership that was ultimately rooted in Roman law; and it had a particular understanding of the relationship of human beings to the land, namely, that if it was not cultivated then it was wasteland and the inhabitants of the land had failed in their duty as human beings. Of course, we now know that The Land was extensively managed by the First Peoples.[73] In the language of section I above, these are all manifestations of the inability to see what is good because of the bound willing of the European nations, Britain in this particular case.

When the British first came to live in Australia, they just came and stayed. It was only in a later legal case, *Cooper v Stuart*, in 1889, that the Privy Council had to explicitly state the basis of the establishment of the legal system in Australia. *Cooper v Stuart* was nothing to do with Indigenous land rights, but it had lasting consequences on the legal system in Australia, and land tenure in particular. In order to make their judgment, the Privy Council had to establish the legal foundation of the colony. European international law allowed colonization under three circumstances, with differing legal consequences: conquest, the land being ceded to the incomers, and taking over an empty land. (It must be remembered that this law was a justification of the actions of those who subscribed to it, not an absolute principle of justice.) The court decision in *Cooper vs Stuart* described New South Wales in 1788 as "practically unoccupied without settled inhabitants," and so the occupation was regarded as the settlement of an empty land. Of course, by the time that the question was considered under English law, it was obvious that this was patently false, even though it may have been thought to have been true before the First Fleet set sail (due to erroneous evidence from Banks, amongst others). This (false and fictional) legal assertion allowed them to assert that common law was applicable in Australia, and that the feudal system of land tenure, where all tenure was derived from the Crown, so that no one could hold title to land unless it could be traced back to a grant from the Crown, held sway.[74]

In the past decades, the term *terra nullius* has entered the legal discourse and debate about land in Australia, as a shorthand name for the legal basis of the founding of the colonies in Australia. This term has been avoided in this book because acrimonious debates about its use have obfuscated the real point at issue, namely, the basis, nature and content of Australian law, and its relationship to Indigenous systems of law. It is hard to give a name to the bundle of consequences of the occupation of The Land, as a shorthand way of referring to it in the rest of this book, that sufficiently captures the dynamics of the situation. In my thesis, I used the term "Foundational Sin," which has value in that it helps us to understand that everything that followed is built on this first act, but it does not capture the dynamic nature of the problem. I do not think that it is helpful to call it the "Original Sin" because this opens up the possibility of confusion with the doctrine of original sin and, as noted above, although it was the first sin against the First Peoples and The Land, it was not original in any sense because it flowed from the cumulative sin of previous generations. In this book, I will draw on the metaphor of a tree, where the tree grows from the roots and is nourished by the roots, and so I will use the term "Root Sin." This at least is able to capture the idea that all that followed from this action continues to be fed from this first action. There has been a lot of work trying to address some of the consequences of the Root Sin—in terms of the metaphor, lopping off some of the branches that have grown from the Root Sin—but it is the failure to address the Root Sin that is continuing to cause so many problems in Australia, and which is the primary focus of this book.

The situation in Australia is most similar to those in Aotearoa/New Zealand and North America (Canada and the United States of America). However, the history of the non-Indigenous occupancy of Australia has some significant differences from these areas. Firstly, the first non-Indigenous outpost in Australia was a penal colony. Secondly, those first non-Indigenous people had wrongly understood that The Land was essentially empty, thinking that there could be no resistance to their occupying it. Thirdly, the Indigenous population was not organized into large-scale units that offered coordinated military resistance to the invaders, because Aboriginal societies were ordered on a much smaller scale, with relationships to particular areas of land;[75] expansion of the occupation was met with skirmishes, which Henry Reynolds has called "frontier wars."[76] Fourthly, no treaties were made with the Indigenous inhabitants.[77] Although First Peoples in Australia compare their experiences with their Indigenous colleagues in Aotearoa /New Zealand, Canada and the USA,[78] the fact that The Land was settled by Europeans as if it was empty is deeply embedded in Australian law and culture, making it much harder for the First Peoples in Australia to make progress in the Australian legal system than their colleagues in other countries.[79] Thus, the situation in Australia merits study as a sort of worst-case scenario for countries in similar situations.

From the standpoint of today, some of the actions of Captain Arthur Phillip, and many things that flowed from that, are seen as wrong. Many believe that, although we recognize this to be the case, we should not blame them for acting as they did, for they were simply living according to the worldview of the Europeans of that time, even if it can now be seen that this was less than good. The theological development so far shows us that we cannot let them off like this: the inability to see through the bound will makes people blind to the damage that they are doing but it does not leave them unaccountable. Furthermore, this Root Sin created further levels of binding of the will of those who were first to come, those who were born into Australia, and those who have subsequently moved to be part of Australia. All of us are caught up, to one extent or another, in continuing the damage that is an inevitable result of Australia's bound willing. This does not mean that there has been no good, for there has been much good in the development of Australia, and many people have heroically struggled to bring good for the First Peoples of The Land, but the problem remains that harm continues to be done to the First Peoples of The Land, even when good is intended.

Three examples will be given of the way that bound willing has worked its way out in Australia, where people were trying to do good but where it caused further problems: equal wages for First Peoples working on cattle stations, unemployment benefits for First Peoples, and medication. These examples have been chosen because they are small enough that they can be explained in a paragraph and yet they show that even the smallest and "obvious" things that are done in order to achieve justice can cause havoc. Each will be briefly discussed in turn. The Intermezzo is an extended case study of how this Root Sin has bound the will of the nation of Australia.

The first example is the granting of equal pay to First People and Subsequent People working in the cattle industry. Although cattle stations were owned and run by Australians and companies from other nations, the First Peoples were able to maintain their connection to their land by working on it and, further, they were able to return to do their ceremonial work during certain seasons when there was no work on the cattle stations. Important Aboriginal business, such as arranging marriages, could be transacted when communities came together, such as at race meetings.[80] When equal wages were awarded, however, most First People were driven out of the cattle industry. The result was that they not only had no income, but they had finally been driven off the land that they regarded as their own.[81] Furthermore, by forcing them onto land which was the responsibility of other First Peoples, connections were built up with the land in the new places. This resulted in conflicts between various groups wanting to make land claims under various pieces of legislation, because now more than one group had connections with particular places.[82]

The second example of the damage being done by policies that seem to be just is the giving of welfare to people in some First Peoples' communities. From about 1999, Noel Pearson began to point out that unemployment benefits were creating a false economy in some Cape York communities: providing income support to able-bodied people is "counter-productive for individuals and it is corrosive of society."[83] Noel Pearson called this "sit-down money" and it has had disastrous consequences:

> Steadily but surely over the past 30 years it has torn our society apart. It has made proud and decent people helpless. It has corrupted a truly wondrous social system, based on reciprocity and care, into social dysfunction. In its daily battles against our traditional values, our culture and our kinship relationships, it routinely overpowers love.[84]

At the other end of the political spectrum, Galarrwuy Yunipingu makes the same point. He notes that the movement back into the homelands that was taking place in the 1970s began to establish vibrant communities, including businesses with set rules, such as "no work, no pay." Then the government introduced a form of welfare. He describes the effects in this way:

> The arrival of welfare demoralised the willingness of local people in every homeland to do things for themselves. This is because of

the way that the government developed the program: you had to be on your homeland to receive the welfare payment but you did not have to work. There was no development agenda and there was no employment. Think about that—the only requirement to get money was that you were on the homeland on a given day. Whether working or not, you still got your payments of $200 or $300 each fortnight. So self-determination and self-management were out the window almost immediately, and later the Community Development and Employment Projects (CDEP) took control of Aboriginal people throughout the Territory—and badly so in East Arnhem Land, where I had a firsthand view of the destructive impact of this government program.[85]

The third example is the provision of medicine to some Yolngu communities. At the invitation of the Rev. Dr. Djiniyini Gondarra, one of the leaders of the Yolngu of Arnhem Land at the time, Richard Trudgen, who had spent more than two decades working with the Yolngu, wrote a book for non-Indigenous people which interprets why the Yolngu have found the dominant culture so debilitating.[86] Richard Trudgen sees that the root problem for the Yolngu has been loss of control, and he lists forty-three factors that have led to loss of control for these people.[87] Besides the foundational causes of taking their land, the destruction of their economy and the introduction of alien diseases, it is clear from reading Richard Trudgen's book that attempts at trying to fix the resulting mess have largely failed because non-Indigenous cultures are so alien to the Yolngu and, on the whole, Subsequent People have not taken the time to, or put the resources into, understanding Yolngu culture and interpreting Subsequent culture to these people. For example, millions of dollars have been spent on medical intervention, with little effect, because the medical model that is being used is alien to the Yolngu, and has never been properly explained. Some ways of trying to teach them, such as using puppets, have treated them like children. When Richard Trudgen has used dialogical teaching methodologies, speaking in their own languages, and with knowledge of their culture, the Yolngu have been able to integrate the new knowledge into their cultural system and then teach it in appropriate ways.

It would be inadequate, however, to read Richard Trudgen's book as arguing that all that must be done is to interpret non-Indigenous culture to the Yolngu. It also implies that Subsequent People need to look at the strangeness of their own culture by looking at it from the standpoint of other cultures. Programs aimed simply at acquiring enough knowledge in order to teach First People to engage with the cultures of Subsequent Peoples are in danger of perpetuating the damaging relationships that have been going on since Europeans first landed in Australia, and they miss the opportunity to be challenged and changed by a real encounter with vibrant and viable alternative worldviews.[88] To allow this to happen will be challenging, but ultimately healing to The Land and its peoples.

Mark Moran gathers together six case studies of how various Indigenous communities have struggled with the continually changing landscape of Indigenous policies in Australia that arise from both Commonwealth and State initiatives.[89] He estimates that the total annual budget for such interventions is about $25 billion and there is little to show for such massive amounts of money.[90] A picture emerges from the case studies of the Indigenous Peoples struggling with very difficult problems whilst also having to find ways of coping with changes of policy, changes of service provider and a huge bureaucratic burden. In one case study, concerning the management of alcohol in Kowanyama, he notes that such problems are called "wicked" in social science, due to their resistance to solution: complex interdependencies mean that an effort to resolve one problem uncovers other problems and creates other problems.[91] Clearly the system is not working and so we must get to the root of the problem. The root of the problem is our inability to see because the will of Australia is bound.

These examples show that even actions that are supposed to bring good can in fact lead to harm. This is because of bound willing. Furthermore, the 1967 referendum resulted in changes for the Indigenous Peoples of The Land. Whilst this is largely understood as giving a voice to the First Peoples in Australia, and it is right that people should have a voice concerning decisions made about them, this has proved to be a weak way for the First Peoples in Australia to have their voices heard, hence the call for the "establishment of a First Nations Voice enshrined in the Constitution" in the Uluru Statement from the Heart. Further, some might find their dual identity very difficult to negotiate, for they are citizens of a nation founded on the denial of their humanity and their connection to The Land.

The focus of this book is about the way that the binding of the will of Australia has worked its way out in history and what must be done to put this right. This may be a new way of thinking for many, for there is a tendency in Western cultures to speak only of individual responsibility:

I am not responsible for what was done in the past. At the heart of the difficulty of comprehension is that we view society as a collection of individuals. These individuals are assumed to have free will to choose how they act in any situation, and are also free to act independently of the history of the society into which they are born. The whole of this First Movement has been showing that this is not an adequate way of thinking.

Because of the difficulty of understanding ourselves as being part of a corporate history, it is hard for Western people to think about disputes that have run over multiple generations. If guilt is reduced to individuals,[92] then it is hard to see how a group of individuals could be guilty of the sins of another group of individuals in the past. There is, however, a stronger cohesion and continuity in the life and actions of a community over time. Alisdair MacIntyre is surely correct when he writes:

> I inherit from the past of my family, my city, my tribe, my nation, a variety of debts, inheritances, rightful expectations and obligations. This thought is likely to appear alien and even surprising from the standpoint of modern individualism. From the standpoint of individualism I am what I myself choose to be. I can always, if I wish to, put in question what are taken to be the merely contingent social features of my existence. I may biologically be my father's son; but I cannot be held responsible for what he did unless I choose implicitly or explicitly to assume such a responsibility. I may legally be a citizen of a certain country; but I cannot be responsible for what my country does or has done unless I choose . . . to assume such responsibility. Such individualism is expressed by those modern Americans who deny any responsibility for the effects of slavery upon black Americans, saying "I never owned any slaves." It is more subtly the standpoint of those other modern Americans who accept a nicely calculated responsibility for such effects measured precisely by the benefits they themselves as individuals have indirectly received from slavery. In both cases, "being an American" is not in itself taken to be part of the moral identity of the individual. And of course there is nothing peculiar to modern Americans in this attitude: the Englishman who says, "*I* never did any wrong to Ireland; why bring up that old history as though it had something to do with *me*?" or the young German who believes that being born after 1945 means that what Nazis did to Jews has no moral relevance to his relationship to his Jewish contemporaries, exhibit the same attitude, that according to which the self is detachable from its social and historical roles and statuses.[93]

We cannot detach ourselves from the history of those amongst whom we dwell and we are shaped by that history so that we continue to sin in ways shaped by our shared history. Everyone who is born into Australia, or joins it from the outside, becomes an inheritor of the guilt of the past actions, and their actions add to the historic burden of wrongdoing towards the First Peoples in Australia. We cannot draw a line under the past and assume that we will be able to do better in the future. We are both shaped by the nation of Australia and also responsible for shaping the future of the nation of Australia by how we respond to what has happened in the past.

Many Australians behave as if the problems faced by First Peoples in Australia were caused by others in the past. However, this is clearly not the case. In some cases, the problems weren't even in the past. For example, the *Bringing Them Home* report[94] highlighted the fact that children of First Peoples were taken away from their families as late as in the 1970s, the beginning of the era of some of the current members of Parliament.[95] No matter how well-meaning government policies of "assimilation," "integration," "self-determination," "practical reconciliation" and so on seeking to solve the "Aboriginal problem" have been, the continuing welfare problems for First Peoples in Australia show that these have not been effective. That is, there has been, and there still is, a continual destructiveness by the Subsequent Peoples in Australia towards the First Peoples in Australia, whether this has been intentional or not.

Even more problematic is the way that the present generation of Subsequent Peoples has a tendency to side with the First Peoples because of what happened in the past, so denying their continuing responsibility, and which also blinds it to the way that it is continuing the same behaviors towards First Peoples. Gillian Cowlishaw writes:

> These histories seem to present with ease a view of our own past that fills us, as readers, with horror at the same time as it distances us from it. How is it that in reading these accounts we position ourselves on the side of the Aborigines and identify our forebears as the enemy? These violent and racist men could be our grandfathers and they certainly left us something, if not the land they took or the wealth they made from it, then the culture they were developing. The call to examine the colonial past is in danger of foundering on the complacency of an imagined distance from the spectacle of blood and violence. Continuity with the past is easily severed and the cultural source of these events is lost. Our disgust and horror at the violence and abusive

racism means we are absolved. Where before, readers were offered no access to the contemporary experience of the anthropologists' timeless Aborigines, now historians immerse readers in an awful past and distract them from contemporary forms of violence and racism.[96]

Deborah Bird Rose recalls the wisdom of Hobbles:

> Hobbles [a member of the Yarralin people from the Victoria River area in the Northern Territory] and other story tellers are concerned to show that invasion is not a process of the past which is now finished. Rather, they go to considerable effort to explain that the process is on-going and is continuing to destroy people and land. The other integral point, which is rarely stated explicitly, is that conquest is based on desire and on the illusion of winners and losers. One wins by disabling not only the opposition but the very life systems in which the opposition is embedded. This is a fatal error, for there are no other life systems. As Riley Young said, "I know government say he can change him rule. But he'll never get out of this ground."[97]

Warnings such as this should alert the Subsequent Peoples to the fact that it is not possible simply to draw a line under the past and to move into the future. The problems of the past are being reproduced in the present and they need to be addressed so that they do not continue to damage the future.

Sarah Maddison gives many more examples of how the errors of the past continue into the present. She too is clear that the problems in Australia are not simply the fault of individuals, but of communities and of the whole nation. She also recognizes that the problem is one that has its roots in the Root Sin (which she calls the "Original Sin") and that the present generation will continue the problems of the past unless our inherited and present guilt is addressed. Policies and practices that seek to address the "Aboriginal problem" have failed because the problem is in ourselves, the Subsequent Peoples, and in our nation. She concludes that,

> it is time to imagine a different approach, one in which non-Indigenous Australians start from a belief that we have the capacity to *change ourselves* and our institutions. Beginning to decolonise the relationship between Indigenous and non-Indigenous people will require—at a minimum—a constitution that recognises Indigenous sovereignty and/or a treaty that

formalises a new relationship between Indigenous and non-Indigenous Australia.[98]

This book goes further than this, firstly by exposing the mechanism—bound willing—by which the guilt is passed and accrues from one generation to another. Maddison does not give a clear definition of the nature of guilt; at some points it seems to be a debilitating (individual and communal) psychological feeling, and at others a failure of a moral or legal nature. Part of the contribution of this book, which is grounded in the earlier work of my thesis, is that it argues that the guilt is ontological, part of our being as a nation, and that we are accountable, before God, for all the damaging actions that have flowed from the way that Australia's will became bound by the Root Sin. Further, we are unable to change ourselves, but change can only come from a deep and radical repentance of the Root Sin. Moreover, it will be argued, the problems cannot be resolved by a treaty or changes in the constitution unless these arise from a repentance that renegotiates the relationship between the conflicting claims by Australia and the First Peoples regarding sovereignty over The Land. As the Overture tried to make clear, it is not helpful to talk about "non-Indigenous Australia" because this obfuscates the fact that Australia itself is the problem; the fact that the First Peoples in Australia have been incorporated as Australians by the granting of Australian citizenship makes it harder to see that their claims to sovereignty over The Land cannot be incorporated into the nation of Australia if it remains founded on the Root Sin.

The theological principle of bound willing helps us to understand the underlying reason why bad things continue to happen for the First Peoples in Australia, even when good is desired. By planting a flag in the soil, claiming ownership of The Land and sovereignty over it for the English Crown, Captain Arthur Philip committed the Root Sin against the First Peoples in Australia. This act did not recognize Indigenous systems of law and thus it recognized neither the sovereignty of the First Peoples nor their relationship to The Land. The incomers assumed that they had the right to settle in The Land and very quickly defended this assumed right by resorting to destructive violence. Although English common law is able to incorporate aspects of the legal systems of countries that were colonized by Great Britain, it failed to do this in Australia, because it did not recognize Aboriginal systems of law. Furthermore, the full humanity of the Aboriginal Peoples was not recognized: they were seen as curious and primitive, suitable for anthropological study. The first incomers almost starved, as they struggled against The Land, rather than learning how to live with the bounty of The Land, and so established a narrative of overcoming and conquering The Land.

Near the end of the discussion, in section I above, of the case study of the Nazi holocaust, it was stated that the Nazis absolutized aspects of their identity, which led to removal of those—the Jewish people and others—who, by their existence and practices, challenged that notion of being a people. There is a resonance with the situation in The Land: although it was probably not intended, the establishment of Australia and its legal system absolutized that understanding of the world, disabling the life systems of those who were already in The Land, stopping them from flourishing, or even preventing their existence in the worst cases. Moreover, just as the attempted destruction of the Jewish people was striking at their vocation to show the world how to live within the plenitude of God, living against all absolutizing of national identity, so too the destruction of the First Peoples and their cultures was the denial of their vocation to know the ways of living in harmony with the plenitude of The Land. Care must be taken here so that their way of living in The Land is not absolutized, for there can be flourishing when different ways of living in the world come together in such a way that generates a new and deeper understanding for all, but this is not what happened in Australia, although there are attempts to do this now.[99] This will be returned to in the Finale.

This section has given three simple examples of the way that bound willing has worked its way out in what turned out to be damaging policies for First Peoples: equal wages for workers on cattle stations, unemployment benefits and medication. It has deliberately steered away from more complex and controversial topics like the Northern Territory Emergency Response and a more careful study of the *Bringing Them Home* report, only because it would have considerably lengthened this book to make a thorough study of them. Nevertheless, it is hoped that the theological resources developed so far, and those to be developed in the Second Movement, will enable the interested reader to study situations like these in a more nuanced way, free from the political rhetoric, and so come to a deeper understanding of them.

The Intermezzo is a much more extensive example of how this bound willing has worked itself out in the history of The Land and law. It will be seen that the Root Sin has become established in the very fabric of the life of the dominant culture. The *Mabo and Others v State of Queensland (No 2) (1992) 175 CLR 1*[100] judgment recognized this in part, with the majority judgment overturning the previous legal precedent that failed to recognize any form of Indigenous ownership of land. It was not able, however, to address the issue of sovereignty, because Australian law itself is founded on this claim to sovereignty.[101]

The concrete practices that lead to transformation will be explored in the Second Movement, Loosing.

Intermezzo

The Land and Law

The First Movement of this book, Binding, introduced the theological concept of bound willing. It was claimed there that there was a Root Sin in the creation of Australia, namely, the failure to recognize the full humanity of the peoples of The Land, their relationships to The Land and their systems of law, and so there was no negotiation of how the incoming peoples could live with those who were already there. It was further claimed that this created a pattern through history where harm was done even when trying to do good. Some simple examples were given of how this had worked itself out in awarding equal wages to all stock workers on cattle stations, in giving unemployment benefits and in providing medication.

This Intermezzo is a sustained attempt to tease out whether this is a helpful way of viewing things. The legal struggles over the status of ownership of parts of The Land has been chosen for this study. I am aware that many have become tired of hearing about this, with saturation from the media at each twist and turn as the process unfolded, and became history and legal precedent. Perhaps this is sufficient reason for coming back to this topic, because the longer perspective allows us to look back on the shape of a long story, noting the critical incidents along the way, much as we get a very different view if we climb a mountain and look down on a river whose details we have intimately known as we canoed along it. It is important for Australians to see the flow of this history because it has shaped all the peoples of The Land in indelible ways.

Land has been chosen as the topic of this case study for a number of reasons. The most important reason is that land is essential to the identities of the First Peoples in Australia, to Aboriginal cultures in particular, and so the approach of Subsequent Peoples to the claims of First Peoples concerning their land is a good indicator of the commitment of Subsequent Peoples to seeking the welfare of the First Peoples. Secondly, some First Peoples have chosen to bring their political struggle to the attention of the Subsequent Peoples by using the Australian legal system to make claims over their land, forcing the Subsequent Peoples to take note of their rights.[102] Thirdly, the struggle has been well documented and so there is plenty of material to work with. Finally, the period in view is over half a century, a significant proportion of the time since the first Europeans arrived to stay, and a sufficient length of time to track changes in a situation where the time needed for change is often measured in generations.

The approach taken in this chapter is to study legislation and court cases in Australia concerning land from the late 1960s until 2005. Starting and ending dates for a study can be somewhat arbitrary. The 1960s have been chosen as a starting point because they saw the beginnings of a change in non-Indigenous Australian attitudes to First Peoples, with, for example, the 1967 referendum that made important changes in the Australian Constitution concerning First Peoples. It also saw the beginning of the court case that, although the Yolngu failed to establish their claim, was the catalyst for a report which resulted in the first land rights legislation for First Peoples in Australia. The end date for this study is perhaps more arbitrary, and was chosen largely to be able to have closure on this chapter. Nevertheless, there are a number of reasons why this choice is not entirely arbitrary. Firstly, it is the year in which I made an extended study visit Australia to meet with people and talk with them about what was happening in Australia. Secondly, the interpretation of the native title legislation seemed to have reached a furthest extreme by that point. Thirdly, plans were being made to change the *Aboriginal Land Rights (Northern Territory) Act 1976* (Cth) in significant ways, which came into force in 2006. Writing further concerning these developments would not have weakened the conclusions of this Intermezzo.

In outline, the Intermezzo proceeds as follows. The first section attempts to describe some of the features of Aboriginal understandings of land. This is necessarily limited in scope, and a description by an outsider, but it is essential to have at least some understanding of some of the common features of the relationship to The Land in Aboriginal cultures in order to comprehend why this is such an important issue for First

Peoples and also to expose some of the ways that the Subsequent Peoples have failed to engage properly with Aboriginal cultures. Section II gives a narrative outline of the history of land through the courts and in legislation since the late 1960s, so that the overall picture is not lost in the more detailed account presented in section III. Picking up the analogy of a winding river again, we will not be looking at all the details of the river, but rather looking at the flow of the river as it met major geographical features. That is, it will focus on those places where there were significant changes in direction and flow. Finally, section IV will assess the history in light of the theological tools of binding and loosing.

I

Land in Indigenous Cultures in Australia

LAND IS VERY IMPORTANT in Indigenous cultures in Australia. Everything is bound up in the relationships between the people and land: artefacts,[103] language,[104] ceremonies, law,[105] knowledge and the process of initiation, conception, birth, life and death. Popular slogans such as "the land does not belong to the Aboriginals but the Aboriginals belong to the land" do not comprehend the complexity of the relationship, not least because it imports the alien category of ownership into a relationship that is about responsibility, sustenance and the gift of life.[106]

It is beyond the scope of this book to try to explain the features of any particular Indigenous culture in Australia. Instead, some key features of the cultures of First Peoples that will help understand the interaction of First Peoples and Australian law will be highlighted. This section will focus on Aboriginal cultures in particular.[107]

Aboriginal People speak of "country."[108] This is not just an area of soil, but the whole package of areas of land, all its geographical and geological features, flora, fauna, people, stories, ceremonies, law and so on. "Country" need not only be land, but can be parts of the sea too. Deborah Bird Rose is helpful here:

> In Aboriginal English, the word "country" is both a common noun and a proper noun. People talk about country in the same way that they would talk about a person: they speak to country, sing to country, visit country, worry about country, grieve for country and long for country. People say that country knows, hears, smells, takes notice, takes care, is sorry or happy. Country is a living entity with a yesterday, today and tomorrow, with

consciousness, action, and a will toward life. Because of this richness of meaning, country is home and peace; nourishment for body, mind and spirit; and heart's ease.[109]

Connection to country is not just to an arbitrary piece of land, but to particular parcels of land. Nancy Daiyi, a member of the Mak Mak people, says:

> When I travel around my country I won't starve. I know I'll find good tucker because I have the right sweat for my country. It'll look after us, because we are one and the same. You only need to call out. Talk to the land, it gives us life.[110]

Indigenous Peoples in Australia had, and continue to have, both a sophisticated understanding of their relationship to land and a system of land tenure.[111] An Aboriginal person may have attachments of varying degrees to multiple countries. Attachments are formed in many ways, for example: through the place of conception, the birth place, through the lines of both mother and father, through marriage and through living in a place for a significant length of time.[112] A person has a whole package of responsibilities, and so there is some flexibility in the system for taking up responsibility for whichever land seems most appropriate according to various criteria.[113] The country for which a person has primary attachment and responsibility depends on making choices amongst the various possibilities, and political issues come into play.[114]

A group can grow so that it needs to split, or a group may decline and so others may take over their land (and songs and ceremonies).[115] Periods of "abandonment" of areas of land were natural in Aboriginal cultures. When country was abandoned for a time, connection to the land was maintained by such things as carrying the objects for that land and remote ceremonial actions.[116] Relationships to the land could also be shaped by times of scarcity.[117]

This natural process has been complicated since the occupation of Aboriginal land in a number of ways. The fact that people have moved or have been moved from their lands means that they begin to build up attachment to the land on which they are living, either through the normal inheritance systems, through the cycle of conception, birth and death, or just through the attachment of living there and getting to know the country. This is further complicated when there have been waves of settlement in a place, so that there are several different groups of First Peoples who have built up land rights in a particular place, whilst maintaining rights to their own countries to a greater or lesser extent.[118] This sometimes results in severe conflicts between people living in the same place,[119] and also severe conflict in land title negotiations under various non-Indigenous laws.[120] It must be remembered that the descendants of the original owners of any country may have maintained their connection to their land, despite multiple disruptions, even in the most surprising circumstances,[121] and that they may not recognize the claims on country by people who have built up their connections in other ways.[122]

Alongside this understanding of land and tenure systems was a well-developed political system with ambassadorial protocols that governed movement over and use of land by other groups.[123]

Women and men have different, overlapping, and interacting responsibilities for country: they may have different songs and stories, places which only women or men are allowed to visit, they share in the process of initiation, and so on. For many decades, half of Aboriginal culture was being overlooked without people really realizing it, namely, the place of women in Aboriginal society and their responsibility for land. The reason for this oversight is obvious: the anthropologists were largely men, who only had access into "men's business" as they could not talk about "women's business," and who only pursued issues from a male perspective.[124] Often, female anthropologists were young, and so were not considered eligible for women's wisdom. With colonization, European models of womanhood were forced onto Aboriginal women, who often became domestic slaves. When land issues were moved to the courts, the courts were largely dominated by men, again making it impossible for women to be heard in the early days, because women could only speak about women's business to other women.[125]

Because of this overlooking of the role of women in Aboriginal society, people were unaware of the complementary nature of the responsibilities of women and men for land, responsibilities that were mutually respected. It was thought that ownership of country went down the male line, but, as was mentioned above, there is a much more complex system of the ways that responsibilities for particular countries can be inherited.

First Peoples manage country, for example, through the use of fire,[126] the introduction of new species, maintaining the stocks of food,[127] knowing when various foodstuffs are plentiful[128] and modification of the environment, such as building dams to catch fish.[129] Some Aboriginal communities built permanent villages, which included substantial structures, farmed the land and managed the animal populations for food.

First Peoples have changed the landscape and kept it fruitful. This does not mean that they are conservationists.[130] Recent studies have helped us to remember just how diverse the Aboriginal communities were and how they managed the fragile environment so that it was fruitful and sustainable, even in what, to the incomers, appeared to be uninhabitable regions.[131] This is significant because one of the ways that Europeans justified taking over land is by claiming that it was "waste land," that is, not farmed in any way,[132] which we now understand to be untrue. This is discussed further below in the section on *Milirrpum and Others v Nabalco Pty. Ltd. and the Commonwealth of Australia* ("*Milirrpum*").[133]

With the multiple disruptions to the lives of many First Peoples, it is no surprise that there are often conflicts over land claims. For example, the fact that whole groups of people were slaughtered by non-Indigenous people means that the normal way of passing on country was disrupted, not to mention the deep trauma that it caused to surviving First Peoples themselves. When First Peoples were forced off their land and had to live on the land of other people, this introduced conflict, both because the people should not have been there and because the newcomers built up some association with the country through living there. Ironically, many First People were forced off the land when a law was passed in 1968 that made it mandatory to pay First Peoples the same as other stock workers, as was discussed in section III of the First Movement. An enforced sedentary existence and exclusion from country meant that vital knowledge was lost, ceremonies could not be performed and initiation processes have dwindled in many cases. With many Aboriginal men now spending time in jail or with drug and alcohol problems, women have taken an increasing responsibility in managing country and deciding who should have responsibility for country when the preferred patterns of passing on responsibility have become disordered.[134] Dianne Bell notes that what were once safeguard mechanisms have become part of the everyday working of the system; what was once latent in the structure of land relations has become consciously articulated principles.[135] With multiple disruptions to their societies, it is possible that different descendants of the same tribal groups may end up with differing knowledge of particular pieces of country.[136] All of these things make basing Australian law on the idea of a "traditional owner" deeply problematic. Historian Patrick Wolfe rightly observes "that to fall within Native Title criteria, it is necessary to fall outside history."[137]

Not only have First Peoples been disrupted, but the environment also has been radically altered. For example, mining has dried up reliable water sources,[138] water sources have been damaged by cattle[139] and introduced species, both flora and fauna, which have no natural predators have explosively multiplied.[140] Some indigenous species have become extinct or are facing extinction, and so the claims of First Peoples to be allowed to do what they want to with the flora and fauna in their country becomes problematic, and local knowledge is no longer sufficient for making these decisions.[141] Maureen Tehan helpfully writes that "the colonization resulted in a complex of power of external origin in charge of a new geopolitical space. New meanings became engraved upon the landscape and in its peoples' consciousness."[142]

When European people first started living in Australia, there were some hundreds of nations and languages and many First Peoples spoke multiple languages. Today there is perhaps a wider spectrum of Aboriginal cultures. However, it would be a mistake to think that connections with the land and with kinship systems and knowledge has disappeared in even the longest settled and most urban of environments: Peter Read, for example, makes a fascinating study of continuing Aboriginal attachment to land in the Sydney area.[143]

The presentation here is not meant to romanticize Aboriginal cultures. In particular, it is not saying that the cultures are just, nor that there was not and is not abuse of power. In closing this section, however, it must be remembered that First Peoples have a much more communal understanding of personhood and their relationship to land than that which has grown up in the Western Enlightenment tradition.

Given this knowledge, the reader may find the recounting of the story of court cases and legislation that is narrated in the next section rather bemusing: if all of this is true, then why did some cases so disastrously miss the point? Part of the reason is that the understanding given here is now freely available to non-Indigenous people, but it has not always been so. This is due to a number of reasons, such as: knowledge only being available to properly initiated people; the predominance of male anthropologists or anthropologists working in a paradigm of male domination, so that women's voices were not heard; the failure to acknowledge the multiple varieties of Indigenous cultures; the failure to understand the categories of Indigenous cultures; and so on. On top of this, there are questions about how to negotiate two conflicting cultures, and conflicting presumed rights that have built up over generations, in a land where one culture is much more powerful than the other. However, judgments such as this must await the drawing together of the threads in telling the story.

II

An Outline Narrative of Land in Recent Decades

So that the overall narrative is not lost in the details, the outline is as follows.[144] The place to begin is always a little arbitrary, but the modern Indigenous land rights movement can certainly be traced back as far as some of the Yolngu people of the Gove Peninsula petitioning the Commonwealth government concerning the grant of a lease to mine bauxite on their land, a petition which was rejected by the government. In response, the Yolngu took the mining company and the government to court, in order to establish the ownership of their land, and to have the actions of the government declared illegal. The presiding judge recognized the existence of Aboriginal law, but was unable to see, in the evidence that was presented to him, an understanding of land ownership that could be recognized in Australian law.[145] Following the Gove Peninsula case, Woodward J. was instructed to produce a more careful report on the relationship of Aboriginal People to the land, and the then Commonwealth Labour government drew up legislation, which was followed through, in a slightly altered form, by the new Liberal-Country Party government in 1976, forming the *Aboriginal Land Rights (Northern Territory) Act 1976* ("*ALR Act*"). As its name implied, it only covered land in the Northern Territory. It introduced the notion of "traditional owner" into government legislation. Most claims under this act have been settled and over 40 percent of the land in the Northern Territory is in Aboriginal hands, with certain provisos, largely concerning mining rights. A later Labour government backed away from an election pledge to make similar legislation

An Outline Narrative of Land in Recent Decades   65

that would be binding on the rest of the Australian continent. In 1982, a Torres Strait Islander, Eddie Mabo, was instrumental in setting up a case against the Queensland government concerning the ownership of land on the island of Mer in the Torres Strait. The case was finally decided in 1992, with a majority in the High Court of Australia adjudging that a concept of "native title" was consistent with Australian common law and that some of the claimants still held this on the island. The *Mabo and Others v State of Queensland (No 2)* ("*Mabo (2)*")[146] judgment recognized that "common law title" could, and had been, extinguished in some lands under Australian law, and indeed by virtue of some Australian and parliamentary and executive actions already taken. To say that any title to any particular land held by the First Peoples has been "extinguished" is to say that this title no longer exists and so cannot be recognized by the courts. Nevertheless, the decision opened the way for other groups of First Peoples to make similar claims about their own lands, which would be expected to be successful. In order to respond to this new situation, which would have led to protracted and expensive legal cases, the Keating (Labour) Commonwealth government, in consultation with groups of Indigenous leaders, introduced the *Native Title Act 1993* (Cth) ("*NT Act*"), which ratified the extinguishment of native title on large tracts of Australia, as per the *Mabo (2)* judgment, and, at the same time, set up a procedure whereby First Peoples could try to have their "native title" recognized on land where it had not already been extinguished. This was the high-water mark of genuine collaborative dialogue between the First and Subsequent Peoples. The act produced a way to fast-track judicial decision-making, provided for mediation of disputes and legal funding for claims, and established a legislative code in relation to native title. This complex yet genuine framework aimed at reducing time and costs and, of course, involved some compromise in relation to outcomes. In other words, it was clear to all that every "Mabo-like" case would be successful, whilst also acknowledging that vast tracts of the continent would not be affected by the decision. Significantly, the preferred process included mediation between the claimants, with the results ratified by the courts. The Commonwealth government changed in 1995 to a coalition led by John Howard, who was distinctly cool about the reconciliation process in general, and land rights for the First Peoples in particular.[147] The following year, 1996, saw another major judgment in the High Court of Australia, in a case between the Wik people and the Queensland government, where the court decided that the existence of a pastoral lease did not necessarily extinguish native title (*Wik Peoples v Queensland and Others; The Thayorre People v Queensland and Others* ("*Wik*")).[148] Famously, John Howard appeared on national television holding up a map of Australia, on which he had marked in black ink what he described as the 70 percent of Australia that might fall into Aboriginal ownership because of "judge-made law" in the *Wik* decision.[149] An orchestrated media frenzy followed, with Deputy Prime Minister Tim Fischer announcing that the government would be amending the *NT Act* so as to achieve "bucket-loads of extinguishment." Access to legal funding was restricted and the benefits of a favorable judicial finding under the act were watered down. The effect was a substantial unilateral rescission of the terms of the accord reached by the Keating government. Subsequent Federal Court judgments gave effect to the clear intentions of Parliament in restricting access to, and the meaning of, the "title" intended to be recognized by *Native Title Amendment Act 1998* (Cth).

In reading this story, it is clear that the key shifts in policy towards First Peoples and land have often been led by the people themselves; they have not been passive observers, rather, it has been the dominant culture which has had to respond to pressure brought by First Peoples within the system of the dominant culture itself. The struggle within the Australian legal system has not exhausted their political struggle, but it was a tactic which forced the Subsequent Peoples in Australia to take note of their claims in a legally enforceable way.[150]

Although this is a story about the dominant Australian legal system, it does not deny the existence of parallel legal systems of the First Peoples, which have, on the whole, never ceded ownership of Indigenous land to others. In fact, for many First Peoples, the Australian legal system is "lawless" and is not wholly assented to.[151]

III

A Narrative About Land in Half a Century of Australian Legislation and Law

The Bark Petition[152]

IN AUSTRALIA, THERE WAS extensive exploration for bauxite because of the shortage of iron during the 1939–1945 war. Deposits were found in Arnhem Land in 1951, around Yirrkala Methodist Mission in particular. When the lease, held by the Methodist Overseas Mission Board,[153] on two hundred square miles of land ran out in 1957, the Commonwealth government replaced it with a "Special Purpose Lease," which allowed mining. In 1958 the Mission board agreed to transfer the land from mission control for mining purposes. There was no consultation with the local Yolngu, and, whilst it was not a secret agreement, it was not publicized.

The Rev. Edgar Wells and his wife Ann arrived soon after, in January 1962. They had both studied anthropology under Adolphus Elkin, and had been missionaries at Milingimbi from 1950 to 1960. Soon after their arrival, the local people, the Yolngu, expressed worries about mining activity. A survey peg appeared on Bremner Island. Edgar Wells wrote to Arthur Calwell, leader of opposition, in January 1963, asking for protection for the Yirrkala Yolngu. On February 18, 1963, Prime Minister Robert Menzies announced a $50 million mining project and large excisions of land of the Aborigines' reserve to Grove Bauxite Corporation (GBC), representing overseas mining interests. On same day, S. B. Dickinson of the GBC attended a meeting of the board of the Methodist Overseas Mission and received rubber-stamp approval. There were no Yolngu at the meeting and they were not informed afterwards.

Edgar Wells received a reply from Arthur Calwell and was shocked to find that the mission land had been reduced to two square miles and later to half a square mile. Under the old lease, the Methodists acted in control of the mission village itself, but it was understood that the Yolngu controlled the rest of the land. Now they were to lose all control over their land.

All this was happening at height of Comalco dispute in Cape York, where the Mapoon people were refusing to leave their land, and GBC wanted no such problem in the Gove area.

Paul Hasluck, the Minister for Territories, defended the mining initiatives on the principle of assimilation. He said that change was happening as part of the move from "protection" to "assimilation" and this would assist in the assimilation of the Yolngu.

In July 1963, Kim Beazley and Gordon Bryant, two Commonwealth parliamentarians, visited Yirrkala. Letters from the Yolngu had received no response and they wanted to petition the prime minister. When Kim Beazley saw Yolngu paintings in the church, he conceived of the idea of a petition being a bark painting. The bark petition was drawn up by group of Yolngu artists and signed by representatives of various clans.[154] It contained a typescript written in both English and Gumatj.[155] Parliament received the petition on August 14, 1963, but Paul Hasluck opposed its presence because it contained only twelve signatures, some of whom were minors, even though only literate young people's signatures had been used. The Yolngu therefore prepared a second petition overnight, with as many signatures as they could get in one night, about one hundred witnessed thumbprints.

Significantly, the images around the bark petition were a presentation of the Yolngu ownership of the land. Howard Morphy writes:

> The genius of the bark petition was that it introduced an Aboriginal symbol into Parliamentary discourse, making it harder for Europeans to respond in terms of their own cultural precedents. Petitions framed in parliamentary language can be dealt with through parliamentary procedures. Petitions framed with bark paintings add a new element. The bark petition emphasised the difference between 'Aborigines' and other petitioners, and it did so in such a way that the issue was likely to be taken up by the media.[156]

Members of Parliament said that the petition was from Edgar Wells and other missionaries, that they were guilty of agitation. This was an old political ploy, dating back to at least 1870s, when no one could believe the First Peoples in Corranderrk, Victoria, were capable of writing letters.

Kim Beazley moved that a select committee be established to investigate the case and this was accepted on September 12, 1963. It interviewed many witnesses, including Edgar Wells and ten Yolngu, men and women. It accepted evidence in the Gumatj language and the investigators acknowledged the intellectual competence of the Yolngu and their grasp of the issues when giving evidence in their own language through an interpreter, where others had assumed otherwise. Whilst accepting the inevitability of mining, the standing committee recommended that: the Yolngu be consulted as soon as possible about important sites, several types of compensation and royalties should be made, and there should be a House of Representatives standing committee to monitor events at Yirrkala for at least ten years.

Within a few days of the release of the report, the board of the Methodist Overseas Mission sent notice to Edgar Wells to move him from January 1, 1964. When he refused, it attracted media attention and he was sacked immediately. In November 1965, Parliament said they would not set up the recommended standing committee.

This story has been told at some length because it has features that come up again and again in the story of land in the next decades: negotiations about land that exclude the First Peoples themselves, creative responses by the First Peoples, investigations whose recommendations are not acted upon, advocacy by some Subsequent People on behalf of First Peoples, the overwhelming power of the Australian parliament and legal system, and the power of the system to destroy those who get in its way.

The Wave Hill Strike

Minimum wages existed for people working in certain industries, but First People were excluded. In 1965 the North Australian Workers' Union supported the cause of the First Peoples in an application to the Conciliation and Arbitration Commission, claiming equal wages for them. The employers opposed it. The commission awarded the wage, but said that employers would not be required to pay it to "slow workers." Following this disappointment, the Gurindji people of Wave Hill, an immense British-owned cattle station owned by Lord Vesty, withdrew their labor. They held out for over a year. Then they "took a step which was to have the most profound influence on the coming general Aboriginal struggle for land rights. They moved onto their traditional lands (part of the Vesty-owned station) and established a settlement there of their own which they renamed—as it had traditionally been known—Daguragu."[157]

On August 16, 1975, after much negotiation with the Vesteys, the Labour government was able to hand the title for part of their land to the Gurindji people. At Kalkaringi on that day, Prime Minister Gough Whitlam addressed Vincent Lingiari and the Gurindji people, saying:

> On this great day, I, Prime Minister of Australia, speak to you on behalf of the Australian people — all those who honour and love this land we live in.
> For them I want to say to you:
> First, that we congratulate you and those who shared your struggle, on the victory you have achieved 9 years after you walked off Wave Hill Station in protest.
> I want to acknowledge that we Australians have still much to do to redress the injustice and oppression that has for so long been the loss of Black Australians.
> I want to promise you that this act of restitution which we perform today will not stand alone — your fight was not for yourselves alone and we are determined that Aboriginal Australians everywhere will be helped by it.
> I want to promise that, through their Government, the people of Australia will help you in your plans to use this land fruitfully for the Gurindji.
> And I want to give back to you formally in Aboriginal and Australian Law ownership of this land of your fathers.
> Vincent Lingiari I solemnly hand to you these deeds as proof, in Australian law, that these lands belong to the Gurindji people and I put into your hands part of the earth itself as a sign that this land will be the possession of you and your children forever.[158]

The photograph of Gough Whitlam pouring a handful of sand into Vincent Lingiari's hand has become an iconic image in Australian history.[159] This story of Vincent Lingiari and his people is also remembered by one of the slivers in Reconciliation Place in Canberra.

Milirrpum: Aboriginal Law Recognized, but Not Aboriginal Ownership

With the failure of their petition, the Yolngu took the company and the Commonwealth government to court in 1968.

In order to comprehend this case, it is necessary to understand some rudimentary concepts from both Australian property law and also the place of land in the life of Aboriginal Peoples. The latter was examined in section I and the key ideas of non-Indigenous property law will be outlined in the following paragraph.[160]

The foundation of Australian law, in its own eyes, depends on the nature of the occupation of The Land by the Subsequent Peoples. At the time of occupation of Australia, European law recognized three ways that a European nation could take over another land: through conquest, through cession, and through settlement of an unoccupied land. Moreover, settlement of an unoccupied land was extended to include the taking over of a land which was inhabited by people who were "so primitive"[161] that they did not have a system of law which could be recognized by European law,[162] nor an obvious claim to sovereignty.[163] Critically, in the third case, it was understood that the law that now held sway over the land was the law that was brought with the incomers.[164] The Australian legal system is based on this extended third case: that when the Crown proclaimed sovereignty over the eastern half of The Land, it also established the legal system that was brought with the first incomers. Although it quickly became clear that this was not the case, this "legal fiction" was firmly established as the basis of Australian law and, in its eyes, binding on all the inhabitants of The Land.[165] With this legal system came an inherited system of property law, with its origins in the feudal system, where all land title was derived from the Crown. Property "ownership" is a relationship and includes the following rights: "the right to exclusive physical control of the property; the right to possess the property; the right to enjoy and use the property; and the right to alienate (that is, transmit, devise or bequeath) the property."[166] Ownership is a bundle of rights and it is possible for several people to have varying degrees of ownership over any particular piece of property at the same time.[167] Ownership is not absolute, but is subject to a relativity principle: any ownership claim has to be proved to be stronger than that of someone else who may assert a claim on ownership.[168] The legal cases and legislation that will be examined in the rest of this chapter arise from trying to work out the implications of this legal foundation and its subsequent development, in the face of the fact that First cultures had, and retain, complex and sophisticated systems of land "ownership."

In his judgment, Blackburn J recognized that the legal foundation of the Australian legal system was contrary to facts, at least as they were now understood, but his judgment had to be "not one of fact but of law" and he was thus constrained to make a judgment within the legal system.[169]

Despite the subsequent attacks on his judgment, Blackburn J comes across as very sympathetic to the Yolngu case in his judgment.[170] The case ultimately failed because Blackburn J could not find, in the evidence put before him, sufficient proof that the Yolngu "owned" the land in a way that could be recognized in Australian law. Whilst the ability to alienate the land might be able to be waived when considering another system of ownership, in the end he could not find sufficient evidence that any of the plaintiffs had the exclusive right to use and enjoy the land in question and the right to exclude others from it.[171] He thus famously concluded that the Yolngu association to the land was "spiritual" rather than "economic," by which he meant that it had been clearly established that certain groups of people had (sometimes overlapping) responsibility for particular ceremonies and sacred sites, but that the same thing had not been demonstrated for ownership of the land.[172]

He also rejected the notion that "native title" could be recognized in common law:

> I have examined carefully the laws of various jurisdictions which have been put before me in considerable detail by counsel in this case, and, as I have already shown, in my opinion no doctrine of communal native title has any place in any of them, except under express statutory provisions. I must inevitably therefore come to the conclusion that the doctrine does not form, and never has formed, part of the law of any part of Australia.[173]

Some believe this to have been a misconception,[174] although others understand that this was an invitation to the High Court to re-examine the issue.[175]

Nevertheless, Blackburn J made a statement about the nature of the system of law the Yolngu people, which was significant for the later *Mabo (2)* judgment. He described the Yolngu system of law as being

> a subtle and elaborate system highly adapted to the country in which the people led their lives, which provided a stable order

or society and was remarkably free from the vagaries of personal whim or influence. If ever a system could be called "a government of laws, and not of men", it is that shown in the evidence before me ... Great as they are, the difference between that system and our system are, for the purposes in hand, differences of degree. I hold that I must recognize the system revealed by the evidence as a system of law.[176]

Stepping back from the judgment itself, there are several observations that need to be made. Firstly, there was a mismatch between what the Yolngu and the non-Indigenous legal system thought that they were doing, arising in part from differing conceptions of dispute resolution. In particular, the Yolngu thought that their primary task was to give knowledge, which would lead to respect and the recognition of their land rights. "They found it difficult to accommodate defense counsel's mode of questioning, and of attempting to elicit from them inconsistent or contradictory responses. Having seen the court situation as analogous to traditional meetings where they expected explanation and persuasion to lead to the expression of consensus, the Yolngu leaders were unprepared for a situation in which Europeans explain only enough to 'win.'"[177] Because Yolngu ways of disputation seek consensus, this put them at a disadvantage in an alien cultural system that emphasized adversarial approaches to dispute.

Secondly, the Yolngu were taking a risk in revealing knowledge and sacred objects that would not normally be available to those who had not reached the recognized stage of maturity in their culture.[178] They therefore had to weigh up how much they were willing to break with their culture, which potentially had dire consequences for those who did so, and what bits they simply would not reveal.[179] So they were in a position where, culturally, they may not have been able to give the information that was needed for the court to make an adequate decision.

Thirdly, and consequently, the court was unable to ascertain that the Yolngu really did have a proprietary interest in the land which could have been recognized in Australian law. This was partly because some important information was not presented:

> they left largely implicit, for example, the procedures of seeking permission to use the resources of lands owned by other groups. They did make statements about permission but, perhaps because of the form in which they expressed them, the court appeared to comprehend them imperfectly or to ignore them.

They also left implicit or only partially interpreted the various categories of subsidiary rights in land, including those of 'sister' clans linked by a common myth and those entailed in the alternative generation *märi-gutharra* relationship, in the interests of describing their relationship to land in terms they hoped would be comprehensible to English speakers.[180]

They were not helped by the fact that the expert witnesses sometimes contradicted the evidence of the Yolngu themselves,[181] and there were problems arising from the fact that the people translating for the Yolngu were not authorized to speak for some of the land in question.[182]

Perhaps the clearest thing from the case and the judgment is that there was no one who was sufficiently versed in both systems of law for there to have been a proper conversation.[183] This is an indictment particularly on the dominant system, which could have taken the time to understand things better, well before the First Peoples had to bring a case like this to court.

As an afterword, Ian McIntosh noted, in 2000, that the mine was earning Nabalco $300 million per year, and yet they paid nothing to the Yolngu. Further, there has been terrible damage to the environment: "toxic waste ponds occupy hunting grounds; alumina dust pollutes the air, and a mining town of 4000 occupies land within view of the Yolngu communities. The processing plant expels chemicals in to Melville Bay, and in 1990 it was discovered that unacceptably high levels of heavy metals, such as cadmium, had been dumped into the harbor, and the Yolngu were warned not to eat shellfish."[184]

The *Aboriginal Land Rights (Northern Territory) Act 1976* ("*ALR Act*")

Following the *Milirrpum* judgment, it seemed that the only way to advance Aboriginal land claims was through explicit legislation, in order to stop the expensive process of making claims through the courts and also to ensure that similar mistakes were not made again. This was the purpose of the *ALR Act*.

After twenty-three years in opposition, November 1972 saw the election of a Labour government under the leadership of Gough Whitlam. In their campaign they promised "to legislate to establish for land in Commonwealth territories which is reserved for Aboriginal use and benefit, a system of Aboriginal tenure based on the traditional right of clans and other tribal groups and, under this legislation, vest such lands in Aboriginal communities."[185] On being elected, the government immediately began to legislate concerning Aboriginal affairs. Within three months, Mr. A. E. Woodward, who had acted for the plaintiffs in the *Milirrpum* case discussed above, and who was now a judge, was appointed to report on "the appropriate means to recognize and establish the traditional rights and interests of the Aborigines in and in relation to land, and to satisfy in other ways the reasonable aspirations of the Aborigines to rights in or in relation to land."[186]

Woodward J reported back in 1974 and his recommendations were broadly taken up in the bill the Labour government presented to Parliament on October 16, 1975 as the *Aboriginal Land Rights (Northern Territory) Bill 1975*. However, the bill was to lapse, for Governor General John Kerr took the unprecedented step of dissolving both houses of the Federal Parliament on November 11, 1975. Nevertheless, a modified bill was re-presented by the incoming conservative (Liberal-Country Party) government, and it became the *ALR Act*. The act created a new form of land title, inalienable communal freehold, and gave the holders of this title some control over mining on their lands.

At the heart of the legislation was the definition in Section 3(1) of "traditional Aboriginal owners":[187]

> "traditional Aboriginal owners," in relation to land, means a local descent group of Aborigines who
>
> a. have common spiritual affiliations to a site on the land, being affiliations that place the group under a primary spiritual responsibility for that site and for the land; and
>
> b. are entitled by Aboriginal tradition to forage as of right over that land.

The act says that only "traditional aboriginal owners" can make a claim, and then they will have rights in relation to the land that others cannot enjoy.[188]

This act has been susceptible to multiple criticisms: it further entrenches the idea in public consciousness, although maybe not in law, of First Peoples having to be "traditional," so making it harder for other groups to have their ownership of land recognized; it was based on a wrong model of patrilineal descent of rights to land;[189] it ignored women's business;[190] it set up a system of land management (land councils) based on male power; these land councils were the mediation point between Australian power and Aboriginal power, but in Aboriginal culture only those associated with a particular piece of country could speak for it;[191] and it took no account of disruption due to the activity of Subsequent Peoples since 1788. Land councils were organized within European male paradigms and inevitably privileged men's knowledge and participation. "Aboriginal women were, and continue to be, active in meetings about community affairs, but the Land Council's agenda was about ceremonial and often sacred knowledge about land which, in Aboriginal society, is sex-segregated knowledge."[192]

Despite the shortcomings of the *ALR Act*, the application of the act was allowed to evolve over time so that it overcame some of these objections.[193] For example, writing from a position of three years' experience of working on land claims under the act, as an employee of the Central Land Council, Meredith Rowell saw how the role of women in land claims became increasingly important.[194] By describing several land cases, she was able to show that there was increasing participation by women, with equal participation in the final case she considered, where the claim book was prepared by both male and female researchers (J. Wafer and P. Wafer), after many years of research. At one point during the hearing of the last case, at the insistence of Ms. Wafer and Ms. Bell, the court was cleared of all but the essential male participants so that women could more freely give evidence. Women's evidence was complete and in no way secondary to that of the men. Moreover, it was clear from the transcript that the claim would have been sufficient on the women's evidence alone. Observations such as these were enough to convince people that, although the definition in the original act was not accurate, because it did not correctly represent the varieties of forms of Aboriginal tenure, the way that the application of the act had developed in practice, with considerable flexibility in the interpretation of "traditional Aboriginal owners," meant that the definition did not have to be revised in subsequent revisions of the act.[195]

The Northern Territory government opposed every land claim made under the act, engaging in litigation that is estimated to have cost over $10 million.[196] Nevertheless, in 1998, about 44.3 percent of the Northern Territory (573,000 square kilometers) had been granted to Aboriginal land trusts for the benefit of Aboriginal Peoples.[197] The act was reviewed by John Reeves QC in 1998,[198] which led to the *Aboriginal Land Rights (Northern Territory) Amendment Bill (No. 2) 1999*. Towards the end of

2005, proposals were being tabled, recommending a radical change in the act in order to allow the mortgaging of land by groups and individuals. This represented a huge shift from the inalienable communal freehold that was established in the act. As was stated in the introduction to the Intermezzo, these developments have not been included here.

The curious reader may be wondering why such a large proportion of the land mass in the Northern Territory escaped having title to it being held by Subsequent Peoples. The reason is that the land itself could not support any sort of Western agricultural industry, so it was useless to Subsequent Peoples. However, it has since been discovered that many parts of this land are rich in minerals and, as has been noted earlier in this section, the title granted under the *ALR Act* does not include ownership of the mineral resources. This means that ownership confers little in terms of participation in the Australian economy, whilst exposing the titleholders to considerable disruption of their land.

It is worth noting at this point that a long journey had been made in a relatively short time: it was only after the referendum in 1967 that First Peoples were counted as people in Australian population statistics and that the Federal Government was given the power to legislate for the First Peoples, and nine years later it was possible for some First Peoples in the Northern Territory to have their ownership of land recognized by Australian law.

These acts were not without cost, for they formalized the extinguishment of the title held by First Peoples on land which could not be claimed under the act. Writing in 1997, Galarrwuy Yunupingu noted that:

> One of the key compromises that Aboriginal leaders agreed to was that all land titles issued between 1788 and 1976 could be validated and made secure. This was an historic gift to the Australian people and a profound statement of our commitment to reconciliation. In return, we argued that we must retain the right to negotiate over future developments on land where native title remained.[199]

Mabo (2): The Recognition of "Native Title"

> It is a terrible thing for us to have to go to this kind of court to prove what we have always known: that these islands are our homes, not something to be bought or sold. But we have no choice.[200]

Henry Reynolds records Eddie Mabo's astonishment and horror when he learned in the late 1970s that, in Queensland law, Mer had been regarded as Crown land since 1879.[201] Like the Yolngu in Arnhem Land, who had been "more or less free to have virtually complete enjoyment of their land rights as they understood them" until about 1969, when plans for a bauxite mine at Gove Peninsula were made,[202] the Meriam had had the Murray Islands more or less to themselves. Again, like the Yolngu, "the possibility of their being ousted was unthinkable."[203] They were not bringing their case to the tribunal of the Crown in a state of mind in which failure was conceivable. The chairman of the Murray Island Council, Ron Day, made this clear both firmly and courteously before the cameras with Justice Moynihan alongside him outside the court at Mer in 1989: the Murray Islanders owned the land from which they grew, something that no judge, no lawyer, no politician—not even the Crown—could take away.[204]

The Mabo judgment in fact was made in two stages because the Queensland government tried to short-circuit the land claim by retrospectively enacting the extinguishments of title from when it took over the administration of the islands in 1879 (*The Queensland Coast Islands Declaratory Act 1985*) and the Mabo defendants agreed that if this stood, they would drop their case.[205] The argument against the action of the Queensland government that proved to be decisive was that the retrospective act contravened the *Racial Discrimination Act 1975* (Cth) ("*RD Act*").[206] It will be seen in subsequent sections below that since this judgment there have been many attempts, some of them successful, to dismantle the *RD Act*.

The second judgment, in a six-to-one majority, upheld the Meriam claim on their land, and so established the concept of "native title" for the first time in Australian common law. With the approval of the other members of the court, Mason CJ and McHugh J, summarized the judgment in the following way:

> In the result, six members of the Court (Dawson J dissenting) are in agreement that the common law of this country recognizes a form of native title which, in the cases where it has not been extinguished, reflects the entitlement of the Indigenous inhabitants, in accordance with their laws or customs, to their traditional lands and that, subject to the effect of some particular Crown leases, the land entitlement of the Murray Islanders in accordance with their laws or customs is preserved, as native title, under the law of Queensland. The main difference between

those members of the Court who constitute the majority is that, subject to the operation of the *Racial Discrimination Act 1975* (Cth), neither of us nor Brennan J agrees with the conclusion to be drawn from the judgments of Deane, Toohey and Gaudron JJ that, at least in the absence of clear and unambiguous statutory provision to the contrary, extinguishment of native title by the Crown by inconsistent grant is wrongful and gives rise to a claim for compensatory damages. We note that the judgment of Dawson J supports the conclusion of Brennan J and ourselves on that aspect of the case since his Honour considers that native title, where it exists, is a form of permissive occupancy at the will of the Crown.[207]

It is worth summarizing the argument of Brennan J in making his judgment, as it will be important later in reflecting on this narrative of land from the point of view of the theological concept of bound willing. The heart of what Brennan J argued was that the High Court is charged with developing a truly Australian law and it has the power to overturn previous judgments.[208] This is particularly applicable where judgments had been made under a developing system of law that was based on treating Australia as if it was empty, without any systems of law, when it was first occupied by Europeans.[209] It was now known that this did not represent the truth of the situation and the existence of Aboriginal systems of law had also been established in Australian law.[210] Previous judgments had assumed that when the Crown took radical title for the land (that is, all ownership of land was legally derived from the Crown), it had also assumed full beneficial title (that is, it really owned the land, so extinguishing all the title of the First Peoples). The question that Brennan J asked was: is it possible to make a judgment that recognized the Crown's radical title, but denied that it held full beneficial title (so that the title of the First Peoples had not been automatically extinguished in Australian law), without fracturing the skeleton of Australian law?[211] His opinion, and that of the majority of the judges in the case, was that it could.[212] Moreover, justice required such a judgment to be made if it could be.[213] Because the Crown still held radical title, wherever it had extinguished the title held by First Peoples, that extinguishment remained sound under Australian law.[214] That is, "native title" was a remnant title and it only existed where it could be proved that it had not been extinguished. "Native title," according to the judgment, did not conform to traditional common law titles, but was unique, or *sui generis*.[215] It was also adjudged that, apart from some small areas which had been subject to leases, the native title to the Murray Islands had not been extinguished.

Clearly, the majority judgment opened up the possibility of bringing other cases concerning the continuing existence of native title. The *Native Title Act 1993*, discussed below, was enacted in order to facilitate this process in such a way that claimants did not face costly legal battles. Also, the case brought by the Wik peoples of Queensland, discussed below, opened up the possibility that native title had not been extinguished in as many cases as had been thought. Before moving on to discuss the act and the Wik case, it is worth considering some of the responses to the *Mabo (2)* judgment.

Any judgment is an interpretation of the material which is brought before the court, and Dawson J, in dissenting from the majority of the bench, argued that the correct interpretation of what had happened in the past was that there was a clear political intention that the Crown held full beneficial title of the land and so all title held by First Peoples had been automatically extinguished at occupation by the British. Even though it was unpalatable to do so, the present court had to uphold this principle, until there was a political change enacted by the government.[216]

Although the majority judgment within *Mabo (2)* was operating firmly within the remit of the law, the judgment by Dawson J rightly points out that the majority judgment had significant social and political consequences, although only over land where it could be proved that native title had not been extinguished. There was an inevitable political furor,[217] some of which was ill-founded because it missed the point that the judgment did not disturb the title of others over land where native title had been extinguished. The primary charge against the majority judgment was that it was an example of "judicial activism," that the court went beyond its remit and made a *political* rather than a *legal* decision.[218] However, this misses the point that the court was operating firmly within the legal framework, and *either* decision that the court could have made was going to have political consequences: if the majority judgment had sided with Dawson J, then it would have had equally radical consequences, effectively ending the possibility for the First Peoples to pursue their rights to land in the Australian legal system. It can be argued that the decision that the court did make was the more just of the two decisions that it could have made, given the present understanding of what has happened in The Land since occupation by the British.

It is important to recall that, although the *Mabo (2)* judgment had an effect on the land rights of all of the First Peoples in Australia, the concept of land tenure in the Torres Strait Islands is significantly different to that in Aboriginal cultures.

It was seen above that the process in the *Milirrpum* case was criticized. In a similar way, the *Mabo (2)* case was criticized, both for the process and also for how the judges understood the evidence. Nonie Sharp had worked in the Torres Strait Islands since 1978 and contributed to the case from its earliest days. Her book, *No Ordinary Judgment*, aims to show that the Meriam people were not heard properly at vital points in the case. She believes that: they were belittled; they were asked questions in a logic which was alien to them, and did not allow for subtle explanation; their metaphorical system of knowledge was not understood;[219] their oral culture, in particular, the oral handing down of property rights, was classed as hearsay and so not properly admissible evidence, even though the written form of documentation that was required by white people, and kept to a certain extent, was understood by the Meriam people as being of less importance than oral instructions; they were constantly interrupted with objections to their evidence by the defense team (for example, Eddie Mabo gave evidence over ten days, which was recorded in 536 pages of transcript and his evidence attracted 289 objections from Queensland[220]);[221] the court would not recognize Malo's law as a valid system of law;[222] and there was incomprehension as to how it could function to solve land disputes, that is, that it could not be a real system of law.[223]

Some people took a creative response to the *Mabo (2)* judgment. An outstanding example of this happened in the Cape York area. In 1994, the cattlemen's convention decided to try to reach a land use agreement with the Aboriginal People. Noel Pearson and some of his fellow First Peoples accepted the invitation to attend the 1995 convention. In November 1995 a working party was established to produce an agreement. After eleven meetings between the Cattlemen's Union and the Cape York Land Council, with the Australian Conservation Foundation and the Wilderness Society joining part way through the discussions, an agreement was reached and signed within three months. It then faced a long delay because the Queensland government refused to ratify it, even though it was supported by successive Commonwealth governments. Finally, when a new Queensland government was elected in 2001, the original signatories were still happy with it, so the government ratified it, and the agreement came into effect.[224]

The *Native Title Act 1993* (Cth): Responding to *Mabo (2)*

The Hawke Labour government was elected in 1983 in part on a platform of implementing national, uniform land rights legislation. The idea was to create national legislation like that of the *ALR Act* in the Northern Territory, but the government abandoned the idea in 1986 due to political pressure.[225] Seven years later, the *Mabo (2)* judgment meant that First People's ownership of land could be recognized under Australian common law, and the consequences of this judgment had to be worked out. It was now possible for First Peoples to pursue the recognition of their ownership of land through the normal workings of the law, rather than needing special legislation, in the limited case that native title had not been extinguished by a superior grant by the Crown.[226]

Labor Prime Minister Paul Keating heralded the *Mabo (2)* decision as "a large step towards reconciliation and away from the injustice dealt to Aborigines over 200 years,"[227] when on December 10, 1992, he launched the International Year for the World's Indigenous Peoples with a speech in Redfern.[228] In this speech, he declared,

> *Mabo* is an historic decision. We can make it an historic turning point, the basis of a new relationship between indigenous and non-Aboriginal Australians. The message should be that there is nothing to fear or to lose in the recognition of historical truth, or the extension of social justice, or the deepening of Australian social democracy to include indigenous Australians. There is everything to gain.[229]

Because pursuing each claim through the courts would be very expensive, a three-staged process was planned as a response to the *Mabo (2)* judgment: land legislation, an Indigenous Land Fund to enable First Peoples to purchase their land where they could not have their ownership recognized under the legislation, and social justice measures.[230] The land legislation materialized as the *Native Title Act 1993* (Cth), and the Indigenous Land Fund was set up,[231] but the social justice measures were not tackled before the Keating government was replaced by the Howard government.

Noel Pearson, an Aboriginal leader and the director of the Cape York Land Council, explained the position of some First Peoples in an article in *The Australian* newspaper on June 8, 1993. It was not, he wrote, sufficient to treat native title the same as other interests:

> Yet to compare Aboriginal rights to the rights of others not discriminated against in the past 200 years is not appropriate. So much has been lost that Aboriginal people are entitled to expect special protection for what remains. There needs to be positive acknowledgement of different treatment of Aboriginal title which reflects the fact that Aboriginal culture is inseparable from the land to which Aboriginal title attaches. The loss or impairment of that title is not simply a loss of real estate, it is a loss of culture . . . The IDC [Inter-Departmental Committee of officials, set up to prepare the legislation] has assumed that to treat Aboriginal equally and "no less favourably" than other titles means Aboriginal title must be treated like "normal" titles. The fallacy of this approach is that strict adherence to the notions of formal equality compounds inequality because it fails to acknowledge the legitimacy of difference, particularly of culturally distinct minorities.[232]

The political process for reaching the *NT Act* was bloody, inflammatory, and vitriolic.[233] Various points in the proposed act were hotly contested by Aboriginal organizations[234] and the act was nearly scuppered by a change of Federal Government, but the Labor Party won an unexpected victory on March 13, 1993. As an example of the degree of hostility to the *Mabo (2)* judgment and the proposed legislation, the premier of Western Australia, Richard Court, suggested that the *RD Act* should be watered down (recall that it was crucial in establishing the first *Mabo* case), and he embarked on a campaign in which he falsely suggested that suburban backyards throughout the state were under threat from *Mabo (2)*.[235] He argued that the "original *Mabo* ruling was flawed and discriminated against all Australians in the State."[236] Playing on fear and fostering the belief that non-Indigenous Australians are victims of policies that wrongly advantage Indigenous Peoples have been recurrent themes in Australian politics.[237] The political move would not be used unless it worked. The mining industry also was particularly vociferous in its opposition to any legislation. "Under the heading *Mabo—Protect Your Children's Future*, it urged that 'all Australians must be equal'; rejected 'special rights and privileges based on race,' and called for the restoration of the 'principle of equality.'"[238]

The *NT Act* received royal assent on December 24, 1993, and largely took effect from January 1, 1994. The act went through a bitter revision process and was significantly revised by parliament in 1998 as a result of the *Wik* judgment. The *Wik* judgment will be discussed in the next section, and the revisions to the act in the following one. Before doing this, there are some important observations to be made about the act and how it was interpreted.

The *NT Act* formally extinguished native title for Crown grants made before January 1, 1994, or through legislation before July 1, 1993 (ss 11, 15).[239]

The act encouraged agreements about land use by mediation and negotiation, rather than resorting to the time-consuming and expensive process of deciding claims through the courts. Under the act, the National Native Title Tribunal (NNTT)[240] was set up to help mediate claims to native title, agreements over the use of Indigenous lands, and future acts.[241] Claimants had to approach the NNTT in the first instance to see if their claim met the conditions for it to be considered. If it did, then it would be registered with the Federal Court. A period of negotiation would then ensue, with the aim that as many claims as possible would be settled by the mediation offered by the NNTT. A handbook about the mediation process was produced for the NNTT.[242]

Several shortcomings have become evident in the working of the NNTT. Firstly, the system is working very slowly. In 2005, Fred Chaney, a deputy president of the NNTT, estimated that it would take another thirty years to clear the backlog at the current rate of working.[243] Not only is this delay frustrating, but death and illness during this period may compromise the ability of some groups to establish native title.

Secondly, it was envisaged that contact between the claimants and other interested parties would be an important part of the process. However, the mediation manual for the NNTT notes that it is increasingly the case that parties are represented by legal or other representatives, and sometimes one person represents more than one party. They note that this goes against the spirit of the process:

> Legal or other representatives may not have instructions or may not be suited to convey their clients' perspectives and emotions in the story telling part of the process. For Indigenous parties, mediation may be understood as an opportunity

to explain and contextualise both their ongoing culture and their cultural loss. The concomitant opportunities for genuine cathartic and cross-cultural communication of indigenous experience may be compromised where the parties are not participating directly in the mediation process. This can have a negative effect on mediation.[244]

Thirdly, the Indigenous parties may be swamped by the number of other interested parties. The NNTT must notify all such parties, and their experience is that they have had to make as few as three notifications, typically between 10 and 200, but in an extreme case in Victoria there were 4,113, and in South Australia there was a case requiring 5,409.[245]

Fourthly, although the process is supposed to be designed to take into account power imbalances and to build the capacity of parties to take a full role in negotiations, it is not clear that this can be done effectively at the moment, especially as the international literature on mediation in situations of gross power imbalance is sparse.[246]

In implementing the *NT Act*, the Australian government departed significantly from what was done both in the United States of America and Canada.[247] There, the vulnerability of native title was seen to need special protection and, initially, protection was provided by giving exclusive jurisdiction concerning native title to the federal governments in both countries. Treaties and agreements were to be made which fully respected native title and its equality before law and the situation was allowed to develop in the natural way of common law. In contrast, the hastily constructed *NT Act*, having explicitly rejected the North American approach,[248] especially after the 1998 amendments, has led, in some cases, to great complexity and a very costly combative and litigious approach. Richard Bartlett concludes that "relying on the common law, without legislation, as in the United States of America and Canada, it now seems, would have been more beneficial to human rights, efficiency and productivity."[249] These observations are noted here, but it is beyond the competence of this work to make an assessment of their validity.

It is important to remember that "native title" is about the continuing existence of some rights over land and is thus significantly different from the ownership of land that was established in the *ALR Act*.

Wik: Native Title Is Not Necessarily Extinguished by the Granting of a Pastoral Lease

The *Wik* judgment was made in the High Court, following the failure of a land claim that had started in 1993. In January 1996, Drummond J, of the Federal Court, had ruled that some pastoral leases had extinguished native title. The appeal to the High Court overruled the Federal Court decision, with a majority of four to three. In summary, the majority *Wik* judgment was:

> The rights and obligations of the grantees of the pastoral leases in question depend upon the terms of the grant of the pastoral lease and upon the statute which authorised it. There was no necessary extinguishment of native title rights by reason of the grant of those pastoral leases. Whether there was extinguishment can only be determined by reference to such particular rights and interests as may be asserted and established. If inconsistency is held to exist between the rights and interests conferred by native title and the rights conferred under the statutory grants, those rights and interest must yield, to that extent, to the rights of the grantees.[250]

Recalling that "ownership" in Australian law is a bundle of rights and that several people may have conflicting rights, as discussed above, the force of the *Wik* judgment is "that the granting of a pastoral lease, whether or not it has now expired (or has been otherwise terminated), did not *necessarily* extinguish *all* native title rights that *might* otherwise exist."[251]

The primary question that the court had to answer was whether the granting of leases over the lands of the Wik and Thayorre peoples extinguished any native title rights that might have existed before the granting of the leases. The basis of the dissenting judgment was that "in the absence of any contrary indication, the use in statute of a term [lease] that has acquired a technical legal meaning is taken prima facie to bear that meaning."[252] Such a lease would normally be understood as including "the right of exclusive possession,"[253] which would necessarily result in the extinguishment of any existing native title.

The majority judgments argued that the nature of the leases in question had to be examined in detail to see their legal implications, rather than relying on the expected legal implications of them being called "leases," for they were a creature of statute, not common law.[254] What had to be determined was the nature of the possession conferred by the leases:

in particular, if this possession excluded the Wik and Thayorre peoples from continuing some forms of possession.[255] There were four principle reasons why the majority believed that the leases did not grant exclusive possession to the lessees, and hence that some of any existing native title interests will have survived the granting of the leases.[256] Firstly, it was argued that the historical documentation proved that a special sort of leasehold was being set up in Australia, which acknowledged Aboriginal rights.[257] Secondly, the leases were limited to "pastoral purposes" only, and so did not cover all the rights over the land in question.[258] There was nothing in the leases which granted the lessees a form of possession which excluded the rights and interests of the Indigenous inhabitants that derived from their traditional title.[259] Thirdly, there were a significant degree of reservation, restriction, and exceptions in the leases, such as: minerals, timber, and other materials; access; and the depasturing of stock upon a stock route.[260] Fourthly, the leases concerned vast areas and so it was unlikely that the intention was to exclude the Wik and Thayorre peoples from the land.[261] In summary, the judgment was based on the *content* of the leases, rather than the *concept* of a lease,[262] and they thus concluded that the legal intention of the leases was not to extinguish all possible native title rights.

The judgment was clear that the legal rights of lessees were not affected by it: "the holders of pastoral leases are left with precisely the legal rights which they enjoyed pursuant to the leases granted under the Land Acts 'for pastoral purposes only'. Those rights will prevail, to the extent of any inconsistency with native title."[263] That is, any clash of rights is automatically resolved in favor of the lessee, against any native title claim.

There was considerable legal debate concerning the significance of the judgment.[264] Potentially, the *Wik* judgment affected large areas of Australia under pastoral tenure.[265]

A practical consequence of *Wik* was that each lease over any parcel of land for which there was a native title claim would have to be carefully interpreted as to the extent that it restricted native title claims. Richard Bartlett notes that at the end of 2002 the High Court decisions in *Wik* and *Western Australia v Ward* ("*Ward*")[266] (see below for a discussion of *Ward*) indicated that most of the above leases did not extinguish all incidents of native title and so came under the *NT Act*. The exceptions were the perpetual leases in New South Wales, as established in *Wilson v Anderson* (2002) 190 ALR 313.[267]

Wik opened a way for negotiated coexistence, but sadly this option has not been explicitly explored in legislation.[268]

The *Native Title Amendment Act 1998* (Cth): "Bucket Loads of Extinguishment"

On March 2, 1996, a Liberal-Country Party government was elected to the Federal Parliament, led by John Howard. Part of its election platform had been the promise to reform the *NT Act*. Plans were prepared for this by October 8 of that year. Following the *Wik* judgment on December 23, 1996, there was a political storm. The furor was then further fanned by Prime Minister John Howard showing a map of Australia with the areas colored in where First Peoples might claim land, playing the fear card again.

The response of the deputy prime minister was to promise "bucket loads of extinguishment."[269] In order to do this, the government introduced its *Ten Point Plan*, outlining ten major changes to the *NT Act*.[270] The proposed changes to the *NT Act* were intended to achieve the following outcomes:

- the validation of non-Aboriginal grants from 1994 to *Wik*;
- certainty for pastoralists;
- "confirmation" of extinguishment by freehold and most leases;
- removal of impediments to the development of municipal services;
- assurance of government powers over water;
- "workability, through removing impediments to development";
- "devolution to the States and Territories"; and
- "speedy and sustainable resolution of concerns and uncertainty."[271]

The bill, reintroduced to the House of Representatives on March 9, 1998, ran to 346 pages to supplement the 147 pages of the original act. Part of the reason for this is that the High Court had ruled (*Western Australia v Commonwealth* (1995) 183 CLR 373) that the *RD Act* took precedence over the *NT Act* where there was any ambiguity, and the government wanted to make it clear that the *RD Act* was being specifically overruled at many points.[272]

The changes will not be discussed in detail here. Rather, we will examine how the interpretation of the revised act has worked out in practice below.

Such are the vagaries of parliamentary politics that the fate of the bill was in the hands of an independent senator, Brian Harradine, for neither party had a majority in the Senate. First Peoples were not included in the political process in the preparation of the *Native Title Amendment Act 1998*. The Aboriginal and Torres Strait Islander Commission (ATSIC), the peak representative body of Indigenous Peoples that was recognized by the government at that time, had no formal part in the process.[273] Mick Dodson said:

> What I see now is the spectacle of two white men, John Howard and Brian Harradine, discussing our native title when we're not even in the room. How symbolically colonialist is that?[274]

Many Aboriginal groups prepared responses to the proposed changes, even though they found it hard to have their voice heard by government.[275]

The United Nations Committee on the Elimination of All Forms of Racial Discrimination expressed concern that the *Ten Point Plan* breached the International Convention on the Elimination of All Forms of Racial Discrimination on four counts: (1) the validation of past acts which were otherwise invalid, (2) the confirmation of extinguishment provisions, (3) allowing primary producers to upgrade and change the nature of their land use without respect to native title interests, and (4) the restrictions on the right to negotiate. These provisions effect widespread extinguishment of native title and allow further extinguishment without negotiation.[276] Australia thereby became the first Western nation to be subject of an "early warning/urgent action" procedure by the United Nations.[277]

The Aboriginal and Torres Strait Islander Social Justice Commissioner argued that the changes were not only a lost opportunity to build on the coexistence envisaged by *Wik*, but were "destructive of the most valuable resource . . . trust."[278] Maureen Tehan concludes that "the overall effect of the amendments was to significantly diminish the area of land and water over which native title might exist and the areas of land or water and types of activities over which indigenous people have meaningful rights in relation to future uses,"[279] a conclusion that seems to have been born out in practice.

Ward; and *Members of the Yorta Yorta Aboriginal Community v Victoria and Others* ("*Yorta Yorta*")[280]: Retreating from *Mabo (2)*

The *Ten Point Plan* and *Native Title Amendment Act 1998* entailed a substantial denial of equality before the law, and the tenor of these changes were carried over to the judicial system.[281]

In order to understand the judgments in the High Court in these two cases, some preliminary observations need to be made. Firstly, the changes brought in by the *Native Title Amendment Act 1998* represented an explicit change in *political* will. Secondly, the government appoints the High Court judges and so, as vacancies appear, it appoints people whom it believes will support government policy. Kirby J made this point very strongly in a lecture in 2005, when he said that "if the *Mabo* case on Aboriginal land rights ... [here he lists other trials] ... had come to the High Court in its present composition, the outcomes would probably have been very different. In the business of judging, much depends on the time of one's appointment and the values of one's colleagues."[282] Thirdly, and as a consequence of this, the judgments turned on the interpretation of "native title" and "native title rights and interests" in s 223(1) of the *NT Act*:

> The expression native title or native title rights and interests means the communal, group or individual rights and interests of Aboriginal peoples or Torres Strait Islanders in relation to land or waters, where:
>
> a. the rights and interests are possessed under the traditional laws acknowledged, and the traditional customs observed, by the Aboriginal peoples or Torres Strait Islanders; and
>
> b. the Aboriginal peoples or Torres Strait Islanders, by those laws and customs, have a connection with the land or waters; and
>
> c. the rights and interests are recognised by the common law of Australia.

Although the clear intention of the Keating government when framing this act was for this to refer to the developing common law concerning native title,[283] in the absence of explicit reference to this in the act, the High Court was free to treat s 223(1) of the act as being the *definition* of *new* concepts called "native title" and "native title interests" (which, coincidentally, and confusingly, had the same name as some different concepts discussed in earlier judgments), the nature of which had to be determined by the court, by close examination of the act. This is how the High Court chose to read the act[284] and the way that the court interpreted these "definitions" in the act in the *Ward* and *Yorta Yorta* cases resulted in a significant curtailment of the way that the common law had been developing. It is worth spending a little time examining these two judgments.[285]

Ward was the first contested mainland native title determination. It concerned an area of 7,900 square kilometers in the eastern Kimberley, overlapping the border between Western Australia and the Northern Territory. The case went before Lee J in the first instance, who made a determination of the existence of native title over most of the claim area. In making his judgment, Lee J continued the development of the common law concerning native title in a way that was sympathetic to the tenor of the *Mabo (2)* and *Wik* judgments, in particular allowing for the transformation of traditional practices.[286] This judgment was largely overturned in the full Federal Court on March 3, 2000. An appeal to the High Court was made in March 2001, and it delivered its judgment on August 8, 2002. The effect of the judgment was to overturn many of the features of the *Wik* judgment. In summary, the key aspects of the judgment were:

- *Frozen rights:* native title was treated as a distinct sort of title. In particular: the customary rights given by traditional laws were not to be counted as equivalent to ownership under common law; it rejected Aboriginal rights over mineral and petroleum resources; it required the statement of which particular rights the people had over the area, rather than granting them a bundle of rights; and the rights were those which existed in 1788, so that the development of rights over time was ruled out.

- *Principles of extinguishment:* the requirement to show that there was a clear and plain intention to extinguish native title in any leases was ignored, instead using an aspect of the *NT Act* (Pt 2 Div 2B) to override this requirement; when there was inconsistency, extinguishment would be to the extent of the inconsistency; and temporary suspension was regarded as equivalent to extinguishment.

- *Vesting of reserves:* the vesting of land in reserves was seen to lead to the extinguishment of title.

- *Pastoral leases:* the court ignored the requirement of the existence of a clear and plain intention for extinguishment in the granting of pastoral leases.
- *The NT Act:* the judgment declared that the *NT Act* was determinative in any native title claim, and in developing common law, rather than the common law judgments of *Mabo (2)* and *Wik* interpreting the *NT Act*.[287]

The claim in *Yorta Yorta* was for various public lands and waters in northern Victoria and southern New South Wales, on either side of the Murray River. In summary, the judgment was that "tides of history" had wiped away the claim.[288]

Like the *Ward* claim, the *Yorta Yorta* claim went through three levels of the court system,[289] but, unlike the *Ward* claim, it was rejected at each level. The first hearing of the case was before Olney J. He was clear that there was no "warrant within the Native Title Act for the Court to play the role of social engineer, righting the wrongs of past centuries and dispensing justice according to contemporary notions of political correctness rather than according to law."[290] The High Court decision was largely in accord with the original judgment by Olney J. The key features of the High Court judgment are that:

- "traditional" in s 223(1) of the *Native Title Act 1993* was interpreted to mean the laws and customs that existed on or before the assertion of sovereignty by the British Crown;
- the society which had these laws and customs must have continued in existence, and that the laws and customs from before the occupation by the British must have continued undisturbed; and
- the onus on proving that the laws and customs had been maintained was placed firmly on the claimants, without any presumption of continuity.[291]

A feature of the judgment was that it left undisturbed the preference shown by Olney J for the written evidence of Europeans over the oral tradition of the Yorta Yorta people, despite the precedent given in the Supreme Court in Canada[292] that oral historical evidence must be "accommodated and placed on an equal footing with the types of historical evidence that courts are familiar with, which largely consists of historical documents."[293] Critically, some written evidence, used in a way that was ignorant of the issues in interpreting historical documents, was crucial in establishing that the practices of the Yorta Yorta people had changed.[294]

In summary, "the combined effect of the three recent cases [*Ward, Yorta Yorta, Wilson v Anderson* (2002) 190 ALR 313] is to drastically reduce the numbers of indigenous people who will be able to successfully claim native title either because native title has been extinguished over land or because of the difficulties in proving the necessary elements said to be required under s 223 of the Act."[295] Richard Bartlett comments further that the end result of the *Yorta Yorta* case "is that native title claimants in remote areas will find proof of native title very difficult, but in the south they are likely to find it impossible."[296] Following *Ward* and *Yorta Yorta*, there is the further possibility that previously successful native title applications will be revisited and have their rights diminished.[297]

As a postscript to the legal debate, the Yorta Yorta people persisted in their negotiations and in 2004 signed the Co-Operative Management Agreement between the Yorta Yorta Nation Aboriginal Corporation and the State of Victoria.

IV

Theological Reflection
Binding and Loosing

THIS BOOK HAS BEEN exploring the explanatory power of bound willing as a way of understanding how the First Peoples in Australia still experience themselves as being under siege even when good is planned. It has been argued that the proclamation of sovereignty over The Land on behalf of the British Crown without regard to the First Peoples was a part of the Root Sin, part of its failure to engage with the First Peoples in their full humanity. This Root Sin had several aspects, including: failure to acknowledge the sovereignties of the First Peoples, failure to recognize their systems of law, and failure to recognize their relationships to The Land, which are very different to the concept of "ownership" in what has become Australian law. What follows is an analysis of how these problems have been perpetuated or deviated from in the legal cases and legislation that were discussed in the previous section.

The discussion in my thesis did not give due weight to the significant movements away from the Root Sin in the above history.[298] It is hoped that this discussion gives a more accurate analysis of what has happened, so honoring all those who worked so generously for the welfare of the First Peoples in Australia.

When the Yolngu took the Commonwealth government to court, what did not happen was an equal discussion between the two systems of law, the law of the Aboriginal People of that land and the Australian law. Instead, the Australian law saw its role as seeing if the claims made by the Yolngu could be recognized within the Australian law; sovereignty could not be discussed. This is a clear perpetuation of the situation that was created by the Root Sin and it immediately limits the possible outcomes. In the argument for his judgment, Blackburn J recognized that the legal foundation of the Australian legal system was contrary to facts, at least as they were now understood, but his judgment had to be "not one of fact but of law" and he was thus constrained to make a judgment within the legal system.[299] His judgment was a partial loosing of the binding in that he recognized, for the first time in Australian law, that the Australian legal system could recognize the laws of the Yolngu. This was a partial uprooting of the Root Sin.

The *Aboriginal Land Rights (Northern Territory) Act 1976* sought to enshrine this judgment in law, so enabling First Peoples to have their ownership of land recognized, where a previous action had not given title to others. At first sight, this appears to be a deliberate turning away from the ownership aspect of the Root Sin. There are, however, significant ways, outlined in the discussion of the act above, in which the act continued the ways of the past:

- It further entrenched the idea in public consciousness, although maybe not in law, of First Peoples having to be "traditional," thus making it harder for other groups to have their ownership of land recognized.
- Any other form of title was seen as overriding the title that could be claimed by the First Peoples and the act ratified large areas where it was not possible for the First Peoples to claim title.
- The act did not take proper account of the complexity of the First People's relationships to land, enshrining inheritance of responsibilities based on patrilinear descent and ignoring the role of women in relationship to land.
- It set up structures to manage the land which were alien to the laws of the people who were given a form of title over it.
- It took no account of the disruption due to the activities of Subsequent Peoples since 1788.

Whilst the third point was ameliorated over time, it remains true that the effect of this act was only a partial turning away from the Root Sin, and then only in quite limited circumstances, whilst also setting up structures which potentially caused harm.

The narratives of all the High Court judges in the *Mabo (2)* judgment make it clear that up until then the series of judgments about land rights had understood that the Crown gained ownership of The Land on the proclamation of sovereignty. The main disagreement between judges was whether they had to continue making the same judgment, perpetuating the Root Sin and its effects, or they could change this in some way. The majority made an ethical decision and said that the Crown did not acquire ownership of all The Land on the proclamation of sovereignty and so "native title" still existed to the extent that it had not been extinguished by some other action of the Crown. The *Native Title Act 1993* sought to enshrine these observations in law. The judgments and the act were picking away at two aspects of the Root Sin, but they did not sever the roots, for the following reasons:

- The act ratified the extinguishment of native title in many areas.
- It was envisaged that native title claims would be established by mediation and ratified by the courts, but every native title claim up until the end of the study had been challenged in the courts, at great cost to the claimants.[300]
- Whether in mediation or in court, First Peoples are working in an alien environment for settling disputes and they tend to have fewer resources than others.[301]
- Decisions in the courts were driven by the political leanings of the judges involved.
- After the *Wik* judgment, there was a deliberate political decision to both raise the bar of proof for claims and also to weaken the package of rights that came with native title, so retreating firmly in the direction of the Root Sin.
- "Native title" is *sui generis*, not the same as the usual title conferred in Australian law, and it has proved to be a weak form of title;[302] it is not the same as ownership.

Although the *Wik* judgment gave Australia a second chance to formally explore what the coexistence of rights might mean, this was emphatically turned down by the politicians of the day,[303] who took the opposite course, without even the pretense of trying to do what was best for the First Peoples.

Some believe that it was a political mistake to put so much resource into this process.[304] As was noted before, pursuing land rights through the courts was always going to be a limited exercise: "native title is all about what is left over. And land rights have never been about the dispossession of the colonizers and their descendants. Whether it be statutory land rights or common law land rights—these land rights have always focused on remnant lands."[305] Graeme Neate, during his office as president of the Native Title Tribunal, rightly said, "It is my view that far too great a weight of expectation has been put on native title to deliver what it was not capable of delivering. There are areas of Australia where native title will deliver little or nothing."[306] Who knows what progress might have been made if resources had not been put into a battle against land claims and a different attitude had prevailed?[307]

Pursuing the recognition of the ownership by First Peoples through the Australian legal system is a limited exercise, because Australian law was based on the nonrecognition of Indigenous systems of law. Gillian Cowlishaw rightly puts her finger on part of the problem when she criticizes the approach of Nancy Williams in her book following the failure of the *Milirrpum* case:

> Perhaps the strongest defence of liberal humanist anthropology still comes from the appeal to knowledge as the source of liberation from oppressive relations. For instance, when Williams alluded to the difficulty of "explaining the concepts of one culture in the language of another"[308] she was trying to improve the chances of the Yolngu in their struggle to gain control over land. Their chances in the original Blackburn case were inhibited, she argues, by the Court's ignorance of their system of land tenure, and Williams's book is intended to overcome this nescience. The good intentions behind such authors' work are clear, but they are vitiated by lack of attention to the context in which their endeavours are situated. Much intellectual energy is expended in explaining and defending Aboriginal culture and little on who it is being explained to and defended from.
>
> It is the humane but naïve face of liberal egalitarianism which assumes that discrimination, domination and exploitation flow from the limited information about the "Other" in the colonial world.[309]

That is, the law is not neutral, but it is part of the dominant culture and was based on an untruth about relationship between First Peoples and The Land, and so pursuing rights through the legal system will only allow a limited change. In the words of Wayne Atkinson, "in the final analysis, it seems that it is not so much a question of the law providing justice for Indigenous people but one of how justice can be achieved against existing barriers ... [the law] becomes the instrument of power that is used to serve the vested interests of settler society and to maintain the status quo. Under these conditions, it is the power dynamics between the dominator and the controlled, and notions of racial superiority that continue."[310] John Bradley and Kathryn Seton write, "whilst acknowledging the relationships between Indigenous people in Australia and the colonizing state have changed over the last few decades, there are still practices embedded within decolonizing institutions that are meant to reverse the colonizing process but, in fact, sustain it ... Thus, we have a situation of what could be called benign conquest and contestation, a situation that will continue as long as the final arbitrator of the legislation is based within white parliamentary structures."[311]

In summary, the Root Sin had several aspects, including: failure to acknowledge the sovereignties of the First Peoples, failure to recognize their systems of law, and failure to recognize their relationship to the land, which is very different to the concept of "ownership" in what has become Australian law. It became clear very early on that the courts and legislature were not going to consider sovereignty over The Land. The acts and legal judgments have recognized the existence of the laws of First Peoples and some remnant title, but this has neither been properly enshrined nor protected in Australian law. At times, there have been vitriolic and hostile retrenchments into the Root Sin. Although the roots may have been damaged, they remain firmly in place.

As a way of concluding this study on a more positive note, although the process of pursuing land rights through the courts has had limited legal results, it could be argued that these long arguments have led to a significant change in Australian culture, which are steps along the road towards repentance, and an indication of a desire for a deeper repentance by the Subsequent Peoples. For example, in his role as deputy president of the National Native Title Tribunal, Fred Chaney has noticed that groups are working outside the statutory structures to create new agreements and relationships that work for them. He has seen a change to a culture of negotiation and agreement-making and some mining companies have made it corporate policy to negotiate agreements with First Peoples groups, focusing on relationships rather than a narrow interpretation of the legislation.[312] Marcia Langton and Lisa Palmer note that "because of the administrative regime, governments are being forced to treat with Aboriginal People in a variety of ways. We thus find that by default Aboriginal people are, through the cumulative effect of native title determinations both by Tribunal and by the Federal Court, being treated as peoples."[313] There have also been some real advances in Indigenous and non-Indigenous people working together on managing land.[314]

Because the discussion in legislation and in the courts has focused almost exclusively on "ownership" as understood in non-Indigenous law, the deeper questions about human relationships to land have been largely unaddressed. It could be argued that some of the damaging changes wrought on the Australian landscape through various economic practices have arisen precisely because of land being seen in an economic rather than spiritual way.[315] The devastating bushfires at the end of 2019 and beginning of 2020 were due in part to the failure to manage the ecosystem in the way that it had been managed for millennia by the First Peoples. Without addressing these issues, the silent conquest of The Land continues.[316] The Aboriginal assertion that the Australian legal system is "lawless" can, in part, be understood in this way.

Second Movement

Loosing

It was seen in the First Movement that bound willing can cause actions that are damaging to others, even when trying to do what is good. It was also seen that turning towards the generosity of God enables the releasing of the bound will. The purpose of the Second Movement is to explore this movement in more detail.

The theological concept of bound willing was introduced in the First Movement, Binding. It was argued there that the failure to recognize the full humanity of the First Peoples and their relationship to The Land bound the will of those Subsequent Peoples, who later became the nation of Australia, so that, even when good was desired, harm was often done. This failure of recognition was called the Root Sin. The theology also helped us see that this could only be understood in reference to the overflowing love of God, where the bound will stops the flow of life that comes from a worshipful response to God, but that we can turn away from those things which have bound us and towards God to be freed from those things which have held us. A bound will does not mean that we become incapable of good, but that there is always the danger of bad coming from good intentions. The Intermezzo was an extended study that looked at how this worked its way out in the history of relationships in legislation and the courts of Australia with their focus on The Land. This study was a big enough example to see how complex the situation is, where there was significant movement in undoing the Root Sin as well as explicitly willed reinforcement of it, continuing the sin of the past into the future. The Second Movement, Loosing, contains further theological development so that we can more clearly understand the process of turning away from those things which have bound our will in order to receive the freedom that God gives.

What can be done when something wrong has been done that cannot be undone? This is a serious question. Even something as trivial as stealing a small item cannot be undone simply by returning the stolen item, because there has been a breach of trust and so the people involved must work to restore the damaged relationship. What can be done, then, for something which happened a long time in the past and still continues to affect the way that we behave today, such as the failure to recognize the humanity of the residents of The Land and their law? Clearly, an apology is not enough, because it does not change the underlying dynamic.

The biblical word for what is needed is *repentance*. Repentance is not just a transaction between human beings and God, for something has to be done about the damage that was caused by our actions. Thus, repentance is more than just apologizing to God, or confession, as it is sometimes called, for it requires actions that seek to put things right with the parties who have been damaged. The goal of repentance is to put things right in such a way that there can be a restoration of the relationships that were damaged. This is a much deeper concept than apology and it involves an openness to an unknowable future, where those involved are willing to be changed by the process, as they seek to make peace with those who have been harmed.

Repentance is one half of the movement. The other is *forgiveness*. Again, this is much more than simply accepting an apology. Things may need to change because of what has been done and those who are forgiving have a voice in what needs to change. The root idea of forgiveness is letting go, of not allowing the future to be determined by the past, so it is not about retribution. God's forgiveness is generative in that it makes it possible to forgive.

In order to break the pattern of behaviors that continue to damage the First Peoples in Australia, the Subsequent Peoples need to repent of the Root Sin of not recognizing both the humanity of the people of The Land and also their law, and the First Peoples need to forgive. It is unlikely that this process can be anything less than a renegotiation of the relationship of the Australian law to the laws of the First Peoples. Some would call this a *treaty*. But care has to be taken when using words like "treaty," because this is a term which is used in many different ways and any treaty will only be safe if it results from the process of coming together in repentance and forgiveness; anything less will continue to perpetuate the effects of the Root Sin.

Many in Australia have talked about and worked for *reconciliation*. The problem with reconciliation is that it has never been properly defined and so people should be wary of anyone pursuing this without defining the term. As has been demonstrated so far in this book, any process which does not come from a place of repenting of the Root Sin is going to further damage the First Peoples, and so all the peoples, in Australia. It was the apostle Paul who first used the word *reconciliation* in Christian theological discourse. He took a word from the political discourse of his day which was used to describe processes where often all that was happening was that the more powerful party was continuing its oppression of the weaker party. Paul introduced several innovations into how he used the word in what he wrote, which completely turned it on its head and also made it a word of hope, because God is at work in the world to liberate the world from bound willing. It will prove valuable to uncover this way of understanding reconciliation as another way of looking at what needs to be done in Australia.

Theologically speaking, reconciliation is prior to *justice*; that is, it is the process of reconciliation that delivers the deepest concept of justice. Loosely speaking, different forms of so-called justice predefine the nature of repentance and how much repentance there can be, and so they are fundamentally limited. For example, a justice system which simply determines whether someone has committed a certain act and then punishes that person if found guilty does not allow for any repentance and has no benefit for either the guilty party or the damaged party. It is in seeking reconciliation, the dance of repentance and forgiveness, that a deep justice arises as a gift of God, a justice that cannot be imagined at the beginning of the process of seeking to be reconciled.

There has been a distinctive change in culture in Australia over the past few decades, so that organizations and individuals are adopting different ways of working, critically listening to First Peoples, and sometimes putting right wrongs of the past. In terms of the metaphor of the Root Sin, these are like lopping off some of the branches which are nourished by the roots. There has, however, been a continual and sustained and conscious refusal to address the Root Sin. This must be born in mind as the theology is developed in the following sections.

Forgiveness and repentance will be explored more fully in section I below. The major purpose of that section is to give a thicker description of repentance, which will set the stage for section III, where we will return to how Australia might repent of the Root Sin of the Australian occupation of The Land.

In order to be able to think even more clearly about how radical repentance might have to be, section II will study Paul's relationship with the church in Corinth, as expressed in his letters preserved as 1 and 2 Corinthians in the Bible.[317] Because of the problems in Corinth, which include enmity and discord, Paul borrows a term from the political discourse of his day, namely, *reconciliation*, but makes several critical changes to the standard meaning of the term when he uses it himself. So the purposes of that section are twofold: firstly, to recover a deeper theological account of what the term reconciliation can mean because it has become so hackneyed and tired in recent Australian history, so much so that people no longer want to hear about it, when, in fact, when properly understood, it is a key concept in the liberation of all the peoples of The Land; and secondly, to give a deeper account of the nature of repentance.

This work will be brought together in section III, where we look at how to respond to the Uluru Statement from the Heart in a way that truly repents of the Root Sin.

I

Forgiveness and Repentance

FORGIVENESS AND REPENTANCE BELONG together; together, they are aimed at the restoration of relationships. Usually, forgiveness and repentance are not a simple, single event, but processes that take time. In a conflict situation, it is normal for both parties to need to both repent and forgive. Miroslav Volf gives a helpful image for the process of forgiveness and repentance, namely, an embrace. At the beginning of the process, both parties are expressing their desire to repent and to forgive, which is like each party opening its arms, ready to embrace. Then there is the move towards each other, which is the process of each party working out what repentance and forgiveness might look like in the particular situation. If this can be agreed, then relationships can be restored, the embrace can take place.[318] Clearly, many situations are extremely complex and have a long history, which may be centuries old, and so there may need to be multiple levels of repentance and forgiveness.

We will look at repentance and then forgiveness. Repentance is often reduced to apology or confession. These are the first steps of the process of repentance, but repentance is a much deeper concept, involving putting right the wrong. God's offer of forgiveness makes human forgiveness possible. Even more, God's offer of forgiveness makes human forgiveness an imperative. Forgiveness sets us free from those things which have bound us and opens the way to the future which is not bound by the past. Forgiveness and repentance are inseparable and there can be no forgiveness without repentance.

Repentance

Repentance is a central theological concept in the Old Testament. The root word is שׁוּב (šwb). Its root meaning is "to turn" and can mean either turning away or turning towards. In some texts it is the turning away which is in view whilst in others the turning to is in view. It is often used in terms of turning away from sin and/or turning towards God. Jeremiah 3:22—4:2 captures all these meanings: acknowledging the lordship of God (3:22, 25); admitting wrongdoing and its delusion (3:23); admission of sin, critically both of the present generation and their ancestors (3:25); admitting, even physically inhabiting, their shame (3:25); and ceasing their former ways in order to live in truth, justice, and uprightness (4:1-2).[319] The prophetic writings in particular are calling people back to live in covenant faithfulness to God, to ways of living that are consonant with the revelation of the Torah. God's gracious action often exceeds people's willingness or ability to repent. Such is God's love that, again and again, God works to bring righteousness in spite of people's failure in their response. Sometimes this is expressed as being because God has compassion on the people (e.g., Jeremiah 31:20), or because of God's honor (e.g., Ezekiel 36:22-38).

The word שׁוּב is also used of God. For example, using this human language of God, Amos list the following sins of the nations for which God will not turn away from judgment: atrocity (1:3), forced removal or peoples from their land and into slavery (1:6), breaking of a treaty and handing over entire communities into slavery (1:9), unforgiveness and violent retribution (1:11), the ripping open of the bodies of pregnant women (1:13), and insulting an enemy by desecration of his remains (2:1). In the case of the people of Judah, they have rejected the Torah, not keeping its statutes, and are being led astray by the same lies as their ancestors (cf. bound willing) (2:4); they exploit and sell the poor; they pervert sexual practices; and they try to invoke the blessing of God by inappropriate means (2:6-8). On the other hand, the repentance of people and nations leads to God's turning away from plans of destructive judgment. This dynamic is explored especially in the book of Jonah.

Repentance allows the flourishing of both human beings and the land (e.g., Hosea 14:4-7), a reversal of the desertification of the land and the healing of humanity (e.g., Isaiah 35), a return to life (e.g., Ezekiel 37), and, where punishment for sin was understood as exile from the land, a return to the land (e.g., Jeremiah 16:15; 31:16; Ezekiel 11:17; 20:34, 41–42; 34:13; 36:24; 37:21; 39:27–28).

Because repentance entails returning to covenant faithfulness, the Old Testament does not always specify the nature of repentance, but it often implies that some form of concrete action must be undertaken.[320] Three examples of repentance requiring some form of restitution will now be briefly examined. They have been chosen because they have resonances with the situation in Australia.

For the first example, consider Isaiah 5:8–10:

> Ah, you who join house to house, who add field to field, until there is room for no one but you, and you are left to live alone in the midst of the land! The Lord of hosts has sworn in my hearing: Surely many houses shall be desolate, large and beautiful houses, without inhabitant. For ten acres of vineyard shall yield but one bath, and a homer of seed shall yield a mere ephah.

Note how sin results in the land becoming unfruitful. In reading this, it is important to recall that God's pronouncement of judgment is supposed to drive people to repentance.[321] The nature of repentance is not specified here, but it is clear that it must be more than refraining from further accumulation of land. Even an apology would be insufficient, because it would leave the people continuing in their state of sin. Therefore, repentance must include undoing the accumulation of land, and this requirement perhaps echoes the jubilee legislation (Leviticus 25).[322]

As a second example of repentance requiring action, consider God's judgment on those who are living a lavish lifestyle that is sustained by the exploitation of the poor (e.g., Amos 4:1–12; 6:4–7). Here God escalates disaster in order to bring people to repentance (Amos 4:10), but the rich are able, to a certain extent, to shield themselves from the disaster affecting others (Amos 6:4–6), not worrying about others (Amos 6:6), and they have not repented (Amos 4:10). Again, repentance means taking action that expresses a genuine grief over what is happening to the land and its people (e.g., Amos 6:6), which can only be achieved by changing the unjust economic system.

As a third and final example of repentance involving doing something, consider Isaiah 58, where the people's fasting does not express repentance,[323] but rather masks a complete lack of repentance (Isaiah 58:3). Here it is very clear that repentance is not just stopping doing wrong, but undoing the results of sin (e.g., Isaiah 58:6–7, 9–10, 13).

Turning to the New Testament, the first words that Matthew records John the Baptist as saying are, "Repent, for the kingdom of heaven has come near" (Matthew 3:2), and the first words of Jesus' public ministry are identical (Matthew 4:17). Similarly, in Mark, John the Baptist appears, baptizing in the wilderness, "proclaiming a baptism of repentance for the forgiveness of sins" (Mark 1:4), and the first words of Jesus are, "The time is fulfilled, and the kingdom of God has come near; repent and believe in the good news" (Mark 1:15). In Luke also, John the Baptist calls people to repentance (Luke 3:3).

Looking more carefully at the text, we see that John the Baptist was calling people to turn away from their sins because of the proximity of judgment (Matthew 3:7–10 // Luke 3:7–9).[324] This was being addressed primarily to people of Israel, for whom these words would have evoked the rich heritage of material in the Genesis to Malachi, which was explored above. That is, in order to understand repentance, we have to turn back to the Old Testament, as previously outlined.

In most cases, Jesus does not specify what it means to repent. Instead, the call to repent invites us to explore the rich vein of material in the Scriptures to which the first gospel readers would have had access, preserved as the books Genesis to Malachi in the Christian Bible. That is, although repenting is an imperative, the nature of repentance can more fully be understood by contemplating the Scriptures of the people to whom the call to repent was addressed. God's call was for people to turn away from their sin, and to return to covenant faithfulness, and to do what needed to be done in order to restore righteousness. Likewise, repentance in the New Testament entails turning away from sin, being (re-)integrated into the covenant community, with a lifestyle shaped by the gospel imperatives of the kingdom of God, and empowered by the Holy Spirit to do so.[325]

One example of where the nature of repentance is spelt out by Jesus is his encounter with a rich young man (Matthew 19:16–30 // Mark 10:17–31 // Luke 18:18–30). The young man asks Jesus what he must do in order to inherit eternal life. In responding to the young man, Jesus appears to quote from the Ten Commandments, sometimes known as the Decalogue, but in the Markan version there is an extra commandment: "do not defraud." Ched Myers notes that

> a closer reading [of Mark's version] reveals that there is . . . a twist in his citation. For one of the statutes listed by Jesus does not in fact appear in the Decalogue! It is "do not defraud". . . and is

dropped by Matthew and Luke.³²⁶ The reference in this addition is clearly to economic exploitation: In the Greek Bible the verb is appropriated to the act *of keeping back the wages* of a hireling ... This is our first indication that much more is being discussed in this story than the personal failure of this one man: judgment is being passed upon the wealthy class ... Judging this man to be affluent, Jesus stipulates that his wealth must be distributed to the poor ... All this emotion [the man departing gloomily] becomes clear in the light of the revelation that "he had much property". . . With this revelation, the story of the man abruptly finishes, as if the point is obvious. As far as Mark is concerned, the man's wealth has been gained by "defrauding" the poor—he was not "blameless" at all—for which he must make restitution. For Mark, the law is kept only through concrete acts of justice, not the façade of piety.³²⁷

Although one may not want to go as far as Myers in judging wealth per se, it is certainly important to note that in this particular case, where the wealth has been obtained through defrauding others, repentance includes making restitution to those who have been defrauded. Further, Jesus invites the man, once he has given away his possessions, to follow him (Mark 10:21 // Matthew 19:21 // Luke 18:22), which is the Markan word for a life of discipleship. That is, this narrative implies that being a disciple of Jesus requires the return of ill-gotten wealth. Although this man does not repent, Luke records the repentance of Zacchaeus, who volunteers to give half his wealth to the poor, and to return fourfold anything that he has taken (Luke 19:1–10).³²⁸

In the gospel accounts, Jesus goes beyond just forgiving people their sins by also, as God does in the Old Testament, bringing a righteousness that undoes the results of sin.³²⁹ Significantly, the first public words of Jesus in Luke are a reading that combines verses from Isaiah 61:1–2 and 58:6 (Luke 4:18–19). Here Jesus is proclaiming that he is going to enact God's liberation (or forgiveness, for recall that "liberate" and "forgive" are the same Greek word). One of the ways that he does this is by healing people, and setting them free from demon possession.³³⁰ That is, Jesus goes beyond requiring simply that others repent by being part of the undoing of the results of sin himself.³³¹ That Jesus sends his followers out to do the same thing (e.g., Mark 6:6b–13 // Luke 9:1–6; Matthew 28:16–20; Luke 24:44–49) means that the role of a follower of Jesus is not only to repent, and so do the things that need to be done for one's own sin, but to work as an agent of redemption in the world.

For those wishing to repent, the situation may be so overwhelmingly bad, that it is hard to know where to begin. Here, the psalms of lament are helpful, for they show how the expression of overwhelmed-ness in the presence of God can lead to clarity of vision, which then allows transformation.[332]

In summary, the biblical material stresses that repentance is imperative, and that often some form of restitution is required as part of the process of repentance, although what has to be done is often left unspecified, but the process of repentance must include paying attention to those who have been affected by what has happened and working with them to seek their welfare. This may be very costly, as it was for the man who was required to divest himself of all of his possessions. What has happened cannot be undone, but there is the hope of new beginnings made possible through repentance. Some authors make the mistake of equating apology with repentance,[333] but the biblical material has shown that repentance usually requires some actions to be taken to address the problems that have been caused.[334]

Although repentance is more than an apology, and an apology is just the start of the process of repentance, it remains the case that real apology is not easy. Geiko Müller-Fahrenholz says that the German term *Entblössung* (literally, "denuding oneself") describes something of the difficulty of apology:

> It identifies a process by which one returns to the point at which the original evil act was done. To revisit this moment implies admitting all the shameful implications of that act. It is painful to enter into this shame. It is more painful still to acknowledge this act in the face of all those who suffered it. All confessions of guilt carry with them an element of self-humiliation which runs counter to our pride and seems to threaten our self-esteem. Nobody likes to be stripped of his or her defences and to appear naked in front of others.[335]

Nicholas Tavuchis makes a similar observation:

> apology expresses itself as the exigency of a painful re-membering, literally of being mindful again, of what we were and had as members and, at the same time, what we have jeopardized or lost by virtue of our offensive speech or action . . . As shared mementos, apologies require much more than admission or confession of the unadorned facts of wrongdoing or deviance. They constitute—in their most responsible, authentic, and,

hence, vulnerable expression—a form of self-punishment that cuts deeply because we are obliged to retell, relive, and seek forgiveness for sorrowful events that have rendered our claims to membership in a moral community suspect or defeasible.[336]

Whilst apology is not the same as full repentance, it can sometimes be very powerful. For example, Martin Graham tells a story of an experience where an apology of the present members of the church for what had happened in the past created a space for the work of the present church to be welcomed, whereas there had been hostility towards it up to that point.[337] The context was a barbecue mission in Tonbridge, Kent. Each morning of the mission, people would hand out invitations to people in the street to come for a free barbecue. During the morning and during the barbecue, worship bands would be worshipping at various places around the town. However, seemingly inexplicably, there was all sorts of disruption to what was going on, a "*spiritual* climate . . . as if the people of the town didn't *like* us."[338] For example, someone hung loud speakers out a window where there was a worship band, and played obscene music; people were gratuitously rude when given an invitation to the free barbecue; and youths cycled through an evening meeting. Things like this had not happened in other towns where similar missions had taken place. A few days into the mission, there was a message in tongues during the morning worship session, which was attended by the 150 members of the team that was drawn from the various churches in Tonbridge. In the interpretation of the message, a picture emerged of what God was saying to the church: "You need to listen to Tonbridge; Tonbridge is hurting; Tonbridge has been hurt by the church."[339] As people there explored what this might mean, it emerged that some hundreds of years ago church authorities in Tonbridge had stolen the poor fund and spent it on themselves. As well, in the mid-nineteenth century, when railway workers had arrived in the town, they had been informed that they were not welcome in the church. There were other stories too, which Graham does not record. Graham concludes that "what became clear was that the contemporary generation of Tonbridge residents had, as it were, 'received' a dislike for the church, without knowing why they should have such an attitude. It was in the DNA of Tonbridge, if you like, that the church was disliked from generation to generation—a 'spiritual stronghold' if ever I saw one."[340] Later that day, when there were about three hundred people eating at the barbecue, Graham felt God say to him that he had to apologize on behalf of the church for what the church had done in the past. He went to the microphone and said, quite simply, that we had been praying and that God had shown us that the church had hurt the people of Tonbridge (I told the story of the railway workers) and that in response to this, we really wanted to say how sorry we were—if they felt able to receive this apology. I was also able to say that, in hurting people in this way, we had misrepresented the image of God and the truth was that, unlike the "no" they had received from the church, there was a "yes" for them from God.[341]

Graham records that "the atmosphere changed instantly. People were ready to receive us—and our message,"[342] and, further, that many people became Christians that day, including some of the youths who had been so disruptive with their bicycles the evening before.

There are several points from this story that are worth noting. Firstly, the story is told of corporate entities: it is the town and the church which have a broken relationship, expressed by the behavior of individuals (e.g., the person who played loud music to drown out the worship) and groups of people (e.g., the youths who cycled through an event). There was something about the way that the people in the town itself were acting as a corporate entity, expressed by Graham as a "spiritual climate." Secondly, the present generation was living out a hatred of the church, even though it may not have been conscious of either its doing so or of the roots of the problem. Graham says that the attitude was "inherited," part of the town's "DNA." Unfortunately, Graham does not explore in this story how the church's sinful history was part of its DNA, and how this worked itself out in the way that the church was continuing to behave. Thirdly, the roots of the antagonism were multiple incidents, some of them a long time ago. As was noted in the second point, there is not enough information to know if the past attitudes of the church were also being lived out in the present generation of the church, or if the offensive incidents were firmly situated in the past. Fourthly, an apology on behalf of the church, in this case by an outsider, was effective in defusing the animosity between the town and the church.[343]

In order to flesh out these ideas of apology and repentance, consider the apology given by Kevin Rudd, when Australian prime minister, in February 2008 to the "Stolen Generations."[344] The *Bringing Them Home* report, on the implementation and consequences of taking Indigenous children from their parents, was published in 1997.[345] The report brought home to many non-Indigenous people in Australia, in a very powerful way, the reality of how some First People had been treated, and the drastic consequences of this. Significantly, it was not something that had happened a long time ago, but a policy that was in place until into the 1970s.

Soon after the publication of the report, there was a large public movement, with "Sorry Books" being inscribed by people across the country, and a national "Sorry Day" was organized,[346] which included well-attended marches across major bridges in Australia as a way of saying sorry to the Indigenous Peoples in Australia. There have been "Sorry Days" on an annual basis since, although in 2005, the name was changed to "National Day of Healing," to emphasize that there is a deeper need than just apologizing.[347]

Recommendation 5a of the report was:

> That all Australian Parliaments
>
> 1. officially acknowledge the responsibility of their predecessors for the laws, policies and practices of forcible removal,
> 2. negotiate with the Aboriginal and Torres Strait Islander Commission a form of words for official apologies to Indigenous individuals, families and communities and extend those apologies with wide and culturally appropriate publicity, and
> 3. make appropriate reparation as detailed in the following recommendations.[348]

Note that the recommendation was not only for an apology, but also that suitable reparation should be made to those who suffered through the policies of separating families; that is, repentance is more than saying sorry. The repeated refusal of John Howard, the prime minister of Australia when the report was published, to make such an apology, despite apologies being issued by the state parliaments,[349] is well documented in the media. John Howard's belief was that the present generation could not be held responsible for what happened in the past,[350] and that a line needed to be drawn under the past and, instead, work should be done towards a better future.[351] However, the exploration of bound willing has shown that the relationship of the past to the future is not that simple.

John Howard's party lost the election at the end of 2007, and he also lost his seat in Parliament. One of the policy pledges of the new prime minister, Kevin Rudd, was that he would make an apology. After much consultation, in front of a carefully selected audience,[352] with a huge media presence, and with giant screens placed in public places across the country, Kevin Rudd made an apology on behalf of the people on

February 13, 2008,[353] the first action of the Forty-Second Parliament of Australia. Significantly, he recognized that the present generation of non-Indigenous Australians bears a historical burden, when he said:

> As has been said of settler societies elsewhere, we are the bearers of many blessings from our ancestors and therefore we must also be the bearer of their burdens as well. Therefore, for our nation, the course of action is clear. Therefore for our people, the course of action is clear. And that is, to deal now with what has become one of the darkest chapters in Australia's history. In doing so, we are doing more than contending with the facts, the evidence and the often rancorous public debate. In doing so, we are also wrestling with our own soul. This is not, as some would argue, a black-armband view of history; it is just the truth: the cold, confronting, uncomfortable truth—facing it, dealing with it, moving on from it. And until we fully confront that truth, there will always be a shadow hanging over us and our future as a fully united and fully reconciled people. It is time to reconcile. It is time to recognize the injustices of the past. It is time to say sorry. It is time to move forward together.[354]

In his speech, he recognized that the apology itself did not solve the problems, and he hoped that it would be the beginning of a new future for all the people in Australia:

> I know that, in offering this apology on behalf of the government and the parliament, there is nothing I can say today that can take away the pain you have suffered personally. Whatever words I speak today, I cannot undo that. Words alone are not that powerful ... But my proposal is this: if the apology we extend today is accepted in the spirit of reconciliation, in which it is offered, we can today resolve together that there be a new beginning for Australia. And it is to such a new beginning that I believe the nation is now calling us.
>
> Australians are a passionate lot. We are also a very practical lot. For us, symbolism is important but, unless the great symbolism of reconciliation is accompanied by an even greater substance, it is little more than a clanging gong. It is not sentiment that makes history; it is our actions that make history. Today's apology, however inadequate, is aimed at righting past wrongs. It is also aimed at building a bridge between Indigenous and non-Indigenous Australians—a bridge based on a real respect rather than a thinly veiled contempt. Our challenge for the future is now to cross that bridge and, in so

doing, embrace a new partnership between Indigenous and non-Indigenous Australians.[355]

In his response to Rudd's speech, the leader of the opposition, Brendan Nelson, although too issuing an apology, continued to stress the Howardian line that the present generation is not guilty for the past actions:

> Our responsibility, every one of us, is to understand what happened here, why it happened and the impact it had on not only those who were removed but also those who did the removing and supported it. Our generation does not own these actions, nor should it feel guilt for what was done in many, but certainly not all, cases with the best of intentions. But in saying we are sorry, and deeply so, we remind ourselves that each generation lives in ignorance of the long-term consequences of its decisions and actions. Even when motivated by inherent humanity and decency to reach out to the dispossessed in extreme adversity, our actions can have unintended outcomes. As such, many decent Australians are hurt by accusations of theft in relation to their good intentions.[356]

There are a number of points that need to be made about these extracts from the speeches of Rudd and Nelson. Firstly, Nelson's speech repeated the proposition that the present generation of people is not responsible for the policy of splitting Indigenous families. Whilst this is not even strictly true, for the policy only ended in the 1970s, this is to miss the point that the Stolen Generations are but one example of bad policies directed towards the Indigenous Peoples in Australia; they are part of a continuing history of problems caused for Indigenous Peoples in Australia by the non-Indigenous governments and the present generation cannot absolve themselves just because they were not directly responsible for this particular policy. As was argued in the First Movement, the present generation is caught up in the sins of the past in such a way that bad things happen even when good is intended; a failure of the present generation to repent for sins of the past will lead to it continuing policies which are destructive for the First Peoples. Secondly, good intentions cannot excuse the policy: although the intentions of many people may have been good, history has shown that the results have been disastrous and so repentance is required for what happened, even if the intentions were good. Thirdly, whilst Rudd's speech was an apology, it did not fulfill recommendation 5a of the *Bringing Them Home* report (see above), because it did not promise any form of reparation. That is, his speech failed to be a full act of repentance. Kevin Rudd, however, did detail some concrete measures to help the people who had been affected by the removals, as well as more general policies to try to tackle the significant welfare problems of First Peoples in Australia. Finally, the nature of repentance cannot be determined by the Subsequent Peoples, but must arise from engaging with the First Peoples. Some of the requirements of repentance for what was done to the Stolen Generations were made explicit in recommendation 5a of the *Bringing Them Home* report, but they were ignored in Rudd's speech. This fails to face the bigger question of what is required of the Subsequent Peoples in Australia in order to repent in full towards the First Peoples. To use an image from Rudd's speech, the Subsequent Peoples in Australia must walk over the bridge constructed by this apology and see whom they find on the other side. Regarding the Root Sin, this has not happened.

More generally, the example of the apology from Rudd shows that repentance is more than making an apology and that the nature of repentance can only be determined by engagement with the injured parties. In the case of the Stolen Generations, the authors of the report specified what they believed was the nature of repentance in this case: recommendations which arose from an extensive engagement with those who had been affected by the policies of taking children away from their families. This is an example of the principle that the nature of repentance is problem-specific, and that it can only be determined by engagement with the injured parties.

The length of a reconciliation process may need to be measured in generations rather than in years. In fact, from his experience of working on reconciliation in conflict situations, John Paul Lederach has two observations that are helpful here in thinking about reconciliation. Firstly, he has a rule of thumb that it takes as long to get out of a conflict as the conflict has been running.[357] This means that reconciliation is a long-term process. Secondly, he has shown that short-term measures only work in a culture where there is trust that they are part of a long-term strategy for reconciliation with which all parties are happy,[358] and there is, understandably, little trust of non-Indigenous people in much of the Indigenous community.[359]

To draw this section to a close, the observations concerning repentance can be summarized in the following way. Repentance is imperative, and it usually requires more than an apology; although the sin cannot be undone, which is what makes forgiveness difficult, some form of action is usually required to resolve the problems caused by the sin. In the biblical examples that were discussed, exactly what needed to be done was not always spelled out; in practice, the nature of repentance can only be determined through engagement with the injured party in the process of seeking reconciliation. The example of the Stolen Generations in Australia shows how complex, difficult, costly, and lengthy the process of repentance is in practice.

Forgiveness

Forgiveness is a concept that has escaped purely theological discourse, and is being explored within political,[360] philosophical,[361] and therapeutic frameworks.[362] In this section, the focus will be on theological formulations of forgiveness.

The life of repentance and forgiveness was an important part of the Torah and it was this conviction which drove the prophets to call the people to repent, for, as we have seen above, repentance by the nation turns God away from the inevitable judgment for its failure regarding covenant faithfulness. This was most graphically received on the Day of Atonement, which included the confession of the sins of the people over a goat, which was then driven into the desert (Leviticus 16).

In the New Testament, two main words are sometimes translated as "forgive." The first is ἄφεσις (aphesis), which has a range of meanings including release, liberation, and forgiveness: "it means to remit an offence, debt, fine or penalty, to pardon, to cease to feel resentment against."[363] The second is ἀφίημι (aphíēmi), which means to let go, leave, leave alone, release, and forgive.[364] Note that all of these are directed towards the other, not towards oneself or one's group.[365] About one-third of the occurrences of ἀφίημι in the New Testament are translated as "forgive," whilst ἄφεσις is used much less, but two-thirds of the uses are translated as "forgive." Word studies are problematic, and a careful study of the idea of forgiveness (rather than just the use of the word), would not only have to include other words from their semantic network, but would have to consider carefully the uses of these two words where they have not been translated as "forgive."[366] For example, in Luke 4:18, ἄφεσις is often translated as "release" but could be translated as "liberate." What would happen if the study of forgiveness were to be widened to consider its relationship to other concepts, such as liberation?[367]

Most of the use of these words appear in Matthew, Mark, Luke, and Acts. Elsewhere in the New Testament, other words are used for what God has made possible in Christ, not least reconciliation, which will be studied in the next section.

Four main things concerning the New Testament material will concern us here: firstly, Jesus forgave sins; secondly, forgiveness as (re-)incorporation into community; thirdly, that forgiveness is not possible without repentance; and fourthly, the imperative for human beings to forgive one another because of the experience of being forgiven by God.

One of the features of the gospel narratives is the way that Jesus forgave sins (e.g., Matthew 9:1–8 // Mark 2:1–12 // Luke 5:17–26). The people present were scandalized by Jesus pronouncing forgiveness, with Mark and Luke explicitly having them ask, "Who can forgive sins but God alone?" Part of the importance of these stories is to make a christological point, that Jesus is able to forgive sins because he is the Son of Man.

Jesus shared table fellowship with many people in the gospel narratives (e.g., Matthew 8:9–13 // Mark 2:13–17 // Luke 5:27–32; Luke 7:36–50; 11:37–54; 14:1–24; 19:1–10). Donald Shriver writes that this is one of the ways that Jesus modelled God's forgiveness.[368] For Luke, however, Jesus' indiscriminate table fellowship is not the enacting of the forgiveness of sins, but rather it is an expression of God's desire to reincorporate all people into the covenant community.[369] Luke has two contrasting narratives concerning table fellowship. In the first, 7:36–50, Jesus interprets the host's actions as failure to take hold of the forgiveness that is on offer, whereas the woman who breaks into the meal has taken hold of this forgiveness. In the second narrative, 19:1–10, Zacchaeus does take hold of forgiveness and so is reincorporated into the community (17:9), critically through his repentance. His repentance involved undoing his participation of the unjust economic practices of the Roman Empire.[370]

In Luke-Acts, forgiveness is dependent on repentance. Near the end of Luke Jesus says that "repentance and forgiveness of sins is to be proclaimed in his name to all nations" (Luke 24:47); that is, repentance and forgiveness are two halves of a process. In Luke-Acts forgiveness, reincorporation into relationship with God and with the community, is nearly always associated with repentance (e.g., Luke 3:3; 24:47; Acts 2:38; 3:19; 5:31; 8:22; 26:18, 20), and the exceptions are not significant.[371] Coming at this from another angle, we see that there seems to be an exception to Jesus forgiving the sins of others when Jesus asks the Father to forgive those who are crucifying him (Luke 23:34a), a prayer also found on the lips of Stephen as he is being stoned to death (Acts 7:60). This raises the question as to why Jesus does not forgive them himself when he has often forgiven people in other parts of the narrative. The difference between Jesus' forgiving sin in Luke 5:17–26 and, say, his handing over of the responsibility of forgiveness to his Father here escapes the notice of the major commentators.[372] In my mind, this is a critical point: Jesus is unable to forgive because the people have not repented, but he is letting go of his desire for vengeance and opening up the way for the people to be forgiven in the future, beyond his death, if they repent.[373]

Luke does not write much about human beings forgiving each other. In Luke 17:3–4, the followers of Jesus are instructed to forgive whenever there is repentance, whilst in Luke 11:4 the disciples of Jesus are instructed to pray, "forgive us our sins, for we forgive everyone who is indebted to us." Matthew, however, is stronger in his insistence on the obligation to forgive: God will only forgive people if they forgive others (Matthew 6:14–15 // Mark 11:25).[374] The foundation for this is given in the parable that Jesus tells in Matthew 18:21–35. In the parable, the king, who represents God, forgives a person a debt that can never be paid, and then that person fails to forgive a much smaller debt that is owed to him by a "fellow servant" (Matthew 18:28). The king then imprisons the person who the greater debt because he had failed to forgive his fellow servant. Jesus concludes with, "so also my heavenly Father will do to every one of you who does not forgive your brother from your heart" (Matthew 18:35). In this parable, it is God who has taken the initiative in forgiving debts, which carries with it the moral imperative for human beings to forgive each other.[375]

Besides the general command to forgive everyone, not only those in the community, Matthew is also concerned for the practice of reconciliation within the community. In Matthew 5:23–24, the worship of God cannot happen unless one is reconciled to someone who has something against one. The imperative also works the other way around, with Jesus giving a process to encourage the reincorporation of the sinner back into full fellowship in the community (Matthew 18:15–20).[376] Such a process is implementing what Jesus spoke of in the same discourse, the Matthean version of the parable of the lost sheep (Matthew 18:10–14).[377] Peter's question about forgiving, and then the parable of the unforgiving servant (Matthew 18:21–35), discussed above, stress that the person sinned against goes into this process in humility, as one who has experienced the forgiveness of God (for an unimaginably greater debt, according to

Matthew). If, in the end, the sinner refuses to be reconciled, then this does not mean that she is ostracized, but rather that she is treated with special care and attention, as someone who needs to hear the good news of Jesus.[378] This resonates with Paul's concern for the Corinthians, which will be explored in section II below.

For human beings, forgiveness is not a transaction between the individual and God, but is worked out in social and political life, within the context of God's eschatological grace.[379] Forgiving does not say that what happened does not matter, nor does it entail forgetting.[380] Rather, forgiveness recognizes that something wrong has been done. The resurrection narratives imply that Jesus was raised as forgiveness, the judgment of forgiveness,[381] and L. Gregory Jones calls forgiveness the "judgment of grace."[382] Human forgiveness implies that the future will not be controlled by the past.[383]

It is important to remember that an offense against another human being, or another community, is also a sin against God, because it is acting in the world in a way that is in opposition to the way that God is working in the world. Thus, in any situation, there are always two levels of forgiveness: the forgiveness being offered by God, and the forgiveness being offered by the party against whom the offense has been committed. It is hard to be specific in speaking about this, because the same term—forgiveness—is used of both, even though they are different, which can lead to confusion. As Volf writes:

> Only divine forgiveness actually removes guilt. When human beings forgive they (1) forgo resentment, (2) refuse to press the claims of injustice against the other and therefore also (3) bear the cost of wrongdoing. As a result of human forgiveness, the guilty is *treated* as if he or she were not guilty (to be distinguished from *defining* forgiveness itself as treating the other as if he or she had not committed the offense). But unless forgiven by God, he or she remains guilty, human forgiveness notwithstanding.[384]

In the language of this book, it is also the case that God's forgiveness sets people free from the bondage of their wills (cf. 1 John 1:8–9).

There is an important implication of this observation in the opposite direction, namely, that it is possible for a person to know forgiveness, the forgiveness of God, even if this is withheld by the offended party or the offended party is dead and unable to forgive. In the case of the offended party being dead, it will still be necessary to seek forgiveness from the surviving descendants.

It can be very difficult for human beings to forgive. Forgiveness may require the victim first of all to repent of the desire for vengeance, to refuse to reply in kind, or to refuse to be shaped by a dominant story, or to refuse to be shaped by what has been done.[385] Within the Jewish and the Christian traditions, the imprecatory psalms provide a resource for the process of reaching a place where forgiveness can win over vengeance. From a Christian standpoint, Volf writes:

> For the followers of the crucified Messiah, the main message of the imprecatory Psalms is this: rage belongs before God—not in the reflectively managed and manicured form of a confession, but as a pre-reflective outburst from the depths of the soul. This is no mere cathartic discharge of pent up aggression before the Almighty who ought to care. Much more significantly, by placing unattended rage before God we place both our unjust enemy and our own vengeful self face to face with a God who loves and does justice. Hidden in the dark chambers of our hearts and nourished by the system of darkness, hate grows and seeks to infest everything with its hellish will to exclusion. In the light of the justice and love of God, however, hate recedes and the seed is planted for the miracle of forgiveness. Forgiveness flounders because I exclude the enemy from the community of humans even as I exclude myself from the community of sinners. But no one can be in the presence of the God of the crucified Messiah for long without overcoming this double exclusion.[386]

The ability to forgive is a gift of God,[387] but it also is a craft, which must be learned. Within the Christian tradition, "forgiveness is at once an expression of a commitment to a way of life, the cruciform life of holiness in which we seek to 'unlearn' sin and learn the ways of God, and a means of seeking reconciliation in the midst of particular sins."[388] The process of forgiveness might involve lament, prophetic indictment, or even rejoicing at the sufferings brought on by faithfulness to Christ.[389]

What makes forgiveness so hard is that, in many disputes, there have been irreversible actions. What makes forgiveness hard is not just the rage at injustice and the desire for vengeance, but the "active suffering of forgiveness."[390] One simply cannot get away from the fact that forgiveness is costly, forever carrying the fact that what has been done cannot be undone.[391] Where this becomes unjust is where one party in the dispute is forced, or chooses, to forgive without an agreed process of repentance taking place. However, forgiveness is about the primary will to be reconciled, or to embrace, which is Volf's metaphor for reconciliation:

attending to justice is a precondition of actual embrace, and the will to embrace is the framework of the search for justice, so that embrace is the horizon of the struggle for justice.[392]

Sometimes, writers on forgiveness make the category mistake that because God has forgiven, human forgiveness must come before repentance in the process of reconciliation between human beings.[393] However, human relationships are a lot more complicated than that: God's offer of forgiveness opens up the possibility of reconciliation, and the process of achieving reconciliation will usually be some sort of dance involving the two parties in processes of forgiveness and repentance. Moreover, in most human conflicts it is unlikely that only one party is guilty. Further, forgiveness, and for that matter, repentance, is unlikely to be a one-off event, but is more likely to be a process.[394] The end goal of forgiveness is the restoration of communion.[395]

As just one example of forgiveness in politics, Shriver narrates the gift of the African American people to all the American people. He asks, "What makes it possible for the politically excluded to include excluders in their own political vision and then to proceed politically to weaken the powers of exclusion? How do they relate now to their political enemies in ways that hold out the possibility that the latter may yet become their civic, political friends?"[396] He argues that the overall history of the African American peoples in America shows how this is done, giving an ethic for enemies: *"the willingness to count oneself as a neighbor and fellow citizen with enemies in spite of the latter's continuing resistance to reciprocating.* In the most practical sense this *is* forgiveness in politics: 'We will be neighbors to you even while you are busy being unneighborly to us. We belong together, and one day you will know it. We will persist until you do.'"[397] This example shows that forgiveness is not necessarily passive, but it can be active in establishing justice.

Desmond Tutu reminds us that it is the present generation which can end the history of suffering by granting forgiveness for all of the past:

> If we are going to move on and build a new kind of world community there must be a way in which we can deal effectively with a sordid past. The most effective way I can think of is for the perpetrators or their descendents to acknowledge the horror of what happened and the descendants of the victims to respond by granting the forgiveness they ask for, providing something can be done, even symbolically, to compensate for the anguish experienced, whose consequences are still being lived through

today . . . If the present generation could not legitimately speak on behalf of those who are no more, then we could not offer forgiveness for the sins of South Africa's racist past, which predates the advent of apartheid in 1948. The process of healing our land would be subverted because there would always be the risk that some awful atrocity of the past would come to light that would undermine what has been accomplished thus far . . . True forgiveness deals with the past, all of the past, to make the future possible. We cannot go on nursing grudges even vicariously for those who cannot speak for themselves any longer. We have to accept that what we do we do for generations past, present and yet to come. That is what makes a community a community or a people a people—for better or for worse.[398]

It is important to emphasize again that forgiveness for all of what happened in the past can only be given if there has been repentance for all of the damage of the past, which includes the desire to be set free from the binding of the will which caused these problems.

The observations of this section about forgiveness can be summarized in the following way. Forgiveness is offered by God. This forgiveness can be received following repentance. God's prior offer of forgiveness makes human forgiveness both possible and imperative, but it does not imply that human forgiveness must come before repentance in resolving conflicts between human beings, although, where the offer of forgiveness does come first, it may be liberating for the offender. Forgiveness is aimed at the restoration of the offender, and at the restoration of relationship with the offender; it is not primarily about the well-being of the offended party, but it is nevertheless necessary for that party's well-being. Forgiveness is inherently difficult because what has been done cannot be undone.

The observations about repentance and forgiveness will be brought together after the next section, which introduces a deeper understanding of the nature of reconciliation and demonstrates that repentance may involve changing the structures of whole societies.

II

Reconciliation and Changing the Social and Economic Structures in Corinth

THE PURPOSE OF THIS section is to give an extended study of a biblical example where true repentance required a fundamental change in the way that the society worked. In order to see this, it is necessary to understand some things about the history of the city of Corinth and about how its social and economic system was organized. This will be sketched in the next few pages. Then three structural problems in the Corinthian church will be explored: factionalism, the patronage system, and the relationship of the church to Paul. These three problems will be discussed in turn. Paul believes that these issues indicate that the Corinthian church has not fully comprehended the gospel and, in fact, that the church is putting itself outside of God's grace. In order to help them to understand the severity of the situation, and because the problems involve conflicts and fractured human relationships, he borrows a term from the political discourse of his day, reconciliation, but changes its meaning significantly in the way that he uses it. The Corinthians need to be reconciled to God because the way that they are living is opposed to the way that God is at work in the world. Paul does not specify what their new social and economic system should be like. In fact, it should not be expected that he could have done so, because the new social and economic system could only emerge as the church in Corinth repented of their sin, turning to God, who would bring justice and righteousness as a gift in this process.

Historical and Social Background to Corinth in the Time of Paul

At the time when Paul visited Corinth, in the middle of the first century CE, Corinth was a Roman colony. In 146 BCE it had been sacked by Rome because of the way that some Roman ambassadors were treated by some or the city's residents. Strabo, who wrote in the last century BCE and the first century CE, records this in the following way:

> The Corinthians, when they were subject to Philip, not only sided with him in his quarrel with the Romans, but individually behaved so contemptuously towards the Romans that certain persons ventured to pour down filth upon the Roman ambassadors when passing by their house. For this and other offences, however, they soon paid the penalty, for a considerable army was sent thither, and the city itself was razed to the ground by Leucius Mummius.[399]

The city was refounded by Rome following a decree of Julius Caesar in 44 BCE. The Latin name for the colony was *Colonia Laus Julia Corinthiensis*, standing as a constant reminder of the grace of Julius Caesar who helped to refound the colony.[400] It was settled largely by war veterans and the urban poor from Rome, many of them freedmen.[401]

One of the fascinating things about the Roman Empire is that it managed to be held together and to function with a very small central bureaucracy. Part of the reason for this is that it appears to have been structured by what scholars call a *patronage system*, which was distributed across the empire.[402] I say "appears" because, as with most history, we mainly have the records of people who held positions of power and so it is difficult to dive into the deep structures of relationships of ordinary people at the time.[403]

The basis of a patronage system is very simple: there are patrons and clients, who are organized in a hierarchical manner, so that a client of one patron may in turn be the patron for clients of her or his own. The patron-client relationship is an asymmetrical one, with the patron and the client having different responsibilities towards each other. For example, in the Roman Empire, clients had to provide political support for their patron; they often had to turn up daily at their patron's household and would have to attend various meals with the patron, where there was even a hierarchical ordering amongst a patron's clients, made obvious in the seating arrangements and the differentiated provision of the food and drink to the guests. In return, the patron provided things like legal protection, sometimes financial assistance, and connections for the client. These connections may be made by writing letters of recommendation from the patron to another patron, praising the client for his or her qualities and asking for patronage from another person. Sometimes clients were freedmen, former slaves of the patron, tied for life to the patron, or sometimes even generations were tied together, which enabled the patron to build up a dispersed business around the empire. The more clients a patron had, the more prestige she or he had. Having a powerful patron enabled a person to have greater access to positions of power and hence to wealth. In the Roman Empire, the ultimate patron was the emperor. The dispersed nature of the empire was held together by the leading citizens of major cities being clients of the emperor or other senior patrons in the empire. The base unit of the patronage system was the *household*, which had a head, usually a man but sometimes a woman, and included wives, children, and slaves.

Corinth was part of the patronage system. The following inscription is dated in the middle of the first century CE, so was contemporaneous with Paul. It was put up by members of the tribe of Calpurnia, clients of Julius Spartiaticus, in order to honor their patron, a contemporary of Paul:

> Gaius Julius, Son of Laco,
> Grandson of Eurycles,[of the tribe] Fabia, Spartiaticus,
> Procurator of Caesar and Augusta
> Agrippina, Tribune of the Soldiers, Awarded a Public Horse
> By the Deified Claudius, Flamen
> Of the Deified Julius, Pontifex, Duovir Quinquennalis twice,
> Agonothete of the Isthmian and Caesar-
> Augustan Games, High-Priest of the House of Augustus
> In Perpetuity, First of the Achaeans.
> Because of his Virtue and Eager
> And all-encompassing Munificence toward the Divine House
> Of the Tribe Calpurnia
> [Dedicated this] to their Patron.[404]

In this inscription, we see that Spartiaticus was patron of one of the tribes, Calpurnia, in Corinth, whilst he, in turn, was a client of an even more powerful patron, the emperor. Amongst other features of his powerful status as a patron, he gave money towards the running of the

Isthmian and Caesar-Augustan Games and he held office in the emperor cult, the official religious ordering of the Empire.[405]

Another feature of Corinth is that it was famed for its factionalism. L. L. Welborn writes:

> Corinth had a history of faction: from the bloody revolution of Cypselus (Herodotus 5.92) to their role in initiating the Peloponnesian War, to the contemptuous act that sparked the revolt of the Achaean League (Strabo *Geogr* 8.5.23). Politics remained a concern of the Corinthians under the empire, though the game was played for lesser stakes. The names of her ambitious citizens, their rivalries, and election promises are known to us from inscriptions recording their donations. We deceive ourselves if we imagine that the Corinthian Christians were innocent of all of this.[406]

Knowing this about the social, political, and economic conditions of the people who lived in Corinth, we can begin to hear echoes of things that Paul has written about in his correspondence with the church in Corinth. For example, the congregations of the church met in various households; the fellowship meals that Paul criticizes in 1 Corinthians 11 were like the meals that patrons held for clients; we read of factionalism, gathering around particular patrons (e.g., 1 Corinthians 1); we read how Paul refused to receive the patronage of members of the Corinthian church by refusing to receive money from them (2 Corinthians 11:7–10), and he criticized the acceptance of other "super apostles" by the Corinthian church on the basis that they carried letters of recommendation (2 Corinthians 3:1).

The more that we know about the situation of the Corinthian church, the richer Paul's correspondence with the church becomes. These sketches are enough, however, for our purpose here, which is to show that Paul believed that some of the ways that the Corinthian society was structured opposed the true nature of what it means to be church and that this could only be resolved by a fundamental change to the way that the society was ordered. The link to the overarching argument of this book is that fundamental changes also need to be made to Australian society in order to achieve justice for all the peoples of The Land.

In order to do this, we will look more closely at three problems that Paul saw in the Corinthian church: factionalism, the church ordered as a patronage system, and the relationship of the Corinthian Christians with Paul himself. These issues will be addressed in turn.

Problem 1: Factionalism

Paul starts his letter to the church in Corinth by making it clear that he understands that there is only one church in Corinth, which is made up of "those who are sanctified in Christ Jesus, called to be saints" (1 Corinthians 1:2). That the one church is made up of those who are sanctified and those called to be saints already indicates that the theme of unity is going to be an important one for this letter. The dual form of identification—the church named as a singular body and then two references to a composite of individuals—is unparalleled in Paul's letters that are preserved in the Bible.[407] It is quite possible that the Corinthian church did not start out as a united entity, but as a number of disparate groups meeting in people's houses. Mitchell is correct, however, when she writes that "Paul's rhetorical stance throughout 1 Corinthians is to argue that Christian unity is the theological and sociological expectation from which the Corinthians have fallen short, and to which they must return."[408]

Whilst it is not necessarily a problem that the church may have been made up of different congregations, meeting in the houses of various members of the church, it is clear that the church was riven with factions: the problem of factionalism in the Corinthian church appears right at the beginning of Paul's correspondence with them, straight after the opening greeting (1 Corinthians 1:10). As was written above, factionalism was a problem in Corinthian society and so it is not a surprise that it was also a feature of the church in Corinth, albeit one which is at odds with being part of the community of people following Jesus.

Margaret Mitchell translates 1 Corinthians 1:10 as follows:

> I urge you, brothers and sisters, through the name of our Lord Jesus Christ, to all say the same thing, and to let there not be factions among you, but to be reconciled in the same mind and in the same opinion.[409]

There is a strong case for translating the Greek word that Paul uses, κατηρτισμένοι (katērtismenoi), as "to be reconciled."[410] Paul also uses this word in 2 Corinthians 13:9, 11, meaning that his correspondence with the Corinthian church, as preserved in the Bible, is bracketed by his concern that the disputing factions in the church be reconciled to one another.

A number of scholars have noticed that the way that Paul argues his case in 1 Corinthians is similar to other political authors of his day who were urging reconciliation in various situations. Many authors focus on chapters 1 to 4, but Margaret Mitchell argues that the whole of 1 Corinthians is an example of a style of writing, the technical name for which is *deliberative rhetoric*, and that the whole letter is a coherent appeal for unity and cessation of factionalism.[411] L. L. Welborn writes that "Paul does not seek to refute a 'different gospel' (2 Corinthians 11:4), but exhorts the quarrelling Corinthians 'to agree completely, . . . to be united in the same mind and the same judgment' (1 Corinthians 1:10). It is a power struggle, not a theological controversy, that motivates the writing of 1 Corinthians 1–4."[412] This is, however, somewhat simplistic, because, for Paul, bad politics is bad theology. L. L. Welborn notes that John Calvin argued that the problem Paul saw in Corinth was partisanship and that Paul exhorts the Corinthians to be united in the same mind and judgment.[413] Anthony Thiselton notes that in "the subapostolic age and in earlier patristic times it was often broadly assumed that the problem of discord and splits to which 1:10–12 alludes featured as the major issue which Paul felt called to address."[414]

1 Corinthians is more than just letter urging unity, but it is rather an argument for the restructuring of society in Corinth in a way that is in accord with the gospel of Jesus Christ; it is an argument for the unity that arises from a proper comprehension (intellectual and lifestyle) of the gospel. That is, the problems in Corinth will not be solved simply by a reorganization of its ecclesiastical structures, even achieving unity, "but by placing the community as a whole under the *criterion and identity of the cross of Christ*. Here a *reversal of value systems occurs* (cf. 1 Corinthians 1:26–31), and as recipients of the sheer gift of divine *grace* through the cross, all stand on the same footing (cf. 1 Corinthians 4:7) . . . not ecclesiology but *a reproclamation of grace and the cross to Christian believers takes center stage.*"[415]

When writing 2 Corinthians, the problem of factionalism still seems to be present, for Paul returns to this at the end of 2 Corinthians (see 12:20—13:11). In particular, the key verb in 1 Corinthians 1:10, which Margaret Mitchell translated as "to be reconciled," is found again in 2 Corinthians 13:9, 11, in noun and verbal form, which indicates that the problems of factions, one of the issues that caused Paul to write 1 Corinthians, was still present when he wrote 2 Corinthians.[416] The fact that this concern about factionalism and even the use of the same term brackets the whole of Paul's correspondence with the Corinthian church means that he is concerned about factionalism in the whole of his correspondence.

Dieter Georgi argues that in Paul's eyes the vices listed in 2 Corinthians 12:20–21 arise from the "unrestrained competition" in Corinth: "In Paul's opinion, the competition exposed the essentially faithless attitude of the Corinthians (and naturally also of the opponents)."[417] Georgi goes as far as suggesting that Paul could "be stating very bluntly that the Corinthians in reality never had become Jesus-believers."[418]

Furthermore, factionalism continued to be a problem in Corinth, even after the writing of 2 Corinthians. For example, in his letter to the Corinthian church about factionalism in Corinth his day, Clement refers explicitly to what Paul wrote in 1 Corinthians about factions (1 Clement 47:1–3), and he uses the terms and he uses some of the same ways of arguing as in 1 Corinthians in his own appeal for the cessation of factionalism in Corinth.[419]

Problem 2: The Incomers[420] to Corinth and the Patronage System

A second problem that Paul saw with the church in Corinth was that it was in thrall to the patronage system. Whilst the focus of 1 Corinthians is on relationships between the members of the church in Corinth, in 2 Corinthians the focus has shifted to the triangular relationship between the Corinthian Christians, Paul, and some people who have come to the church in Corinth from elsewhere, who have exerted significant influence on it.[421] This does not mean that the incomers were a new phenomenon, for, from 1 Corinthians 1–4, it is clear that some incomers were already present when Paul wrote 1 Corinthians and were possibly a catalyst for, or even a cause of some of the factionalism, as people grouped themselves around particular leaders.[422]

As the present-day reader only has access to what Paul has written, there is no certainty about who the incomers were and what they taught and did. However, it will be argued here that one aspect of their teaching and lifestyle was a continuation of the patronage system, which Paul roundly rejects as being antithetical to his understanding of the gospel. Again, this problem was already present in 1 Corinthians 1–4, 9, and 11.[423]

Margaret Thrall gives a helpful summary of the main scholarly views about who the incomers were and what they taught.[424] She divides theories into three main classes: those that argue that the incomers were some type of Judaizing party, those that see them as teaching some sort of elevated "spiritual" status, and some combination of the two viewpoints. Thrall herself argues that the incomers might have had Palestinian connections, with links to Jesus' original disciples. They are miracle-workers, they are probably visionaries, who boast of their visions, and they claim apostolic status. As missionaries, they claim their right of material support from the Corinthians. Paul queries their right to work in "his area," both because he has done all the groundwork and, perhaps, because of an agreement made with the Jerusalem apostles about areas of missionary responsibility.[425] The different Jesus that they preach focuses on the post-resurrection glorious figure, rather than the crucified Christ, and the different gospel stresses obedience to the teaching of the earthly Jesus, perhaps with some measure of Torah observance.[426] These hypotheses, however, do not take sufficient account of the social dynamics in the Greek East of the Roman Empire.

It is significant that, unlike other churches established by Paul, there seems to have been little friction between the church in Corinth and the wider society. For example, Corinthian Christians take disputes to the civil courts (1 Corinthians 6:1–6), Christians are invited to meals at the homes of unbelievers (1 Corinthians 10:27), and non-Christians might come to a home where Christian worship is taking place (1 Corinthians 14:24–25).[427] Paul, however, is uneasy about both the degree of integration of the Corinthian Christians with the surrounding society and also their corresponding failure to see the church as the place of their primary and dominant relationships.[428] "In the Corinthians' easy dealings with the world Paul detects a failure to comprehend the counter-cultural impact of the message of the cross."[429] "Their perception of their church and of the significance of their faith could correlate well with the life-style which remained fully integrated in Corinthian society."[430]

In particular, it will be argued here that the Corinthians fitted happily within the patronage system and that one of the problems that the church had with Paul was that he could not be captured into their patronage system, whereas the incomers sat easily with the patronage system, and so the Corinthians were more at ease with them than with Paul.

Recall that Graeco-Roman society was shaped and held together by the patronage system. The patronage system was an asymmetrical system of exchange, where one party had more control over resources, and would bind other parties to itself by the giving of benefaction in return for something beneficial to the higher-status party. The receiving of benefaction tied the client to the patron. One of the roles of a patron was the writing of letters of recommendation. One of the obligations of clients was to attend meals given by their patron, which were an opportunity for the host to show off wealth and status. Roman satirists protested about the way that the good food and wine and seating was saved for the guests of honor, whilst the poorer clients had poorer food and places to sit.[431] The fact that these are exactly the issues raised by Paul in 1 Corinthians 11 shows that the church in Corinth was heavily influenced by the patronage system.[432] Recall that the church in Corinth met in homes, where the host/ess had an automatic patronage role, so it was not easy to break away from the patronage system.[433]

Giving and receiving money are key parts of the patronage system, and they are important issues in the relationship between the Corinthian church and Paul. Peter Marshall has argued that Paul's refusal to accept money from the Corinthians was the root cause of the breakdown in his relationship with them.[434] Paul's refusal to receive money from the Corinthians for his own support was a problem already when he wrote 1 Corinthians (1 Corinthians 9) and this continued to be a problem in 2 Corinthians (2 Corinthians 2:17; 11:7-12; 12:13-18), a problem heightened by the fact that, although he did not accept money for himself, he did want to collect money for the saints in Jerusalem (2 Corinthians 8 and 9).[435] If Marshall is right that the issue of money was at the root of the cooling off of the relationship between the Corinthian church and Paul from the Corinthian end, then the fact that Paul refers to the monetary issue so many times in 2 Corinthians would strengthen the case that restoring his relationship with the Corinthians was at the forefront of Paul's mind in 2 Corinthians. It would also suggest that the use of reconciliation as a metaphor is particularly appropriate, because he had become their enemy, and he wanted to establish peace. Paul's relationship with the Jerusalem church had also been difficult, and it is conceivable that the collection was also a reconciliatory gesture on his part towards them.[436]

Why did Paul not accept money from the Corinthians when he had accepted money from the Philippian church when he was in Corinth (2 Corinthians 11:8-9; Philippians 4:14-16)?[437] It may have been the case that the factions in the Corinthian church centered around the homes in which members of the church congregated, perhaps with the householder acting as the patron of the particular congregation,[438] and so, perhaps, Paul refused financial aid because he did not want to become aligned with a particular faction. However, it is more likely that Paul was concerned about the patronage system itself.[439] For Paul, part of the sociality of the gospel was to follow Christ in his becoming poor that others might become rich (2 Corinthians 8:9), a sort of inverse of the patron-client relationship. Paul expresses many times how he has become "poor" so that the Corinthians might become "rich" (e.g., 1 Corinthians 4:6-13; 9:19-20; 2 Corinthians 1:6; 4:5, 12; 12:15; 13:6-7, 9). Perhaps Paul was confident to receive money from the Philippians because he saw them suffering as he did,[440] whereas the Corinthians have failed to fully carry through the socioeconomic distinctions that follow from their faith (2 Corinthians 6:14—7:1; cf. 1 Corinthians 10:23—11:34). Further, it seems that Paul made it a policy not to receive money from people whilst evangelizing in their city (1 Thessalonians 2:9; cf. 2 Thessalonians 3:7-9),[441] but once he was confident of their understanding of the gospel and their relationship with him, then he expected them to send him on to new places (2 Corinthians 10:15-16), presumably with financial support for the work in the new situation.

In his discussion of financial support for himself, Paul shifts the metaphor to say that he is acting as a parent to the Corinthians as children (2 Corinthians 12:14). Some see in this a claim that Paul is acting like a patron to them, albeit that what is on offer is the gospel, and that he is offering the Corinthians the opportunity to become patrons of the Jerusalem church by taking part in the collection.[442] Whilst Paul does use some of the language of benefaction, it is unlikely that he would have been encouraging people to think in this way. Rather, other dynamics seem to be in play: becoming poor that others might become rich (2 Corinthians 8:9); giving as an act of grace, flowing from the grace of God (2 Corinthians 8:6-7; 2 Corinthians 9:13-14); generosity (2 Corinthians 8:2, 15; 9:6); a response of thanksgiving to God (2 Corinthians 9:12); and the requirement that abundance should be shared with those who are poor (2 Corinthians 8:13-15); not to mention the benefits that will flow to the Corinthians (2 Corinthians 9:10-11, 14).[443]

In summary, Paul believed that the patronage system is antithetical to the lifestyle that flows from the cross of Christ. He is worried by the way that the Corinthians fit too easily into their cultural environment and he accuses the incomers of being supporters of the patronage system, as they pride themselves on three key aspects of the system: they accept money for their work (2 Corinthians 2:17; 11:7-11; 12:13-18); they came recommended and require recommendation (2 Corinthians 3:1-3; 4:2; 5:12; 10:12, 18);[444] and they fitted easily into hierarchy of the patronage system (2 Corinthians 11:20-21). In fact, it could have been the refusal of

Paul to fit into the Corinthian construal of the patronage system that led to his perceiving that the relationship between him and the Corinthians had broken down, which means that the desire to restore the relationship with the Corinthians is more than just an issue of the relationship between him and the Corinthians. This does not exhaust Paul's critique of the message and lifestyle of the incomers, but it is sufficient to show that Paul believes that the Corinthians must at least repent of their taking part in the patronage system.[445]

Problem 3: Relationships between the Corinthians and Paul

The final problem that Paul saw in Corinth that will be highlighted here is the relationship between the Corinthians and Paul. There is widespread scholarly agreement that Paul was already facing opposition in Corinth when he wrote 1 Corinthians.[446] Nils Dahl argued that slogans "I belong to" (1 Corinthians 1:12) should be understood as declarations of independence from Paul. If there are already problems in his relationship with the Corinthian Christians, then there are many features of 1 Corinthians that could have made things worse. In this letter, Paul criticizes almost every aspect of the lives of the Corinthian Christians: what they wear; how they worship; what, when, where and with whom they eat; what they do with their bodies; how they settle disputes; and so on. Not only does Paul criticize a wide range of aspects of their lives, but sometimes he also addresses them in a diminutive fashion. Margaret Mitchell writes that "Paul interprets [the Corinthian's] factional activity as indicative, not of political sophistication, but of childishness and renunciation of their precious freedom, through their alignment behind various missionaries. Paul's response is his replacement slogan which stresses their common allegiance to Christ (1 Corinthians 3:23)."[447] Paul refers repeatedly to the Corinthians as children, even babies, which could imply that their behavior is like children (1 Corinthians 3:1; 4:14; 13:11; 14:20).[448] Paul may see some of these references as being a positive development of his metaphor of his being in a father-child relationship with the Corinthians, but in others they are definitely derogatory, and Paul sees them ultimately as signs that people are enslaved to some other power (e.g., 1 Corinthians 6:19–20; 7:23).

A striking feature of 2 Corinthians as a whole is "how much attention Paul gives to his relationship with the community at Corinth."[449] For example: he hopes that they will fully acknowledge "us,"[450] as they have partially acknowledged "us," and that they will boast of "us" on the day of the Lord Jesus (1:13–14); he refrained from visiting Corinth so that there would not be further pain in the relationship (1:23; 2:1–4); "we" are working together with the Corinthians (1:24);[451] he left an opportunity to preach the gospel in Troas because his heart was troubled because he wanted to hear from Titus about how Titus's visit to Corinth on his behalf had gone (2:12–13); he is enabling the Corinthians to boast about "us," so that they might answer those who boast about outward appearance and not what is in the heart (5:12); "our" heart is wide open, but the Corinthians have restricted their affections, and he calls them to widen their hearts (6:11–13), and to make room in their hearts for "us" (7:2–4); the report from Titus showed that Paul had received some of the restoration of relationship that he had hoped for (7:6–13); and he calls the Corinthians "brothers" (1:8; and also 8:1; 13:11).[452] R. Bieringer also argues that naming them specifically in 6:11 ("We have spoken freely to you, Corinthians; our heart is wide open"), being one of the only three places that he does so in his undisputed letters (the others being Galatians 3:1; Philippians 4:15), makes the statement highly personal, making sure that the readers realize he is talking to them and no one else.[453] The Macedonians are held up as an example of giving themselves to Paul (8:5), and the collection is seen by Paul as a test of the Corinthians' love (e.g., 8:8, 24); he does not want to have to act in boldness when he gets to Corinth (10:2), waging war (10:3–6; cf. 13:1–4); he hopes that as the faith of the Corinthians increases, so will "our" area of influence increase amongst them (10:15); he fears he might not find them as he wishes when he visits them again (12:19–21); and he prays for their restoration (13:9, 11). Paul is eager for the relationship between himself and the Corinthians to be restored. He stresses that his love for them has been constant, and that he has always acted out of love for them (e.g., 2:4; 6:11; 7:3; and also 11:11; 12:15, 19), and he wants the Corinthians to respond with love towards him (e.g., 6:12–13; 7:2); he wishes to be reconciled with the Corinthians. Paul has to say these things because he feels that some people in the Corinthian church have rejected him, and he has been humbled (2 Corinthians 11:7; 12:21), even humiliated (2 Corinthians 9:4) before them.[454]

It is clear from the structure of the argument in 2 Corinthians 5:1–7:2 that Paul interprets the Corinthian response to him as a rejection of himself and his understanding of the gospel. In Paul's mind, this is a serious offense, because they are rejecting God's ambassador, and so are rejecting God. But, unlike the Romans when the Corinthians mistreated their ambassadors, God does not come to sack the city, but, through Paul, urges the Corinthians to be reconciled to God. Part of that reconciliation to God is to open their hearts to Paul again (6:1, 11–13; 7:2), that is, they must be reconciled with Paul as part of their being reconciled to God. Fitzgerald writes:

> The first and foremost of these additional appeals in 2 Corinthians 6–7 is the call for a full reconciliation between himself and the Corinthians (6:11–13 + 7:2–4). Indeed, since there can be no reconciliation with God apart from a reconciliation with Paul as God's ambassador, this appeal constitutes the real point of the apostle's earlier exhortation to be reconciled to God (5:20). Like the heart of the God who entrusted him with the message of reconciliation, Paul's own heart stands wide open to the Corinthians (6.11); he has done nothing to harm them (7:2) or to present an obstacle (6:3) to their opening wide their hearts (6:13) and making room for him (7:2). There is thus no impediment to their reconciliation; there are no reparations to be made. And just as God had taken the initiative in reconciling Paul to himself, Paul now takes the initiative in trying fully to reconcile the Corinthians to himself.[455]

It is important to note that Paul makes a plea as an ambassador; he does not command the Corinthians. If ambassadors went from the defeated party to the dominant party in order to plead for reconciliation,[456] then we have here an admission from Paul of his weakness before the Corinthians, and he must plead with them to be reconciled to him.[457]

What does not seem to have been noticed by other commentators is the parallel between Paul's experience on the road to Damascus and his fears concerning what the Corinthian church is doing. Paul was once a persecutor of the church, but the question posed to him by the risen Christ, in the encounter on the road to Damascus, was, "Saul, Saul, why are you persecuting me?" (Acts 9:4).[458] That is, whilst Paul's action is against the church, it is received by the risen Christ as being persecution of himself. From this, Paul understood that his behavior towards the followers of Jesus was sinful, and he had also alienated himself from God, but Christ was calling him back into relationship with God, which became the pattern of his ministry as an ambassador of reconciliation.

Regarding his relationship with the Corinthians, Paul fears that in rejecting him, the Corinthians are making exactly the same mistake that he did in persecuting the church, so that they risk alienating themselves from God. In the letter Paul had already sent to the Corinthians, he refers to the fact that he persecuted the church (1 Corinthians 15:8–9).[459] But Paul says that God's "grace towards me was not in vain" (1 Corinthians 15:10).[460] The Corinthians, however, are in danger of having received the grace of God in vain (2 Corinthians 6:1) because they have restricted their relationship with Paul (2 Corinthians 6:11–13; 7:2), and so they must be reconciled with God (2 Corinthians 5:20). Paul fears that the Corinthians have not only moved away from him, but are also moving away from his understanding of the gospel, and so they will be "led astray from a sincere and pure devotion to Christ" (2 Corinthians 11:2–6).

Seeking Reconciliation in Corinth

This section has highlighted three of the problems that Paul saw in Corinth, namely, factionalism, participation in the patronage system, and the breakdown of their relationship with Paul. Two of these, factionalism and the patronage system, were deeply rooted in Corinthian society and the Church in Corinth could see no problems with them, but Paul says that they are opposed to the way that God is at work in the world. In the language of this book, these are further examples of bound willing, where people continue to live in the damaging ways of the past and cannot see what is good. The church in Corinth has fallen out with Paul because they could not fully understand what he was trying to tell them and to live out amongst them. Instead, they felt more comfortable with teachers who were themselves part of the patronage system. Again and again, Paul returns to the cross in the Corinthian correspondence, tellingly in 1 Corinthians 11, where he says that their meals together should not simply continue the patronage system but should reflect the fact that they are proclaiming the death of Christ.[461] Paul is deeply concerned for the church in Corinth because the ways that they are living are opposed to the ways that God is at work in the world and so they are treating God as their enemy, just as he had done in persecuting the church. In this situation, Paul says that they must seek to make peace with God and they can only do this if they fundamentally change the way that they live. Paul borrows from the political language of his day, saying that the Corinthians must be reconciled to God, but, critically, he makes several changes to how the word was used. We will look at how Paul uses reconciliation below, but for now we note that the Corinthians do not need to appease an angry and powerful enemy that is seeking to maintain the current politics of oppression, but instead they find God coming towards them, seeking their welfare, urging them to take hold of the reconciliation that God both offers and provides the power to take hold of it.

What is easy to miss, because it is not there, is that Paul does not tell the Corinthian church how it must reorder its social structures in order to be reconciled with God; he only says that ordering itself on the patronage system is living in a way that is opposed to how God is at work in the world. This is probably because neither the church nor Paul can imagine a different social ordering to the one in which they find themselves. The closest that we get to this is Paul's commendation of the church in Philippi because their life in God had led them to economic suffering and so it bore something of the cruciform lifestyle of the church. This is critically important when we come to consider the situation in Australia, where it seems impossible to imagine how we would go about repenting of the Root Sin or what the world would look like if we really repented of it. Even more, we may be afraid to imagine it because of the benefits and privileges that may need to be sacrificed. Nonetheless, we can be encouraged by what Paul has written, for it is in turning to God in repentance, in seeking to receive the overflowing love of God that exchanges sin for righteousness as a gift, that the new world can come into being.

Reconciliation

We have been using the term *reconciliation* without carefully looking at how Paul used this term. One of the problems with the idea of reconciliation is that it is often used without definition and so this imprecise meaning allows it to be used in such a way that it avoids the importance of pursuing justice. Susan Dwyer expresses this well when she writes:

> The notable lack of any clear account of what reconciliation is, and what it requires, justifiably alerts the cynics among us. Reconciliation is being urged upon people who have been bitter and murderous enemies, upon victims and perpetrators of terrible human rights abuses, upon groups of individuals whose very self-conceptions have been structured in terms of historical and often state-sanctioned relations of dominance and submission. The

rhetoric of reconciliation is particularly common in situations where traditional judicial responses to wrongdoing are unavailable because of corruption in the legal system, staggeringly large numbers of offenders, or anxiety about the political consequences of trials and punishments. Hence, a natural worry, exacerbated by the use of explicitly therapeutic language of healing and recovery, is that talk of reconciliation is merely a ruse to disguise the fact that a "purer" form of justice cannot be realized.[462]

This is a fair and right criticism. It will be seen below that the way that the word "reconciliation" was used by those before and contemporaneously with Paul failed in ways that are not dissimilar to those that concern Dwyer. When Paul picked up the word, he made several significant changes, turning the concept on its head, so critiquing the politics of his day as well as giving a new vision of the way that God is at work in the world. It is hoped that this will show that reconciliation is a much deeper concept than that which is rightly criticized by Dwyer, and that the process of reconciliation achieves a deeper justice than can be imagined before the process of reconciliation has been embarked upon.

The English word "reconciliation" is derived from Latin, but Paul wrote in Greek. We have already seen that Paul used the word κατηρτισμένοι when he was urging the Corinthian Christians to be reconciled to one another (1 Corinthians 1:10; 2 Corinthians 13:9, 11). When urging the Corinthians to be reconciled to God, Paul uses the noun καταλλαγή (katallagē), which is translated in our Bibles as "reconciliation" (Romans 5:11; 11:15; 2 Corinthians 5:18, 19), and its related verb, καταλλάσσω (katallassō), translated as "reconcile" (Romans 5.10 (used twice); 1 Corinthians 7:11; 2 Corinthians 5:18, 19, 20). Standard dictionaries note that the words καταλλαγή and καταλλάσσω are compounds of ἀλλάσσω (allassō), which means "to alter" or "to exchange." In turn, ἀλλάσσω is based on ἄλλος (allos), meaning "other." From the time of Herodotus, the usage of ἀλλάσσω moved from meaning "to change" or "to exchange," to meaning "to reconcile." The prefix κατα (kata) in καταλλάσσω is understood as having no effect on the meaning,[463] and so the compound καταλλάσσω "generally denotes in classical Greek the restoration of the original understanding between people after hostility or displeasure."[464] "It was used figuratively for the 'exchange' of hostility, anger, or war for friendship, love, or peace; it thus designates reconciliation in the human or political realm."[465] The religious use of καταλλάσσω was rare in classical Greek literature, and it is not used of the relationship between God and his people in Jewish literature until 2 Maccabees 1:4; 5:20; 7:33; 8:29. In fact, it appears that it was Paul's use of the term which was the motivating factor for a radically increased use of καταλλάσσω and its cognates in Greek literature, with these words appearing an "inordinately larger" number of times in the church fathers, especially John Chrysostom.[466] Interestingly, Plutarch described Alexander the Great as "reconciler of everything," sent by God to unite humanity into a world state.[467]

Paul's use of these words in 2 Corinthians is their first occurrence in the Bible and so it is important to see how he uses them.

Paul was very creative in the metaphors he chose in order to help his readers understand the riches that are theirs in Christ. Sometimes we can be lazy when we read the Bible and collapse all the images or ideas into one overriding concept so that we miss out on the rich web of meaning that Paul is creating for us in his writings. It is a valuable exercise to look at each of the metaphors in turn to see the vistas that they open up for us.[468] When considering reconciliation, it must not simply be equated with other terms that Paul uses. In particular, Cilliers Breytenbach has conclusively demonstrated that "reconciliation" and "atonement" come from two completely different semantic fields and so they have no intrinsic relationship to one another.[469] That is, a deeper and richer understanding of what God has done in Christ can be found by studying what each of these terms brings. It is especially unhelpful to see reconciliation simply as the overarching concept in Paul's theology.[470] Both treating the terms that Paul uses as being interchangeable and seeing reconciliation as the overarching concept in his theology mean that the distinctive ideas that Paul is trying to bring to the fore, when he uses a particular term, are missed. An exercise like this needs to see the word in its full context and also the web of other terms that Paul brings into relationship with it in order to fully understand it.

Whilst the source of Paul's reconciliation terminology is the political sphere,[471] it would seem that it was Paul's experience of meeting the risen Christ that was foundational in his understanding of the nature of enmity towards God and reconciliation with God.[472] Using the terminology from the First Movement of this book, in his encounter with the risen Christ, Paul discovered that his will had been bound so that he was acting in the world against God, even though he had been zealously doing what he thought that God required (cf. Galatians 1:13–16). His actions caused severe harm to others and were a sin against God. He discovered that

God had not come to destroy him but had come to set him free from his bondage to sin and to also call him to proclaim this message of the gift of freedom from the bondage of sin to others. Paul understood this experience as being reconciled with God. With this in mind, it is now possible to explore how Paul reconstructs the idea of reconciliation.

Not all the Greek and Roman writers thought that reconciliation was a good idea. For example, "in early Greek literature, friendship and enmity are strongly contrasted in the traditional maxim, that one ought to do everything 'to help a friend and harm an enemy.'"[473] In Aristotle, revenge upon an enemy, rather than reconciliation, is a noble act: "for to retaliate is just and that which is just is noble."[474] "A man's virtue consists in outdoing his friends in kindness and his enemies in mischief."[475] Although later writers reacted against this, it remained part of popular ethics.[476] Some thought that it was possible to make friends with those who were formerly enemies. Reconciliation was not only the province of noble conduct, but could be pursued for reasons of patriotism, expediency and self-preservation.[477]

John Fitzgerald lists five features of the standard way that reconciliation was in used Greek literature:[478]

1. The rule of thumb was that those responsible for the strife were to take the initiative in ending it, and that the offended party should show goodwill by accepting the offer of reconciliation.

2. The guilty party's initiative in reconciliation usually took the form of an appeal, typically introduced by a word of entreaty.[479]

3. Appeals for reconciliation are often accompanied by some indication of the guilty party's affection and concern for the estranged person or group.

4. In many cases, pleas for forgiveness were not sufficient, and some reparation had to be made. This was a standard precondition in the reconciliation of warring nations, and the severity of the demands by the more powerful nation often prolonged the conflict.

5. Although the desire for reconciliation often began with the guilty party, reconciliation brought benefits for both parties, and those who had been reconciled were expected to live in renewed concord with one another.

This understanding of reconciliation is deeply problematic. Anthony Bash notes that embassies were often sent from a weaker group to a group which had power over them[480] and Fitzgerald notes that the large reparations that were required of the vanquished party often extended the conflict.[481] This completely sidesteps the issue of moral responsibility in the conflict: it may sometimes be the case that one party is seeking reconciliation with another party not because they have done anything ethically wrong, but simply because they have not done what the more powerful party required.[482] Here "reconciliation" means no more than a temporary cessation of armed conflict whilst sanctioning and enabling the continuation of the oppressive relationships between the two parties. This is far from the meaning of the word "reconciliation" when it is used in the Bible, where Paul turns many of these ideas on their heads.

We have seen that Paul argues that the Corinthians have become estranged from God by their behavior. The first and key shift change that Paul has made in the reconciliation paradigm is that it is God, from whom the Corinthians have alienated themselves, who takes the initiative in reconciliation. That is, it is God, the offended party, who takes the initiative in reconciliation, making reconciliation possible between Godself and the offending party.[483] I. Howard Marshall conjectured that this was the first time that καταλλάσσω had been used this way in Greek literature[484] and Stanley Porter demonstrated it.[485] The result of this shift is the radical and new understanding of God as the one who has taken responsibility for reconciliation because human beings were either unwilling or unable to take the steps necessary for reaching reconciliation.[486] God is not an angry god who has to be appeased by humanity, but the one who desires that humanity be reconciled to Godself and who removes all barriers that stop this from being a possibility, as was argued in the First Movement of this book.

A second shift is that Paul has taken terminology from the domain of relationships between human beings and he has applied it to God. Reconciliation was the exchange of enmity for friendship and so "Paul's use of this term in conjunction with the divine-human relationship means that he is depicting God as the One who makes friends of his adversaries."[487] This is expressed winsomely in the Good News Bible translation of 2 Corinthians 5:18–20:

> All this is done by God, who through Christ changed us from enemies into his friends and gave us the task of making others his friends also. Our message is that God was making the whole

> human race his friends through Christ. God did not keep an account of their sins, and he has given us the message which tells how he makes them his friends. Here we are, then, speaking for Christ, as though God himself were making his appeal through us. We plead on Christ's behalf: let God change you from enemies into his friends!

A third shift is that it is not the guilty party, the Corinthians, who is making expressions of affection and concern for the estranged party, but Paul, as Christ's ambassador, who expresses his love for the Corinthians many times in 2 Corinthians (e.g., 2:4; 6:11; 7:3; 11:11; 12:15, 19). Related to this reversal and the key change discussed above, is that, according to the standard reconciliation paradigm, Paul should have been an ambassador for humanity, making supplication to God, but instead he is an ambassador for Christ, calling the Corinthians to be reconciled to God.[488] This same shift has been made in the way that the term "ambassador" has been used. Usually, it was the party that was seen as at fault that sent its embassy in order to petition for peace, but in 2 Corinthians 5:20 the embassy is addressed to humanity, not from humanity.[489]

The fourth shift is that, unlike the Romans, who sacked Corinth following the mistreatment of its ambassadors, God does not act in immediate judgment because of the mistreatment of his ambassador by the Corinthians. There is a delay, perhaps to the Day of Judgment, of the consequences of the failure to receive the message of reconciliation (2 Corinthians 5:10; 6:1 and seen more clearly in Romans 5:9).[490]

A final shift that Paul makes in the use of the term "reconciliation" is that there is no need for the guilty party to make reparation. Instead, Paul makes the astoundingly simple claim that it is all gift:

> For our sake [God] made [Christ] to be sin who knew no sin, so that in him we might become the righteousness of God.

Note that the focus here is on the exchange that has been made: Christ becomes sin and we become righteousness; there is no discussion of the mechanism by which this is done. That is, Paul is only interested here in the exchange, not the mechanism of the exchange. Recall that the word that is translated in 2 Corinthians as "reconciliation" is a compound word whose root idea is exchange, and gradually its meaning changed to being used figuratively for the exchange of enmity for friendship, and this idea of exchange is being carried over from verses 18–20 into verse 21.[491] In particular, this cannot be read as a cryptic reference to substitutionary atonement because there is no sacrificial language in 2 Corinthians 5: Christ's death in verse 14 is not sacrificial, but participatory (all have died in Christ); and the exchange of righteousness and sin in verse 21 focuses on the fact of the exchange, not on how it works.[492] Reconciliation, and the exchange of righteousness for sin, is a free gift, a new creation.

One important and final observation remains to be made, which hints at the relationship between reconciliation and justice. In Greek, justice and righteousness are the same word, and so 2 Corinthians 5:21 suggests that righteousness and justice are established as a gift of God in the process of reconciliation; God takes our sin and replaces it with righteousness and justice. The idea of exchange, which is foundational in the word (translated as) "reconciliation" itself, is carried over from verses 18–20 to verse 21. God has made possible two exchanges: that of enmity for friendship, and that of sin for "justice." The point is that justice is not achieved by pursuing it; rather, it is a gift of God that comes from the process of seeking to make enemies into friends through the process of reconciliation.[493] Further, righteousness is relational in Hebrew thought, and so the meaning of the phrase "the righteousness of God" would be understood as "God's activity in drawing individuals into and sustaining them within the relationship, as 'the power of God for salvation'" (cf. Romans 1:16–17), thus continuing the idea of reconciliation that is present in the immediately preceding verses (2 Corinthians 5:18–20).[494]

It is beyond the scope of this book to fully consider the nature of justice, but I hope that this is suggestive of the fact that there is a deeper notion of justice than that found in most philosophical accounts of justice: justice is about putting things right and the restoration of relationships. For those of us who live in the West, "criminal justice" is most often about establishing if someone committed a crime and then punishing him if he did. In that notion of justice, there is no possibility of repentance and the victim is not involved in the process. Punishment restores neither the victim nor the offender; it does no good for anybody.

Reconciliation: The Process of Repentance and Forgiveness

It is now possible to draw various theological strands of this book together. The binding of the wills of human beings, organizations, societies, and nations leads to damage being done, to the inability to always see and do what is good. It has been seen that not only is damage done, but these actions are opposed to the way that God is working in the world, blocking the plenitude that overflows from the love of God for the world, and that such action further embeds and solidifies the binding of the will. Paul expresses this as behaving as enemies of God. God, however, is actively resisting this resistance to God. If the language of enemies is being used, then God is offering and making reconciliation possible. If the language of forgiveness is being used, then God is offering forgiveness. The forgiveness and reconciliation of God are generative because they can take the situation now and bring something new and good out of it, which neither denies the past nor continues the damaging ways of the past. This is seen most clearly in the death and resurrection of Jesus.

God's forgiveness is generative because it makes repentance possible, leading to the liberation of the bound will. Repentance is the appropriate human response—individuals, communities, and nations—to the possibility of the forgiveness of God. Repentance has several aspects to it. It is, first of all, a full confession of both the wrongdoing and also a recognition of how the will is bound, of the confusion that arises from desiring to do good but finding that harm is done, and not knowing what to do about it, of being powerless to do anything about it. Secondly, repentance expresses a desire to be liberated from bound willing and so to be able to live in ways in the future which are not continuing to damage others in ways that arose from the binding of the will. Thirdly, repentance is a willingness to take concrete actions to undo those things which have been a consequence of the bound will. This can only happen if the binding of the will itself is addressed.

God's forgiveness is also generative because it enables human forgiveness. Human forgiveness can be offered but cannot be given until there has been repentance. There are two levels of forgiveness. The first is the forgiving of a particular wrong action, when there has been repentance for that action. Unless there has been a full repentance, an unbinding of the will, this sort of forgiveness will need to be given again and again. At the same time, such forgiveness continues to name and condemn the actions which are taking place, whilst also taking measures to keep safe, as much as possible, that is, taking actions which attempt to disable further damage being done and refusing an easy relationship until there has been a full repentance. For example, an individual may flee from domestic abuse, refusing any further relationship, by initially taking refuge in a specialist hostel. Such action is very difficult when there is an overwhelming power imbalance, or in situations involving whole groups of people embedded in another nation. The deepest forgiveness comes when the repentance is for the binding of the will, which leads to the establishment of good relationships, where the victim is no longer in danger from this particular way of damaging them, because repentance has taken hold of the transformative forgiveness of God, which liberates the binding of the will.

Repentance and forgiveness are unlikely to be single actions, but processes that take considerable time. As was seen in the case of the church in Corinth, discussed above, repentance might require changing the very foundations of how a society or nation works. At the beginning of this process, it will be impossible to imagine what the end might look like, because it has never existed before. What can be known, however, is that seeking to repent and seeking to be able to forgive, that is, seeking reconciliation, is taking part in the active work of God in the world to liberate people from their bondage to sin (those repenting) and their bondage to its consequences (those forgiving). Moreover, that the gift of God is to bring something new, that cannot be imagined from the beginning, and which is recognized as being just; God has exchanged sin for justice and righteousness, and reconciliation has happened.

There is one major issue that I have skirted around in the presentation so far and that is whether God has to be explicitly acknowledged in the processes of repentance and forgiveness. That is, does repentance of the bound will require an explicit understanding that the binding of the will results in ways of living in the world which are opposed to the ways of God, along with an explicit call on God to be liberated from the binding of the will, and does forgiveness require an experience of the forgiveness of God in order to be able to forgive? I have to confess that I do not have the theological resources at the moment—but this does not mean that they do not exist—to give an adequate account of my belief and experience that God is at work in the world to bring reconciliation even if not named in the process: the gift of God is such that taking part in the processes which express repentance and forgiveness are sufficient to allow God to bring the restoration of human relationships that comes from release from the bondage of the will and the liberation of forgiveness. I see this again and again in things like attempts at restorative justice, which are approximations to the full theological process of reconciliation. It would be breaking confidence to tell any of their stories, but I have seen that people who are willing to open their arms to begin to engage in the process of reconciliation, are surprised by a result that they could never have imagined from the beginning of the process, truly a gift of God.⁴⁹⁵

III

The Risk of the Future in Australia

To continue living as we have been living will continue to damage all the peoples in Australia and The Land itself. This is not sustainable. Instead, we must take the risk of addressing the past so that the future can be different.

This book has ranged over what might seem to be a disparate number of topics, but I hope that there have been enough waymarks along the road to hold its inner logic together. This final section will first of all draw together the argument of the book, as it applies to Australia, before considering the Uluru Statement from the Heart, which has an independent life but also forms part of the *Final Report on the Referendum Council*, published in June 2017.[496] I do not want to make an extended critique of this offer to the Australian nation. Rather, what is offered by this book is the key question that must be asked of any proposed way into the future: is it repenting of the Root Sin and so can it be part of what can be called a truly reconciliatory process? Without repentance of the Root Sin, the future will continue to be bound to repeating the damaging ways of the past.

Sin—acting in ways that damage ourselves, others, and the whole of the ecosystem; living in ways that are contrary to the ways that God works in the world; and blocking the flourishing that comes from the overflowing love of God—lays down patterns in ourselves so that our wills become bound. Our wills become so bound that even when we try to do good, we end up causing further damage because we do not even know what good is.

Australians find it hard to think about corporate responsibility and the continuing of the sins of the past in the present day, so an extended example of this dynamic was given in a study of the book of Ezekiel. Ezekiel is one of the most sustained arguments in the Bible that the present generation were continuing the sins of the past, even if they either refused to admit that they were sinning, or, more likely, they could not see the ways in which they were continuing to sin as their ancestors had done. This was an important case study because the book of Ezekiel is often read as being part of a trajectory from corporate to individual responsibility, which it clearly is not, for it continues to be focused on corporate responsibility, with especially harsh judgment of the various forms of leadership in the nation at the time.

With this groundwork done, the Root Sin of Australia could be examined: its failure to recognize the humanity of the First Peoples, including their relationship to The Land, and so coming to live in The Land as if it was unoccupied. This has shaped relationships between the First and Subsequent Peoples ever since, to the continuing detriment of the First Peoples and The Land. Three simple case studies were given that showed how bound willing disabled our ability to see what is good, where what appeared to be the obviously just action caused further problems for those for whom it was supposed to help: equal wages for Aboriginal cattle workers, welfare payments, and medication. The extended case study on land and the law showed that, whilst there were some judgments and legislation that addressed part of the Root Sin, recognizing the ownership or other rights over areas of land by some First Peoples, this process was subject to the whims of the judges and politicians of the time, often deliberately further embedding the Root Sin into Australian law and culture. Further, it was only looking at a small corner of the Root Sin as it could not conceive of negotiating between the sovereignties of the First Peoples and the Subsequent Peoples.

Whilst it is true that there has been a cultural shift towards making agreements and resolving local issues, the Root Sin of Australia still remains unaddressed. The only way that Australia can stop continuing to damage the First Peoples is if it repents of the Root Sin—all of it. We have seen that repentance starts with recognition and full confession, both of what was done and also how this has continued to cause damage up until today. But repentance is much more than an apology. In the case study of Paul's correspondence with the church in Corinth, it was seen that repentance may require the fundamental reordering of society in ways that cannot be imagined at the start of the process.

Personally, I cannot see that repentance of the Root Sin can be anything less than a negotiation between the sovereignties of the First Peoples and the Subsequent Peoples, or Australia, as the sovereignty of the Subsequent Peoples of The Land is called. This is exactly what Judges in the *Mabo (2)* case were unable to do: they could not step outside the law in order to discuss the sovereignty of the Australian law and so their judgment and all subsequent legislation and court cases were hamstrung by this.

What must be required of Australia in any reconciliatory process is that it repents of the Root Sin; this is the test of whether it is truly a reconciliatory process or not. This must include a willingness to look at its legal foundations and claims to sovereignty, to lay them alongside the claims of sovereignty by others, and to see how they can be transformed so that the sovereignties of all the peoples of The Land are somehow negotiated and so there is a full recognition of the humanity of all the peoples of The Land. I understand that we cannot conceive of how this can be done, for it is questioning the very foundations of the Australian legal system and it is impossible to see what the outcome of such a process would be. Nonetheless, the risk must be taken, for otherwise the Root Sin will remain firmly in the ground and all the peoples of The Land will continue to be damaged by it. Although it seems like a huge risk, such a process is a true repentance, a turning towards God, seeking the gift of God that will bring the new and unimaginable things that we will all recognize as just, and there will be peace in The Land.

I would like to go further than this, in a slightly speculative direction. There have been many interventions that have been trying to solve the problems faced by the First Peoples in Australia. This book, however, has argued that the main problem is Australia itself, as currently lived out by us, the Subsequent Peoples. Taking this further, the problems faced by the First Peoples in Australia are not only symptoms of the problem of Australia, but also are a way of Australia resolving its own inner tensions, its deep sense of illegitimacy. Drawing on the work of René Girard, it is possible to read the narrative of the person possessed by a "legion" of demons in Mark 5:1–20 as an account of the unresolved issues in a community that has been colonized by the Roman Empire. That is, somehow this person contains the disorder of the whole community, which arises in part from colonization. It is in the interest of the community that this person remains thus possessed. When Jesus heals the man, the community asks Jesus to leave because they are afraid, for there has been no repentance, and so they are now faced with the unresolved disorder of their community without knowing what to do with it.[497] In a similar way, there is a sense in which the disorder of some First Peoples in Australia is an ontological necessity in order for Australia to continue to exist without repenting of the Root Sin. I am not saying that this is good—rather the contrary—but simply stating that this is the reality of the situation if there is no repentance of the Root Sin. If repentance comes, I believe that a large shadow of spiritual oppression will be lifted off the First Peoples, resulting in significant changes, such as less violence and a decrease in addictive behavior because some people will have been set free from their oppression by the repentance of Australia, without the need for any intervention programs. That is, what Mark Moran called "wicked problems"[498] really are wicked, but they will begin to resolve themselves when Australia repents of the Root Sin.

The First Peoples in Australia have made yet another statement of what they require from Australia in the *Final Report of the Referendum Council*, part of which is the Uluru Statement from the Heart. Two of the things that it is asking for are: "a First Nations Voice to be enshrined in the Constitution," and a *makarrata* commission. Galarrwuy Yunupingu writes about how he understands the work of such a commission[499] and maybe this would be modeled on the Waitangi Tribunal and Office of Treaty Settlements in Aotearoa/New Zealand.[500] How are we to understand this within the theological framework that has been developed in this book? The Uluru Statement from the Heart can be understood as an offer of forgiveness, an opening of the arms in order to walk towards the embrace of reconciliation. It states what Australia must do in order to be able to be forgiven; that is, it is a statement by the First Peoples in Australia concerning the nature of repentance. If accepted, then there can be a move towards *makarrata*, in the words of the Yolngu people, or "reconciliation," if we are to use the word that Paul transformed and imported into Christian political discourse.

I deeply honor the process of consultation that has resulted in the report of the Referendum Council, giving a voice for the first time to multiple First Peoples across the whole of The Land. We, the Subsequent Peoples, must listen to what they have requested and act upon it. Nevertheless, I am deeply concerned that it is not asking for enough because it does not require repentance for the Root Sin: in seeking what is believed to be politically possible,[501] in order to protect the First Peoples from continuing to be ravaged by Australia, I fear that it will not deliver what is hoped for, because it does not appear to require repentance of the Root Sin as part of the process. Whilst I understand that the recommendations of the Referendum Council were chosen because it was felt that this was what might be politically possible, there is a huge political risk in pursuing this policy: if, as I believe, the practical outcomes of the requested changes are disempowered because it has not been preceded by a real repentance of the Root Sin, then the opportunity will have been lost for another generation or more, for people will say that what was requested was given. Without repentance of the Root Sin, a First Nations voice would prove ineffective. The very fact that the statement was reduced to asking for what was thought politically possible is an acknowledgement that the First Peoples in Australia are not safe to ask for everything that is needed in order for them to flourish in The Land. Only repentance by Australia will make the safe space that is required to state and receive all that is needed, to enable a deep forgiveness, to allow reconciliation, to allow flourishing.

Finale

This is my photograph of a sculpture by Fr. Rory (Gregory) Geoghegan, SJ, which is installed in the grounds of St. Bueno's Jesuit Spirituality Centre in North Wales. It is a response to the fifteenth station of the cross, "Resurrection." Fr. Rory said that he was inspired by the way that Olympic athletes celebrate their victory by draping a flag from their country around themselves. Here Jesus is shown throwing off the grave clothes which have held him in his death. The image has been chosen here to represent the joy of the freedom that comes being loosed from the bondage to sin that was discussed in the First and Second Movements of this book. It has been rendered in black and white so as to emphasize the freeing of the First Peoples, in particular, from the oppression that has resulted from the bound willing of the Subsequent Peoples. In their freedom comes the freedom of all the peoples of The Land. (I am grateful to Fr Rory for giving me permission to publish this photograph.)

"One of the things that I've learned to appreciate more as the President is that you are essentially a relay swimmer in a river full of rapids, and that river is history," [Barack Obama] later told me. "You don't start with a clean slate, and the things you start may not come to full fruition on your timetable. But you can move things forward. And sometimes the things that start small may turn out to be fairly significant . . . I think that we are born into this world and inherit all the grudges and rivalries and hatreds and sins of the past . . . But we also inherit the beauty and the joy and goodness of our forebears. And we're on this planet a pretty short time, so that we cannot remake the world entirely during this little stretch that we have."[502]

God is the power of the future contradicting all history
that wishes to build its future out of its present.[503]

What do you do when you don't have a shared name for a place?
You have possibility.[504]

AUSTRALIA IS ENGAGED IN a conscious process of myth-making, of finding a way of telling its story that holds together the complex, interconnecting stories of those who have been and are now living in The Land: the First Peoples, who, "according to the reckoning of [their] culture, from the Creation, according to the common law from 'time immemorial', and according to science more than 60,000 years ago"; those who came with the First Fleet; and those who have been born in or migrated to The Land in the two and half centuries since.[505] There is a desire to hear everyone's story, to find some way of comprehending the past that acknowledges the depths of both the pain and the joy, whilst trying to find a way into the future which does not repeat the damage of the past. This is the message from the cochairs of the Referendum Council in their foreword to the final report. This myth-making was explicit in the television advertisement that was screened in the weeks leading up to January 26, 2020, which I encourage you to watch and ponder.[506] The advertisement begins with a still with the text "Australia Day Presents" and the image of a young girl, who starts the narrative with the first sentence, "The story of Australia." It continues with the following words, each phrase with a carefully selected image of people drawn from across the peoples of The Land, each speaking their lines: "The story of me. It's the story of you. It's the story of we. In parts it is painful. In parts it is raw. In others, it's beautiful, inspiring great awe. It tells of many people, from far and wide, and those who've been here since the beginning of time. It brings us together and tears us apart. We all have our views, so where do we start? By listening to each other and sharing our part." It finishes with a voice-over of the text "We're all part of the story" and then a final image of a multicoloured graphic of Australia and the words "Australia Day. Respect. Reflect. Celebrate."

So, where do we start? In the ten years since I finished my thesis, much has changed in Australia, not least the much greater awareness by all the peoples in Australia of the First Peoples, of the complex and often shameful history since the arrival of the First Fleet, and that our complex "contemporary identity cannot be separated from Aboriginal Australia,"[507] along with a genuine desire to try to put things right, to build a future which does not repeat the damage of the past. This change has been brought about by many things, not least by the First Peoples pursuing land rights through the Australian courts, the increasing numbers of autobiographical narratives being published by First Peoples, and seminal books like Bruce Pascoe's *Dark Emu* and Bill Gammage's *The Biggest Estate on Earth: How Aborigines Made Australia*, which have opened the eyes of many people to the connection of the First Peoples to The Land and how they live with it.

Nonetheless, it remains the case that, despite all the changes and seeming advances, the situation does not seem to have changed at some deep level. This book opened with quotations from two well-known leaders of the First Peoples, which I repeat here. Jackie Huggins writes:

> We older leaders were young and energetic once, but we have grown weary from repeated defeats. The tiredness sets into our bones. Our hearts ache to think of our elders who lived through small wins only to see even greater losses. What we gain we do

not grasp for long. For Indigenous people, powerlessness and impermanence go hand in hand.[508]

Part of Galarrwuy Yunupingu's powerful lament in 2008 reads as follows:

> I am seeing now that too much of the past is for nothing. I have walked the corridors of power; I have negotiated and cajoled and praised and begged prime ministers and ministers, travelled the world and been feted; I have opened the doors to men of power and prestige; I have had a place at the table of the best and the brightest in the Australian nation—and at times success has seemed so close, yet it always slips away. And behind me, in the world of my father, the Yolngu world is always under threat, being swallowed up by whitefellas.
>
> This is a weight that is bearing down on me; it is a pressure that I feel now every moment of my life—it frustrates me and drives me crazy; at night it is like a splinter in my mind. The solutions to the future, simple though I thought they were, have become harder and harder to grasp. I have learnt from experience that nothing is ever what it seems.[509]

This book has been trying to help us understand why so much can seem to have changed and yet, for many First Peoples, it remains essentially the same, whilst also helping us see that this is not a hopeless situation, for there is a way into the future which is not bound by the ways of the past. The following summary stands back in order to see the whole picture presented in this book.

In claiming sovereignty over The Land, the British Crown failed in several ways: firstly, it did not recognise the relationship of the First Peoples to The Land, a relationship which was much more complex than the British concept of sovereignty and ownership; secondly, it was a unilateral declaration, but the rights of the First Peoples over The Land were not given up; thirdly, it did not recognize the systems of law of those inhabiting The Land; and fourthly, even in British law, ownership is a bundle of rights, and so it missed an opportunity to negotiate what a shared coexistence might look like. The incoming did not recognize any of the following for the First Peoples: their identities as peoples, their territorial lands, their languages, and their culture.[510] In summary, this action failed to engage with the full humanity of the First Peoples. These failures were part of the very conception of what eventually became known as the nation of Australia. The will of Australia was bound at its conception, so right from the beginning the Subsequent Peoples could not see clearly about how to relate to the First Peoples.

The First Movement, Binding, introduced the theological concept of *bound willing* by using two case studies from the work of Alistair McFadyen. The first, the sexual abuse of children, introduced the essential dynamics of bound willing, and the second, the Nazi holocaust, showed how the will of whole nations could be bound. A study of the biblical book of Ezekiel showed how the dynamic of bound willing could affect a whole nation over many generations. Particularly problematic is the fact that the binding of the will affects the ability to know what is good so that, even when it is desired to choose what is good, damage can be done, damage that has been shaped by the actions of the past.

The Intermezzo explored how the dynamic of bound willing could help us to understand the history of The Land in the courts and in legislation since the 1960s. When the Yolngu brought their case to the Australian courts concerning their relationship to the land in the Gove Peninsula, what did not happen was a negotiation between two systems of law. Instead, the Australian court took the view that its role was to see if any of the claims of the Yolngu could be recognized in Australian law. This approach was fundamental to the ensuing history of The Land in the courts and legislation. Up until the *Mabo (2)* case, the interpretation of Australian law was that the Crown took both the ownership of The Land and also the right to give title to others. The *Mabo (2)* judgment was significant because it made a moral decision that, although the Crown took the right to give title to others, the law need not be interpreted as the Crown having also taken ownership of The Land. The consequence of this is that where the Crown had given title had given to others, that extinguished the rights of the First Peoples to that land to the extent of the title that was granted, and so there was some remnant title to the parts of The Land that could be claimed by the First Peoples. The *Wik* judgment extended this by deciding that some forms of lease did not necessarily extinguish all title rights of the original inhabitants to the land covered by the lease. This was only a partial turning away from the Root Sin, for it was inherently limited by the fact that the law is incapable of changing its own foundations. Changing the foundations of the law is the role of government. We saw in the narrative that the government did not seek to change the foundation of the law, but it did seek to enshrine the partial repentance of the *Mabo (2)* and judgments by legislating the *Native Title Act 1993* (Cth), to make the process of claiming the residual rights much simpler. It was seen how the implementation of this act was fraught with difficulties, but gradually a deeper process emerged. Following the *Wik* judgment, however, there was explicit political action to rescind the changes allowed by *Mabo (2)* and *Wik*, changes which were cemented by the judgments of the courts, which had a different political make-up from those which had made the *Mabo (2)* and *Wik* judgments. In theological terms, this was an explicit continuation of the Root Sin.

Given that human beings and nations are bound to sin, what hope is there for the future? Already in the First Movement, it was seen that the overflowing love of God is acting in a transformative way in the world, a love that is blocked by the bound will, but that the bound will can be set free by turning towards God. This movement of turning towards God was explored in the Second Movement, Loosing, which examined the concrete processes that can result in the freeing of the will, so that good can be chosen, and so that the future no longer needs to be bound by the past. The concepts of repentance and forgiveness were explored. Critically, repentance is usually more than an apology, involving seeking to put things right. Repentance can be met by forgiveness, which is a choice to let go of retribution so that the future does not need to be determined by the past. There can be no forgiveness without repentance. Repentance and forgiveness are intertwined processes and it is in the deep examination of one's actions, listening to the victims of the actions, that the nature of repentance and forgiveness can arise. The fact that in Australia some of this self-examination is happening, and also that the stories are being told by those who have been adversely affected by this history, is an encouraging sign that we have started down the journey of repentance, but we must be extremely wary of closing off that process too soon, of trying to create a national story that bypasses a true and full repentance. The Second Movement also had an extended biblical case study of the letters of Paul to the church in Corinth. The reason for this study was to show that the whole of their culture was bound by the patronage system and that the only way to repent was to lay open the entire foundations of their culture in repentance. In a similar way, nothing less than repenting of the Root Sin of Australia will enable us all to go into the future in a way that does not continue the damage of the past. Critically, Paul does not tell the people in Corinth how they should restructure their society. In fact, he probably could not see this himself, for he was bound up in that society too, although trying to help the churches shift from their bound willing towards freedom in God. That is, the outcome of the process of repentance is usually not clear at the beginning of the process of repentance, but only emerges in engaging with the victim. It comes as a gift of God, beyond the imagination of those who are embarking on the process together. A byproduct of this study is a deeper understanding of reconciliation: reconciliation is this process of repentance and forgiveness, a radical uncovering of the sins of the past, creating the space for the victim to be able to state everything that is needed for the safety of the future, and an openness to the gift of God that establishes a justice that is deeper than can be imagined at the outset of the process. This radical openness to the future is a risk, but it is an assured risk because we are working in the way that God is working in the world.

The Second Movement finished by looking at the Uluru Statement from the Heart. In the language of this book, this is a statement from the victims of the Root Sin concerning the nature of the repentance that is required of Australia, and it is also an implicit offer of forgiveness. I remain deeply concerned by this, for it is possible for all the requested features to be given without repentance of the Root Sin. Repenting of the Root Sin can be nothing less than examining the whole foundations of Australia, including negotiating the relationship between Australian law and the systems of law of the First Peoples. Without this repentance, it will be inevitable that this offer, too, will be colonized by the dominant system of Australia.

Australia is in the process of myth-creation, of trying to tell a story about its past so that it can go into the future without continuing the damage of the past. We have a complex history with multiple layers of interconnection to each other and to The Land. Those who have are descended from those who came with the First Fleet or subsequently have built up these layers of connection. This myth creation can only be done if we stop trying to create a narrative of Australia, for Australia is indelibly shaped by the Root Sin. Instead, we need to tell a story about The Land and its peoples. In order to have a story which does not continue the damage of the past, that history must include Australia repenting of its Root Sin, which is to be met by forgiveness. Then the gift of God will be a true reconciliation between the peoples of The Land, and the creation of new ways of living with The Land which will also enable The Land to flourish.

I will finish with a story of hope from my own experience, an experience of new and unimaginable life brought to the land. Many years ago, I was participating in a quiet day led by my bishop. In one of his talks, the bishop was encouraging us to be curious, and so I set off on a walk in order to help me pray, consciously seeking to be curious in openness to God. We were in Cornwall, in the area which has been mined for china clay over the centuries. All over the landscape there are piles of waste—the rocks and imperfectly collected clay—that were left behind when the clay was washed out of the rocks. As I was walking past a decades-old abandoned mound of waste, from before the era of mechanization, I noticed that there were lots of birds flying around the face of the clay tip. Curious, I stopped to look and I noticed numerous round holes in the face of the waste tip, where the birds had made nests and they were coming to feed their young. As I looked more carefully, I became aware that shrubs and small trees and other vegetation were also now growing on what was once a pile of stones and imperfectly collected clay. I experienced God speaking to me through this land about the nature of the work of God in the world: that God takes the mess that we have made, even that which has been abandoned as waste and useless, and brings new life into it. It is really important to note that this gift did not pretend that the past did not happen; it did not bulldoze the rubbish into a hole and make it flat, but rather the life had come in what was left in the present from the past.

For me, this has become a definitive metaphor for the work of God in the world, of understanding how the resurrection of Jesus impacts on the life of the world. The Land is not what it once was. The peoples of The Land have been formed by their interactions with each other and with The Land itself. Repentance, forgiveness, and reconciliation do not return us to a pristine past, but enable the development of new ways of living at peace with The Land and with each other that draw on old ways of knowing whilst also allowing new knowledge to emerge.[511] The work of God in this process is why I do not despair about what seems to be an intractable situation in Australia, where huge resources, including time and energy and love, have delivered some benefits, but not delivered all that was hoped for. It is also why we can take the risk of trying to find the root of these problems, not because we want to blame someone or because we want to make people feel guilty, but because we need to understand the reality of the situation in which we find ourselves trapped, for only then can we seek a way out.

The situation in The Land is complex. There are many who are pursuing a national identity which denies or downgrades the errors of Australia, or who claim that they lie firmly in the past.[512] On the other hand, there is a real heart in Australia to come to terms with the whole of the history of all the peoples of The Land, in a way that does not privilege one narrative over another and which does not lose important strands of the narratives. We want all the peoples of The Land to flourish, gathering all of this together in such a way that the past is no longer damaging the present. This book has shown that this cannot be done by simply drawing a line under the past, saying that we, the Subsequent Peoples, are different from our forebears, for we are caught up in ways of living and responding which have been shaped by how we have lived in the past and so we cannot even always see what is good: the will of the Australia has been bound by what, herein, has been called the Root Sin, coming to live in The Land as if it was empty, without taking account of the First Peoples, their identity as a people, their connections to The Land, and their languages and their cultures.[513] It is only by recognizing this and fully understanding the depth of the pathology that has arisen from this that we can begin the long process of repenting of the Root Sin and its consequences through history. At the end of this process, it will be recognized that justice has been done and there will be space for all the peoples of The Land, and The Land itself, to flourish.

I opened this book, inviting the reader to do the "slow work of listening, reflecting, deliberating"[514] because "time is precisely what you need to think of things that are new—things that exceed the conventional wisdom."[515] I hope that you have been able to do this and that the journey has been worth the work. After all, "God is the power of the future contradicting all history that wishes to build its future out of its present."[516]

Endnotes

1. Due to Aboriginal cultural sensitivity concerning the photographing and naming of people who have died, I have refrained from including the performers in the photograph.

2. The 2006 season of the Australian Ballet included a production of "Gathering," a collaboration between the Australian Ballet and the Bangarra Dance Theatre, an Indigenous dance company. The erasure of First Peoples seems to unconsciously assert itself, as displayed in the poster, even when other events seemingly engage with them. I wrote to the Australian Ballet, sending them my photograph and what I had written because I did not want to inadvertently misrepresent them. I had the following helpful response from Rose Mulready, content expert for the Australian Ballet, on December 12, 2018:

> In the world of classical ballet, the *ballet blanc* is a centuries-old tradition that encompasses such canonical works as *Swan Lake*, *Giselle*, *La Sylphide* and *La Bayadère*. The vision of flocks of ballerinas dressed in white tulle is an intrinsic part of this heritage art form. Playing off the audience's love of these kind of ballets to market a triple bill would probably have been the only thinking behind this billboard in 2005. Obviously there are other cultural meanings to the use of this name, as the culture-jamming you have captured in 2005 demonstrates.
>
> In 2018, we would certainly hope that other thoughts would arise when putting together the marketing for one of our programs. Certainly, with a range of non-white company members, including Indigenous dancers, The Australian Ballet is becoming a more accurate reflection of today's nation.
>
> Another thing that may be of interest: for the past 14 months, The Australian Ballet has been working on the development of a Reconciliation Action Plan with Reconciliation Australia. The process compels us to reflect on every aspect of the company and furthermore, to plan a future where The Australian Ballet operates in partnership with, and connection to Aboriginal and Torres Strait Islander Peoples and culture. We are excited by this process and look forward to speaking about the RAP in more detail when the process is complete.

3. Colermajer, "Is Speed Worth the Moral Cost?," quoted in Megan Davis, "Self-Determination," 133.

4. Colermajer, "Is Speed Worth the Moral Cost?," quoted in Megan Davis, "Self-Determination," 133.

5. Huggins and Little, "Rightful Place," 160.

6. Yunupingu, "Tradition, Truth and Tomorrow."

7. Commonwealth of Australia, *Final Report of the Referendum Council*.

8. Megan Davis, "Self-Determination and the Right to be Heard," 131.

9. Langton, "Finding a Resolution," 32.

10. It is worth reading the increasing number of books narrating people's lived experiences of negotiating these layers of identity. A good place to start is Grant, *Talking to My Country*; and Heiss, *Growing Up Aboriginal in Australia*.

11. These four elements are taken from Pearson, "A Rightful Place," 17, 109, expressing the common grievances of indigenous peoples around the world.

12. Commonwealth of Australia, *Final Report of the Referendum Council*, 1.

13. Commonwealth of Australia, *Final Report of the Referendum Council*, 1.

14. McFadyen, *Bound to Sin*.

15. Burn, "Reconciliation and Land in Australia."

16. This is widely attributed to one of William Faulkner's characters, but I have not managed to find the original quotation, nor its context.

17. Baldwin, "White Man's Guilt," 42–43, author's italics. Thanks to Anna Burn for drawing my attention to this.

18. See, e.g., Moran, *Serious Whitefella Stuff*.

19. McFadyen, *Bound to Sin*.

20. McFadyen, *Bound to Sin*, 19–21.

21. McFadyen, *Call to Personhood*, is helpful on the construction of personhood.

22. McFadyen, *Bound to Sin*, 21–22.

23. McFadyen, *Bound to Sin*, 59.

24. McFadyen, *Bound to Sin*, 62–74.

25. From my own experience of working with abused people, I would add spiritual to the list of aspects of reality that are distorted by abuse.

26. McFadyen, *Bound to Sin*, 78–79.

27. Using the language of "survivor" rather than "victim" is important: it highlights the fact that the abused person exercised some agency in the situation, however limited, but it is also hopeful, because that person can exercise agency in choosing those thigs which will overcome the damage of the abuse. McFadyen, *Bound to Sin*, 123.

28. McFadyen, *Bound to Sin*, 124.

29. McFadyen, *Bound to Sin*, 120–25.

30. Bauman, *Modernity and the Holocaust*.

31. McFadyen, *Bound to Sin*, 116.

32. The fact that the underlying passionate commitment to the ideology was suppressed probably made the disavowal of emotions and irrationality even more dangerous.

33. McFadyen, *Bound to Sin*, 82–85.

34. McFadyen, *Bound to Sin*, 85–88.

35. McFadyen, *Bound to Sin*, 89.

36. McFadyen, *Bound to Sin*, 88–91.

37. McFadyen, *Bound to Sin*, 91–93.

38. McFadyen, *Bound to Sin*, 93–95.

39. McFadyen, *Bound to Sin*, 95–98. The italicized quotation is attributed by the author to Bauman, *Modernity and the Holocaust*, 21–22.

40. McFadyen, *Bound to Sin*, 98–103.

41. McFadyen, *Bound to Sin*, 230, author's italics.

42. McFadyen, *Bound to Sin*, 119.

43. McFadyen, *Bound to Sin*, 128.

44. McFadyen, *Bound to Sin*, 208, author's italics.

45. McFadyen, *Bound to Sin*, 210.

46. McFadyen, *Bound to Sin*, 211.

47. McFadyen, *Bound to Sin*, 214–15.

48. Cf. McFadyen, *Bound to Sin*, 210–11.

49. Wink, *Unmasking the Powers*, 95, quoted in McFadyen, *Bound to Sin*, 244.

50. Some examples of such readings can be found in Joyce, *Divine Initiative*, 36.

51. Joyce, *Divine Initiative*, 36.

52. Joyce, *Divine Initiative*, 46, my italics.

53. Kaminsky, "Sins of the Fathers." He makes the same point about the presence of corporate responsibility in parts of the Hebrew Bible that were written late, arguing that its presence in 2 Kings was the result of a number of postexilic redactions of the material. Kaminsky, *Corporate Responsibility*, ch. 2.

54. Barton, "Gospel According to Matthew," 123–24.

55. Howley, *Breaking Spears*, 103, 184.

56. Donovan, *Christianity Rediscovered*, 92.

57. Mbiti, *African Religions and Philosophy*, 141.

58. Maurice Halbwachs has argued that human beings have very few memories that do not depend on being part of a group of some sort. This is noted in Parker, *Healing Wounded History*, 40–41. Alistair McFadyen also argues that personhood is inherently communal and that individuals are formed by their relationships with others. *Call to Personhood*.

59. Westerman, *Creation*, ch. 1. See also Hardy, "Created and Redeemed Sociality."

60. Zimmerli, *Ezekiel*, 377.

61. Joyce, *Divine Initiative*, 38.

62. Joyce, *Divine Initiative*, 52.

63. Kaminsky, *Corporate Responsibility*, 164–65.

64. Paul Joyce writes, "Ezekiel's concern is to discuss the causes of a particular historical disaster, the defeat of the nation and the deportations which followed it, but he advances his argument by drawing on analogies from the realm of criminal law. Recognition of the reapplication of this language is crucial to the understanding of the chapter" (*Divine Initiative*, 41).

65. Joyce, *Divine Initiative*, 163. Joel Kaminsky writes that it "is highly unlikely that this language was employed in order to proclaim a new theology of retribution in which God judged each person as an autonomous entity" (*Corporate Responsibility*, 165).

66. Kaminsky, *Corporate Responsibility*, 165.

67. Kaminsky, *Corporate Responsibility*, 166. Moshe Weinfeld asserts that the same is true of the deuteronomistic historians, namely, that the "conception that God only requites the sins of the fathers on the children only if the latter propagate the evil ways of their fathers is, in effect, the underlying view of the concept of retribution in the deuteronomistic history" (*Deuteronomy and the Deuteronomistic School*, 318). Nevertheless, in the deuteronomistic history, it does seem that God's punishment is being held back, so that, even though the generation being sent into exile was being punished for its own sins, it also appears to be being punished for the accumulated sins over the generations. Kaminsky, *Corporate Responsibility*, 42, 44–45.

68. Kaminsky, *Corporate Responsibility*, 166–68.

69. Joyce, *Divine Initiative*, 53.

70. Sakenfeld, "Ezekiel 18:25–32," 296.

71. Technically, the legal establishment of the colony may have been when Captain Philip caused his second commission to be read on February 7, 1788, and may have included earlier actions as far back as the activities of Captain Cook. See, e.g., *Mabo v Queensland (No 2)* (1992) 175 CLR 1, [3], [32] (Deane and Gaudron JJ). The numbering of the paragraphs comes from the version on the web page: http://www7.austlii.edu.au/cgi-bin/viewdoc/au/cases/cth/HCA/1992/23.html.

72. I have reformulated this following the helpful criticisms of Nigel Biggar, one of the examiners of my PhD thesis. I do not know if he would be satisfied with how it now stands.

73. Gammage, *Biggest Estate on Earth*.

74. http://www.mabonativetitle.com/info/cooperVsStuart.htm and discussions with Pat McIntyre. I remain responsible for any errors in interpretation.

75. Broome, *Aboriginal Australians*, 30–31.

76. Reynolds, *Frontier*.

77. Belgrave et al., *Waitangi Revisited*; Benion, "New Zealand"; Sean Brennan et al., *Treaty*; Buick-Constable, "Indigenous State Relations"; and Kawharu, *Waitangi* show how the Waitangi treaty has been important for Maoris in Aotearoa/New Zealand.

78. See, e.g.: Bartlett, "Canada: Indigenous Land Claims"; Bartlett, *Native Title*, 3–9; Benion, "New Zealand"; Chartrand, "Aboriginal Peoples in Canada"; De Costa, "Treaties in British Colombia"; Dorsett and Godden, *Guide to Overseas Precedents*; Morse, "Indigenous-Settler Treaty Making"; Tehan, "Co-Existence of Interests in Land"; and Rhiân Williams, "Native Title Mediation Practice."

79. Richard Broome writes:

> So it was that while the Indians of North America or the Maoris of New Zealand, who built villages, tilled the soil and had chiefs were offered treaties and some recognition of rights by the British, the Aborigines were not given any of these rights. This fact of dispossession was the crux of the future race relations problems in Australia, for it meant that injustice was sanctioned by the state and there could be little possibility of any fruitful human relations being formed with the Aborigines. (*Aboriginal Australians*, 31)

Legally, the First Peoples in Australia found themselves in a related, but importantly different position from these other nations. For example, in the United States of America, the Indigenous Peoples were regarded as "domestic dependent nations" (*Milirrpum and Others v. Nabalco Pty Ltd and the Commonwealth of Australia* (1971) 17 Federal Law Reports, 141, 215; *Mabo v Queensland (No 2)* (1992) 175 CLR 1, [135], [164] (Dawson J)). As another example, the legal history of land in New Zealand has been informed by the Waitangi treaty (*Mabo v Queensland (No 2)* (1992) 175 CLR 1, [137] (Dawson J)).

80. McGrath, *Born in the Cattle*, 170. See also Willis, "Riders in the Chariot," 316.

81. Keefe, *Paddy's Road*, 200–201; Olive, *Karijini Mirlimirli*, 12.

82. See further Pearson, "Aboriginal Disadvantage," 167–68.

83. Pearson, "Aboriginal Disadvantage," 168.

84. Pearson, "Aboriginal Disadvantage," 167–69. He outlines his political philosophy in his "Rightful Place." He is also a founder of the Cape York Partnership, which describes itself as "an Indigenous policy reform and leadership organisation dedicated to empowering Cape York Indigenous people" (https://capeyorkpartnership.org.au). We await the results of the work of this organization, but I would argue that the outcomes are going to be limited. The reason is that Pearson is just choosing a different set of tools that are still part of

the system, where the problem is the system itself. Of course, having to live in an overpoweringly powerful, dominant system means that one has to find a way of living within the constraints of the system, but it is only the changing of the system itself which will enable the overcoming of Aboriginal disadvantage.

85. Yunupingu, "Rom Watangu," 23, reproduced in Commonwealth of Australia, *Final Report of the Referendum Council*, 53–54.

86. Trudgen, *Why Warriors Lie Down and Die*.

87. Trudgen, *Why Warriors Lie Down and Die*, 221–22.

88. On a small scale, Richard Trudgen writes that the educational methods that he uses often result in "the people [taking] the educator to a new level of understanding about the subject being discussed" (*Why Warriors Lie Down and Die*, 238).

89. Moran, *Serious Whitefella Stuff*.

90. Moran, *Serious Whitefella Stuff*, 182.

91. Moran, *Serious Whitefella Stuff*, 37.

92. E.g., Weber, "Guilt," 19.

93. MacIntyre, *After Virtue*, 220–221, author's italics. Cf. Wendell Berry: "Once you begin to awaken to the realities of what you know, you are subject to staggering recognitions of your complicity in history and in the events in your own life . . . a historical wound, prepared centuries ago to come alive in me at my birth like a hereditary disease and to be augmented and deepened in my life" (quoted in Parker, *Healing Wounded History*, 83).

94. Commonwealth of Australia, *Bringing Them Home*. A significant part of the report is the record of the experiences of many Indigenous people.

95. These people are sometimes called the "Stolen Generations." The term "stolen" was used as early as 1915 by Hon. P. McGarry, who strongly opposed the NSW government *Aborigines Protection Amending Act 1915*, which gave it total power to separate children from their families without having to establish in court that they were neglected . . . According to McGarry it allowed the Board "to steal the child away from its parents" (*Bringing them Home*, pt. 2, ch. 3.) It was used in the title of Peter Read's report on the taking of children in NSW ("The Stolen Generations"). Bain Attwood also discusses the generation of this disputed term. He notes that "this narrative accrual could not have happened had there not been an appropriate cultural and political milieu for it" ("Learning About the Truth," 196). Mark McKenna notes that

> Bain Attwood has described how, in three decades between 1970 and 2000 a gradual process of "narrative accrual" has seen the work of indigenous writers, academic historians, novelists, film-makers, play-wrights, feminists and journalists constitute the Stolen Generations narrative as a site of "collective memory" for Aboriginal Australians. With the release of *Bringing Them Home* in 1997, this narrative had become central to the identity of Aboriginal Australians. In turn, three decades of increased political activism by Aboriginal people and their non-Aboriginal

supporters had begun to alter the way Australians were remembering their past. Just as Aboriginal people, imbued with a greater sense of cultural pride, mourned their historical experience in settler Australia as one of subjugation and oppression, non-Aboriginal Australians began to question the moral legitimacy of their national past. For both Aboriginal and non-Aboriginal Australia, the past was being reimagined. (*Looking for Blackfella's Point*, 209)

Heidi Norman, however, must be right when she observes that the term "Stolen Generation" does not do justice to the complexity of Aboriginal child removal, nor of the wider violent dispossession of the Aboriginal people. "Examination of the Limitations," 14.

96. Cowlishaw, "Studying Aborigines," 27.

97. Rose, *Dingo Makes Us Human*, 191.

98. Maddison, *Beyond White Guilt*, 176, author's italics.

99. See, for example, Baker et al., *Working on Country*; and Walsh and Mitchell, *Planning for Country*.

100. I am using the conventions for citing legal material as set out in the 4th edition of Melbourne Law Review Association's *Australian Guide to Legal Citation*, https://law.unimelb.edu.au/__data/assets/pdf_file/0005/3181325/AGLC4-with-Bookmarks-1.pdf.

101. In his judgment in the *Mabo and Others v State of Queensland (No 2)* (1992) 175 CLR 1 case, Justice Brennan repeatedly made statements along the line of, "in discharging its duty to declare the common law of Australia, this Court is not free to adopt rules that accord with contemporary notions of justice and human rights if their adoption would fracture the skeleton of principle which gives the body of our law its shape and internal consistency" (*Mabo and Others v State of Queensland (No 2)* (1992) 175 CLR 1, [29]).

102. I am grateful to Joe McIntyre for helping me think about this angle on the struggle.

103. These include such things as objects that demonstrate relationships to the land, and paintings which tell the sacred stories. See Morphy, *Aboriginal Art*, especially chs. 3–5; and Morphy, "Now You Understand."

104. Nancy Williams, *Yolngu and Their Land*, 62–72, 96–97.

105. "Law" in Aboriginal English is much closer to the Jewish idea of Torah than to understanding law as a set of rules. Thus, Deborah Bird Rose writes:

> Doug Campbell, one of the senior Yarrali men, explained to me early on in my time there that I must observe Aboriginal rules because there could be no exceptions under the Law:
>> You see that hill over there? Blackfellow Law like that hill. It never changes. Whitefellow law goes this way, that way, all the time changing. Blackfellow law different. It never changes. Blackfellow Law hard—like a stone, like that hill. The Law is the ground.

> Law is often expressed as rules about behaviour. But what Law seems most fundamentally to be about is relationships. Dreamings determined sets of moral relationships—country to country, country to plant and animal species, people to country, people to species, people to people. Individuals of any species come and go, but the underlying relationships persist. Law is a serious life and death business for individuals and for the world; it tells how the world hangs together. To disregard the Law would be to disregard the Root of life and thus to allow the cosmos to fall apart. (*Dingo Makes Us Human*, 56)

106. See. e.g., Memmot, "Social Structure," 40; and Fred Myers, "Always, Ask," 184–85. Cf. Larry Lanley, who wrote: "It all goes back to the land, that is why land rights are so important to us. We need the land to be Aboriginal in our minds . . . Take away our land like the Queensland Government is trying to do and we're nobody, we will die out, finish. The land gives the true meaning to Aboriginal life . . . At the heart of everything is land—it is the way we feel and think about the land that makes us Aboriginals . . . It is the only way to keep our culture, and without it we are scattered into a country that is not ours, where we feel hunted, like wild kangaroos and dingoes . . . There are the things we need to help us keep the head and body alive until we are given back our land, and the land can make us whole again" (quoted in Memmot, "Social Structure," 61–62).

107. Torres Strait Islander cultures are quite different from those of the First Peoples on mainland Australia and some information about these can be found in Becket, *Torres Strait Islanders*; and Sharp, "Malo's Law."

108. Richard Moyle records that the use of term "country" has been necessitated by conversing with whites: there is no equivalent word in the Alayawarra language, and the Agharringa men say they cannot conceive of a situation requiring it. Moyle, "Songs, Ceremonies and Sites," 68.

109. Rose et al., *Country of the Heart*, 14.

110. Rose et al., *Country of the Heart*, 41.

111. Strictly speaking, the understanding of land and tenure systems is not uniform across the country, but is shaped by the terrain. For example, the country owned by the Yolngu is organized in a chequerboard fashion, according to the two moieties of the people, whilst in the Pitjantjatjara country, the sacred sites are more point spaces and the presence of water and how far one can walk in a day from the main watering places in one's country shape the mental map of space. Richard Layton, "Pitjantjatjara Processes." Even the concept of a boundary varies from culture to culture. Moyle, "Songs, Ceremonies and Sites," 71.

112. Ten ways that Aboriginal people can have responsibility for a particular piece of land are given in Choo and O'Connell, "Historical Narrative and Proof," p. 16, n. 10. Similar points are made in McKenna, *Looking for Blackfellas' Point*, 67; and Nancy Williams, "Boundary Is to Cross," 128–41.

113. See, e.g., Sutton and Rigsby, "People with 'Politicks,'" 161; N. Williams, "Yolngu Concepts," 103; Gumbert, *Neither Justice nor Reason*, ch. 5.

114. For example, Peter Sutton and Bruce Rigsby write: "An important point that emerges from these and other case studies is that many Aboriginal people, including adult women, have a choice as to their territorial attachments. Their forbears may have willed land (and other property) to them, but they need not accept it in all cases and they may be able to invoke or create a range of 'facts' to establish new attachments to other land ... The changing political interests of individuals having different sets of paternal and maternal kinsmen, birth places, and the like, may also account for some of the variety in previous accounts of who has what attachments to which lands" ("People with 'Politicks,'" 167–69). See also N. Williams, *Yolngu and Their Land*, 184–85.

115. Layton, "Pitjantjatjara Processes," 24; Myers, "Always Ask," 24; N. Williams, "Yolngu Concepts," 104; Nancy Williams, *Yolngu and Their Land*, 181–85.

116. Veth, "'Abandonment' or Maintenance of Country."

117. Richard Gould, writes: "Since rainfall is scarce and unpredictable throughout the Western Desert, the key to overcoming or mitigating this particular constraint is long-distance social networks that permit families to move from their own foraging areas during periods of extreme drought to other, better favored areas. Elaborate social institutions foster this kind of contact and movement, including second-cross-cousin marriage and subsections. Each of these mechanisms operates to restrict the number of eligible spouses a person will find within his or her local area, compelling him to look farther afield for potential marriage partners. This tendency is increased by the widespread occurrence of polygyny, which results in multiple in-law relationships over long distances in all directions. These long-distance kin ties involve obligatory sharing of food, material goods, and access to key resources" ("To Have," 72).

118. Land tenure systems are discussed at length in Peterson and Langton, *Aborigines, Land and Land Rights*. They are also discussed in Sutton, *Native Title*. Changes in responsibilities are discussed in Langton, "Grandmother's Law".

119. As a concrete example, Sarah Maddison cites Wadeye, four hundred kilometers southwest of Darwin, where the Kardu Diminin people share the town with members of nineteen other clan groups, and, where the Kardu Diminin people would have traditionally spoken for the country, they now find themselves a minority in the organization being set up by the government, where all clans have a say on issues concerning the township. This conflict has its roots in people being brought together from off their own lands, and is exacerbated by the government trying to treat the disparate clans as one "community." Maddison, *Black Politics*, 151–53.

120. See, e.g., Edmunds, "Conflict in Native Title Claims"; Pearson, "Where We've Come From;" McIntosh, *Aboriginal*, 20; and Neate, "Turning Back the Tide?"

121. Maddison, *Black Politics*, 162; and Read, *Belonging*.

122. E.g., see the debate recorded in Maddison, *Black Politics*, 154–56.

123. Fred Myers, "Always Ask," 188–89; Reynolds, *Fate of a Free People*, 140–57; and Nancy Williams, "Boundary Is to Cross."

124. Bell, *Daughters of the Dreaming*, 25–29. Significant early exceptions to this are the anthropologist Catherine Berndt, who worked with her husband, Ronald Berndt; Phyllis Kaberry, "Life and Secret Ritual of Aboriginal Women"; and Olive Pink, "Land Ownership among the Aborigines."

125. Bell, "Aboriginal Women and Religious Experience"; and Keeley, "Women and the Land."

126. R. Jones, "Fire Stick Farming;" and Lewis, "Fire Technology and Resource Management."

127. Rose, "Sacred Site," 101–3.

128. Broome, *Aboriginal Australians*, 14; Rose, *Dingo Makes us Human*, 97–99; and Walsh and Mitchell, *Planning for Country*, 60–61.

129. Maddison, *Black Politics*, 64.

130. Adams and English, "Biodiversity," 87; Herbert, "Reconciliation"; and Horstman, "Black."

131. See, e.g., Gammage, *Biggest Estate on Earth*; and Pascoe, *Dark Emu*.

132. Cf. *Mabo and Others v State of Queensland (No 2)* (1992) 175 CLR 1, 33 (Brennan J): "Another justification for the application of the theory of terra nullius to inhabited territory—a justification first advanced by Vattel at the end of the 18th century—was that new territories could be claimed by occupation if the land were uncultivated, for Europeans had a right to bring lands into production if they were left uncultivated by the indigenous inhabitants."

133. (1971) 17 FLR 141 ('*Milirrpum*').

134. Marcia Langton writes:

> It is increasingly acknowledged by anthropologists that amongst Aboriginal groups which have endured rapid population loss as a result of frontier violence and disease, forced removals or other impacts of colonialisation, the senior women of the relevant land tenure corporations take on a special role in succession arrangements to land where the original land-holding corporation has not survived. (Grandmother's Law," 86)

and:

> The paradigm in which men's evidence is the cornerstone in proving the existence and rules of customary land corporation will be less efficacious in native title claims in those areas where the massacres, epidemics, forced removals and impact of alcohol abuse, imprisonment, employment in the pastoral industry and itinerant labouring have resulted in a female gerontocracy of the remnant clans and of amalgamated customary land corporations such as "tribes." ("Grandmother's Law," 92)

Langton claims that senior Aboriginal women had power over marriage arrangements, which were essentially about distributing kin across various "countries," and that this role has come increasingly to the fore because of the problems mentioned in the above-quoted paragraphs. The women tend to outlive the men, and so they become increasingly important in their preservation of knowledge.

135. Bell, *Daughters of the Dreaming*, 140–41.

136. A situation such as this arose with the Hindmarsh Bridge development. At the heart of the dispute were two groups of Ngarrindjeri women, one of which claimed that a sacred area connected to women's fertility would be destroyed by the development, and the other which said that there was no such area. For a narrative of the events, see Broome, *Aboriginal Australians*, 249–53. Bell made an analysis of the case in her, *Ngarrindjeri*. See also her "Word of a Woman." Bell's analysis is contested by Richard Kimber, who finds the book "severely flawed" ("Diane Bell," 232). He makes lots of detailed criticisms, but he is also concerned that Bell's feminist stance is not value-free, to the point of ignoring difficult evidence ("Diane Bell," 217, 227), importing concepts from native Americans ("Diane Bell," 206, 213, 231), and even having been instrumental in telling the women some things they did not know ("Diane Bell," 220–21), to the point that reasonably knowledgeable readers will "be likely to feel . . . that they've occasionally been misled" ("Diane Bell," 217). The final twist of the case happened after the publication of the book. Justice John von Doussa of the Federal Court ruled that the women's knowledge was not fabricated, although by then the bridge had been built. Richard Broome writes:

> What is clear is that this disagreement was manipulated in a battle over the development at Goolwa and those who wished to discredit Aboriginal custodial claims in native title deliberations. This affair also revealed the continuing gap between European and Aboriginal systems of knowledge and belief, and the politics and manipulations that flourish in that gap. The media gave the issue plenty of space. The public, who were bewildered by the conflicting claims of the women, anthropologists, politicians and inquiries, probably followed their existing prejudices. Those sympathetic to the Aboriginal cause believed the secrets were true, while those who were unsympathetic believed it was a case of mere fabrications preventing legitimate development. Despite the recent vindication of von Doussa's decision in the compensation case, Aboriginal cultural claims across the country have been harmed by the case. (*Aboriginal Australians*, 253)

137. Quoted in Atkinson, "Reflections on the Yorta Yorta," 6.

138. E.g., Olive, *Karijini Mirlimirli*, 77.

139. Deborah Rose recalls stopping at the side of a road in 1986 to film some of the most spectacular erosion in the Victoria River District. She asked her Aboriginal teacher/friend Daly Pulkara what he called that country. He said, "It's the wild. Just the wild." "He then went on to speak of quiet country—the country in which all the care of generations of his people is evident to those who know how to see it. Quiet country stands in contrast to the wild: we were looking at a wilderness, man-made and cattle-made. This wild was a place where the life of the country was falling down into the gullies and washing away with the rain" ("Sacred Site," 117). Quiet country was the result of the organizational "management" of the land by his ancestors. Daly said that the damage in wild country was killing both life and time, "'We'll run out of history,' he said, 'because

kartiya [Europeans] fuck the Law up and [they're] knocking all the power out of this country'" (Rose, "Sacred Site," 118). See further: Rose, *Reports from a Wild Country*, especially ch. 4.

140. Besides sheep and cattle, some famous examples include rabbits, cane toads, water buffalo, and mimosa pigra. Rose et al., *Country of the Heart*, 127–32.

141. Nesbit et al., "Cooperative Cross-Cultural Biological Surveys." Nic Gamold gives examples of the importance of using of both Aboriginal and non-Aboriginal knowledge in wildlife management. Gambold, "Role of Traditional."

142. Tehan, "Hope Disillusioned," 524.

143. Read, *Belonging*. See also, Hinkson, "Exploring 'Aboriginal' Sites in Sydney." Richard Baker et al. write, "for a high proportion of indigenous people, the opportunities to look after country are very limited—their country has largely been alienated and it is likely that they have been physically excluded even from visiting it. Under such circumstances it is astonishing that indigenous residents of major cities like Sydney or Melbourne have retained so much knowledge of where their country is and strong feelings about the need to look after it" (*Working on Country*, 14). Related to this is the long memory of genealogies. Feary, "Moving Towards Joint Management," 288.

144. This narrative bears the marks of heavy revision by Pat McIntyre, for which I am extremely grateful.

145. *Milirrpum* (n 133) 167, 168, 170, 171, 272, 273.

146. (1992) 175 CLR 1 ("*Mabo (2)*"). The numbering of the paragraphs comes from the version on the webpage: http://www7.austlii.edu.au/cgi-bin/viewdoc/au/cases/cth/HCA/1992/23.html.

147. He had opposed the *Aboriginal Land Rights (Northern Territory) Act 1976* when a member of the Frazer government.

148. (1996) 187 CLR 1 ("*Wik*").

149. This event has entered Australian folklore, but I have yet to track down a definitive reference to it.

150. Joe McIntyre, personal communication.

151. Langton, "Medicine Square," 218.

152. This information on the bark petition is largely taken from Harris, *One Blood*.

153. Note that the "overseas" mission board was operating in Australia.

154. This was not the first petition from First Peoples. For example, the First Peoples on Flinders Island petitioned Queen Victoria in February 1846, the petition arriving in March 1847. Reynolds, *Fate of a Free People*, 7–14.

155. Images of the petition and some discussion of its history and significance can be found on the webpage: https://www.foundingdocs.gov.au/item-did-104.html.

156. Morphy, "Now You Understand," 115.

157. Gumbert, *Neither Justice nor Reason*, 22; Broome, *Aboriginal Australians*, 145.

158. Whitlam, "Speech at the Gurindji Land Ceremony."

159. It can be seen, for example, in Perkins and Langton, *First Australians*, 355, or on the webpage: https://collection.maas.museum/object/344580. The webpage records that the photograph was taken by Mervyn Bishop, the first Koori press photographer.

160. Besides reading the judgments, I have been greatly helped in understanding these principles through my discussions with Pat McIntyre and Joe McIntyre, and in reading Hepburn, *Principles of Property Law*, chs. 1–3 and 6.

161. Quotation marks are used here to emphasize that this is the value judgment of those who made it, rather than a statement of fact.

162. See, e.g., *Milirrpum* (n 133) 201.

163. In fact, the thinking was turned on its head, so that the European nations not only had a right but also an obligation to occupy such countries, because the indigenous populations had failed in their responsibility to make the land productive. Duchrow and Hinkelammert, *Property for People*, ch. 3.

164. *Milirrpum* (n 133) 200.

165. This was established in *Cooper v Stuart* (1880) 14 App. Cas. 286 (*Milirrpum* (n 133) 242).

166. Hepburn, *Principles of Property Law*, 3. Cf. *Milirrpum* (n 133) 272.

167. Hepburn, *Principles of Property Law*, ch. 2.

168. Hepburn, *Principles of Property Law*, 34.

169. *Milirrpum* (n 133) 244.

170. I recognize that this is a value judgment by a legal lay person, but it seems to me that Blackburn J was willing the plaintiffs to convince him that the Yolngu had a proprietary interest in the land in question.

171. *Milirrpum* (n 133) 167, 168, 170, 171, 272, 273.

172. *Milirrpum* (n 133) 167.

173. *Milirrpum* (n 133) 244–45. See further, e.g., Merlan, "Regimentation of Customary Practice," 65; and Ritter, "Rejection," 14.

174. Bartlett, *Native Title*, 10–13; and Chaney, "Developments."

175. Pat McIntye, personal communication.

176. *Milirrpum* (n 133) 267–68.

177. Nancy Williams, *Yolngu and Their Land*, 159. The Yolngu believed that if they showed the court the emblems of their ownership, then the court would understand that the land was theirs. Sharp, *No Ordinary Judgement*, 71. W. E. H. Stanner, however, had already warned them that this was unlikely to be the case. Sharp, *No Ordinary Judgement*, 278–79.

178. Brennan J acknowledged the privilege of being shown these objects.

Milirrpum (n 133) 167.

179. McIntosh, *Aboriginal Reconciliation and the Dreaming*, 67–71.

180. Nancy Williams, *Yolngu and Their Land*, 159. She states that "I also argue that the facts I set out, which include some unknown or incompletely understood by non-Aborigines at the time of the Yirrkala land case, and a reinterpretation of certain others demonstrate that the Yolngu system of land tenure both defines and regulates proprietary interests in land and that the Yolngu clans' claim of continuous occupancy in that case was correct, although not as stated" (*Yolngu and Their Land*, 7).

181. Gumbert, *Neither Justice nor Reason*, 78–81, 93–95.

182. Pat McIntyre, personal communication.

183. Pat McIntyre, personal communication.

184. McIntosh, *Aboriginal Reconciliation and the Dreaming*, 126.

185. Gumbert, *Neither Justice nor Reason*, 93.

186. Quoted in Gumbert, *Neither Justice nor Reason*, 93.

187. Nancy Williams says that this definition was a result of the Yolngu simplification of their land tenure system in the *Milirrpum* (n 133) case. *Yolngu and Their Land*, 7. Mark Gumbert claims that it was because Woodward J based his definition on the anthropological advice of Berndt, rather than the Yolngu themselves. *Neither Justice nor Reason*, 95.

188. Gumbert, *Neither Justice nor Reason*, 95.

189. This is the primary criticism raised by Mark Gumbert, who argues, rightly, that land tenure organization is much more complex. *Neither Justice nor Reason*.

190. J. Jones, "We May Have the Spirit;" and Rose, "Women and Land Claims."

191. Edmunds, "Conflict in Native Title Claims," 3.

192. Johnson et al., *Placebound*, 172.

193. E.g., see the discussion of a claim for land around Katherine in Merlan, "Regimentation of Customary Practice."

194. Rowell, "Women and Land Claims."

195. Neate, *Aboriginal Land Rights Law*, 82, 87, 89–91.

196. Maddison, *Black Politics*, 65.

197. Neate, "Review of the Northern Territory Land Rights Act."

198. Reeves, "Building on Land Rights," found at: https://www.aph.gov.au/Parliamentary_Business/Committees/Committees_Exposed/atsia/reeves/inquiryinf. It is summarized in Neate, "Review of the Northern Territory Land Rights Act." See also Altman, "Economic Development of the Indigenous Economy," 107.

199. Yunupingu, "From the Bark Petition," 14.

200. Flo Kennedy, quoted in Sharp, *No Ordinary Judgement*, 29.

201. Reynolds, *Law of the Land*, 185–86.

202. Stanner, "Yirrkala Land Case."

203. Stanner, "Yirrkala Land Case."

204. Nonie Sharp has paraphrased Ron Daly's words, in *No Ordinary Judgement*, 38.

205. Bartlett, *Native Title*, 15–21; Sharp, *No Ordinary Judgement*, 46–48; and Young et al., "Into the Fray Again."

206. See Bartlett, *Native Title*, 17; Sharp, *No Ordinary Judgement*, and Young et al., "Into the Fray Again," 57–62.

207. *Mabo (2)* (n 146) [2] (Decision). Recall that the numbering of the paragraphs comes from the version on the webpage: http://www7.austlii.edu.au/cgi-bin/viewdoc/au/cases/cth/HCA/1992/23.html.

208. *Mabo (2)* (n 146) [29] (Brennan J):

> Australian law is not only the historical successor of, but is an organic development from, the law of England. Although our law is the prisoner of its history, it is not now bound by decisions of courts in the hierarchy of an Empire then concerned with the development of its colonies. It is not immaterial to the resolution of the present problem that, since the *Australia Act 1986* (Cth) came into operation, the law of this country is entirely free of Imperial control. The law which governs Australia is Australian law . . . Increasingly since 1968 . . . the common law of Australia has been substantially in the hands of this Court. Here rests the ultimate responsibility of declaring the law of the nation.

209. *Mabo (2)* (n 146) [58] (Brennan J).

210. This was recognized by Blackburn J in *Milirrpum* (n 133) 267, 268, as discussed above.

211. *Mabo (2)* (n 146) [29] (Brennan J):

> In discharging its duty to declare the common law of Australia, this Court is not free to adopt rules that accord with contemporary notions of justice and human rights if their adoption would fracture the skeleton of principle which gives the body of our law its shape and internal consistency.

Mabo (2) (n 146) [43] (Brennan J):

> However, recognition by our common law of the rights and interests in land of the indigenous inhabitants of a settled colony would be precluded if the recognition were to fracture a skeletal principle of our legal system. The proposition that the Crown became the beneficial owner of all colonial land on first settlement has been supported by more than a disregard of indigenous rights and interests. It is necessary to consider these other reasons for past disregard of indigenous rights and interests and then to

return to a consideration of the question whether and in what way our contemporary common law recognizes such rights and interests in land.

212. *Mabo (2)* (n 146) [51] (Brennan J):

By attributing to the Crown a radical title to all land within a territory over which the Crown has assumed sovereignty, the common law enabled the Crown, in exercise of its sovereign power, to grant an interest in land to be held of the Crown or to acquire land for the Crown's demesne. The notion of radical title enabled the Crown to become Paramount Lord of all who hold a tenure granted by the Crown and to become absolute beneficial owner of unalienated land required for the Crown's purposes. But it is not a corollary of the Crown's acquisition of a radical title to land in an occupied territory that the Crown acquired absolute beneficial ownership of that land to the exclusion of the indigenous inhabitants. If the land were desert and uninhabited, truly a terra nullius, the Crown would take an absolute beneficial title (an allodial title) to the land ... there would be no other proprietor. But if the land were occupied by the indigenous inhabitants and their rights and interests in the land are recognized by the common law, the radical title which is acquired with the acquisition of sovereignty cannot itself be taken to confer an absolute beneficial title to the occupied land. Nor is it necessary to the structure of our legal system to refuse recognition to the rights and interests in land of the indigenous inhabitants. The doctrine of tenure applies to every Crown grant of an interest in land, but not to rights and interests which do not owe their existence to a Crown grant. The English legal system accommodated the recognition of rights and interests derived from occupation of land in a territory over which sovereignty was acquired by conquest without the necessity of a Crown grant.

Mabo (2) (n 146) [52] (Brennan J):

Recognition of the radical title of the Crown is quite consistent with recognition of native title to land, for the radical title, without more, is merely a logical postulate required to support the doctrine of tenure (when the Crown has exercised its sovereign power to grant an interest in land) and to support the plenary title of the Crown (when the Crown has exercised its sovereign power to appropriate to itself ownership of parcels of land within the Crown's territory). Unless the sovereign power is exercised in one or other of those ways, there is no reason why land within the Crown's territory should not continue to be subject to native title. It is only the fallacy of equating sovereignty and beneficial ownership of land that gives rise to the notion that native title is extinguished by the acquisition of sovereignty.

213. *Mabo (2)* (n 146) [39–42] (Brennan J):

The theory that the indigenous inhabitants of a "settled" colony had no proprietary interest in the land thus depended on a discriminatory denigration of indigenous inhabitants, their social organization and customs. As the basis of the theory is false in fact and unacceptable in our society, there is a choice of legal principle to be made in the present case. This Court can either apply the existing authorities and proceed to inquire whether the Meriam people are higher "in the scale of social organization" than the Australian Aborigines whose claims were "utterly disregarded" by the existing authorities or the Court can overrule the existing authorities, discarding the distinction between inhabited colonies that were terra nullius and those which were not . . . The fiction by which the rights and interests of indigenous inhabitants in land were treated as non-existent was justified by a policy which has no place in the contemporary law of this country . . . Whatever the justification advanced in earlier days for refusing to recognize the rights and interests in land of the indigenous inhabitants of settled colonies, an unjust and discriminatory doctrine of that kind can no longer be accepted. The expectations of the international community accord in this respect with the contemporary values of the Australian people.

214. *Mabo (2)* (n 146) [63] (Brennan J):

The dispossession of the indigenous inhabitants of Australia was not worked by a transfer of beneficial ownership when sovereignty was acquired by the Crown, but by the recurrent exercise of a paramount power to exclude the indigenous inhabitants from their traditional lands as colonial settlement expanded and land was granted to the colonists. Dispossession is attributable not to a failure of native title to survive the acquisition of sovereignty, but to its subsequent extinction by a paramount power.

Mabo (2) (n 146) [83] (Brennan J):

Where the Crown has validly alienated land by granting an interest that is wholly or partially inconsistent with a continuing right to enjoy native title, native title is extinguished to the extent of the inconsistency. Thus native title has been extinguished by grants of estates of freehold or of leases but not necessarily by the grant of lesser interests (e.g., authorities to prospect for minerals).

215. *Mabo (2)* (n 146) [22] (Deane and Gaudron JJ); and Neate, "Turning Back the Tide?," 8. Also, Maureen Tehan writes:

The title was outside the common law's tenurial system, but it encompassed rights that were recognised and protected by the common law, although those rights were not part of the common law itself. In fact, the title was said to be *sui generis* and the precise nature of the title and where it sat within the broader property system was unclear. Was it proprietary or was it merely a usufructuary right? Was it a right to exclusive occupation or was it a lesser right and, if so, what did that right conceptually entail? ("Hope Disillusioned," 534–35)

These were resolved in a particular way by the *Native Title Act 1993*, and several key decisions, including *Ward* and *Yorta Yorta*, discussed below.

216. *Mabo (2)* (n 146) [42–48] (Dawson J):

Therefore, the policy of the Imperial Government during this period is clear: whilst the aboriginal inhabitants were not to be ill-treated, settlement was not to be impeded by any claim which those inhabitants might seek to exert over the land. Settlement expanded rapidly, and the selection and occupation of the land by settlers were regulated by the Governors in a way that was intended to be comprehensive and complete and was simply inconsistent with the existence of any native interests in the land . . . There may not be a great deal to be proud of in this history of events. But a dispassionate appraisal of what occurred is essential to the determination of the legal consequences . . . The policy which lay behind the legal regime was determined politically and, however insensitive the politics may now seem to have been, a change in view does not of itself mean a change in the law. It requires the implementation of a new policy to do that and that is a matter for government rather than the courts. In the meantime, it would be wrong to attempt to revise history or to fail to recognize its legal impact, however unpalatable it may now seem. To do so would be to impugn the foundations of the very legal system under which this case must be decided.

217. Maureen Tehan has a helpful discussion of the types of response, and further pointers into the literature, in "Hope Disillusioned," 526–27.

218. Gibbs, "Foreword," xiii.

219. Nonie Sharp writes that "evidence was not always presented in a form which the judge could understand, and this was not primarily a problem of language. For example, the mythical-religious idiom of many fundamental truths for the Meriam is one of metaphor and analogy, and hence not readily accessible to the literal mind" (*No Ordinary Judgement*, 74).

220. Keon-Cohen, "Some Problems of Proof," 200.

221. Sharp, *No Ordinary Judgement*, 76, 105–8, 112–24.

222. Sharp, *No Ordinary Judgement*, 94–95.

223. Sharp, *No Ordinary Judgement*, 139–44, 154.

224. Broome, *Aboriginal Australians*, 256; Foley and Watson, *People's Movement*, 101–5; Herbert, "Reconciliation in Cape York Peninsula"; and Horstman, "Black Shadows."

225. Gunstone, "Responses of Australian Governments to Indigenous Challenges," 11; and Jennet, "Aboriginal Affairs Policy," 254–57.

226. Merlan, "Regimentation of Customary Practice," 65.

227. *The Australian*, October 17, 1992.

228. Redfern is an inner-city area of Sydney, with a large population of First Peoples.

229. Keating, "Redfern Park Speech," 64.

230. Bartlett, *Native Title*, 34; Patrick Dodson, "Unfinished Business," 39–40; Ridgeway, "Mabo Ten Years On," 186; and Tickner, *Taking Taking a Stand*, 221.

231. Robert Tickner was the Federal Minister for Aboriginal and Torres Strait Islander Affairs during this period, and he gives his personal account of this process in *Taking a Stand*, 191–200. For his comments on the act, see 191–200, and for the land fund, 221–36. See also Bartlett, *Native Title*, ch. 3.

232. *The Australian*, June 8, 1993.

233. Richard Bartlett summarizes some of the types of opposition from the states, mining companies, and pastoralists, including saying that First Peoples were "too primitive" for it to be possible to make a treaty with them, calling them "Stone Age" people, and saying that unless *Mabo (2)* was rescinded, Australians would revert to the Stone Age. *Native Title*, 35–39.

234. Bartlett, *Native Title*, 39.

235. *The West Australian*, June 19, 1993; June 21, 1993; June 24, 1993.

236. *The West Australian*, July 20, 1993.

237. Cf. the perceptive observation of Ann Curthoys:

> Many non-indigenous Australians have difficulty in seeing themselves as the beneficiaries of the colonisation process because they, like so many others, from the United States to Canada to Israel and elsewhere, see themselves as victims, not oppressors ... [For the victim], the legacy of the colonial past is a continuing fear of illegitimacy. ("Mythologies," 13, 37)

238. Bartlett, *Native Title*, 39. He is quoting an October 1993 advertising leaflet from the Association of Mining and Exploration Companies.

239. Bartlett, *Native Title*, 40.

240. The National Native Title Tribunal has an excellent website: http://www.nntt.gov.au. It contains, for example: information about the process of making a native title claim, information about making an indigenous land use agreement or an agreement about a future act, the current status of negotiations about these issues, maps, and so on. They have also produced a video/DVD *Native Title Stories*.

241. The provision for future acts allowed registered native title claimants and holders the "right to negotiate" about use of the land for which they were claiming, or held native title.

242. National Native Title Tribunal, *Mediating Native Title Applications*.

243. Personal communication in an interview on 28.5.05. This was confirmed

in an interview with Jenny Macklin, the Federal Indigenous Affairs Minister, on May 21, 2008: "Ms Macklin says it would take at least 30 years to resolve the backlog of outstanding claims under the current system and some of the burden should be removed from the courts" (http://www.abc.net.au/news/stories/2008/05/21/2251850.htm).

244. National Native Title Tribunal, *Mediating Native Title Applications*, 179.

245. National Native Title Tribunal, *Mediating Native Title Applications*, 73.

246. Cf. Patrick Dodson, "Unfinished Business." A study of the experience of mediation from the perspective of mediators can found in R. Williams, "Native Title Mediation Practice."

247. Bartlett, *Native Title*, 39.

248. Draft report of the Interdepartmental Committee of Officials, para. 33.

249. Bartlett, *Native Title*, 39.

250. *Wik* (n 148) 2–3. This was the judgment of Toohey, Gaudron, Gummow, and Kirby JJ, with Brennan CJ, Dawson, and McHugh JJ dissenting.

251. Hiley, "Introduction," 1.

252. *Wik* (n 148) 76 (Brennan CJ).

253. *Wik* (n 148) 78 (Brennan CJ).

254. *Wik* (n 148) 115–16 (Toohey J).

255. *Wik* (n 148) 120 (Toohey J).

256. Bartlett, *Native Title*, 46–47, 49.

257. The research of Reynolds Dalziel was critical here, arguing that the instructions from Lord Grey concerning leases at the foundation of the colony of South Australia led to this interpretation ("Aborigines and Pastoral Leases"). This interpretation is not without its challengers, such as James Fulcher, who argues, amongst other things, that Reynolds has misinterpreted the documents by reading them in the context of today rather than the context in which they were written ("Sui Generis").

258. *Wik* (n 148) 122 (Toohey J).

259. *Wik* (n 148) 122 (Toohey J).

260. *Wik* (n 148) 154 (Gaudron J):

> The strongest indication that a pastoral lease granted under the 1910 Act did not confer a right of exclusive possession is to be found in those provisions of the Act conferring rights on persons authorised in that behalf to enter upon land the subject of a pastoral lease to remove timber, stone, gravel, clay, guano or other material (s 199) denying the lessee the right to ringbark, cut or destroy trees (s 198) and also denying the lessee power to restrict authorised persons from cutting or removing timber or material within the holding (s 200). There is a similar indication in the provision permitting others to depasture stock if a stock route or

road passed through the holding (s 205). And, of course, there were the reservations in the Leases as required by the prescribed form of lease. In particular, there were the identical reservations in both Leases of "the right of any person duly authorised in that behalf . . . at all times to go upon the said Land, or any part thereof, for any purpose whatsoever, or to make any survey, inspection, or examination of the same."

261. *Wik* (n 148) 130 (Toohey J). Cf. *Wik* (n 148) 154 (Gaudron J).

262. Bartlett, *Native Title*, 47. *Wik* (n 148) 2–3 (Toohey, Gaudron, Gummow, Kirby JJ).

263. *Wik* (n 148) 250 (Kirby J); cf. *Wik* (n 148) 132 (Toohey J).

264. See, for example, Frank Brennan, *Wik Debate*; David Byrne, "Sharing Country"; and the papers in Hiley, *Wik Case*.

265. Bartlett, *Native Title*, 50.

266. (2002) 213 CLR 1 (*"Ward"*). The case is variously known by two short titles: *Mirriuwung Gajerrong* and *Ward*. It will be referred to as *Ward* hereafter. The full text of the High Court judgment can be found on the webpage: http://www.austlii.edu.au/au/cases/cth/high_ct/2002/28.html.

267. Bartlett, *Native Title*, 50.

268. Spindler, "Programme for Practical Reconciliation"; and Tehan, "Co-Existence of Interests in Land." Cf. *Wik* (n 148) 102 (Toohey J).

269. Fischer, "Interview."

270. Bartlett, *Native Title*, 52–64; Broome, *Aboriginal Australians*, 255–62; Butt and Eagleson, *Mabo Wik & Native Title*, 109–13; and Tehan, "Hope Disillusioned," 554–55.

271. This summary is from Bartlett, *Native Title*, 54.

272. Richard Bartlett writes that "examination of the substance of the Native Title Amendment Act 1998 reveals that it is a substantial, complex, and *specific* disapplication of the protection of the *Racial Discrimination Act 1975* (Cth)" (*Native Title*, 55, author's italics).

273. McGlade, "'Not Invited to the Negotiating Table,'" 97–100. ATSIC collected some responses to native title developments. With its disbanding in 2005, its website has been archived, but the relevant webpages can be found: http://pandora.nla.gov.au/pan/41037/20050516/www.atsic.gov.au/issues/land/native_title/Default.html.

274. Brearly and Nason, "Long Division," quoted in McGlade, "'Not Invited to the Negotiating Table,'" 100.

275. For example, Native Title Representative Bodies, the Aboriginal and Torres Strait Islander Commission, the Indigenous Land Corporation, the Aboriginal and Torres Strait Islander Social Justice Commissioner, and the National Aboriginal and Islander Legal Services Secretariat met together for a series of workshops and formed the National Indigenous Working Group on Native Title

(NIWG) to represent the wider group, with the mandate to develop a position on proposed amendments to the *NT Act* and present this to government. During 1996, members of the NIWG attended meetings with industry groups convened by the Council for Aboriginal Reconciliation to seek an agreed position on the government's proposed amendments to the *NT Act*. Unfortunately, no agreement was reached. Their position paper, "Coexistence—Negotiation and Certainty," can be found in the National Library of Australia, with catalogue reference: https://catalogue.nla.gov.au/Record/1515643.

276. Decision of the Committee on the Elimination of Racial Discrimination, 54th Session, CERD/C/54/Misc.40/Rev.2. Point 8 of the report states that "these provisions raise concerns that the amended Act appears to wind back the protections of indigenous title offered in the Mabo decision of the High Court of Australia and the 1993 Native Title Act. As such, the amended Act cannot be considered to be a special measure within the meaning of Articles 1(4) and 2(2) of the Convention and raises concerns about the State Party's compliance with Articles 2 and 5 of the Convention." See also CERD/C/55/Misc.31/Rev.3, August 16, 1999. See also McGlade, "'Not Invited to the Negotiating Table,'" 101.

277. McGlade, "'Not Invited to the Negotiating Table,'" 100.

278. Aboriginal and Torres Strait Islander Social Justice Commissioner, Native Title Report 1998, 9, quoted in Tehan, "Hope Disillusioned," 556.

279. Tehan, "Hope Disillusioned," 555.

280. (2002) 214 CLR 422 ("*Yorta Yorta*").

281. I am particularly grateful to Michael O'Donnell who first explained to me the implications of these various decisions. The following have also been helpful: Bartlett, *Native Title*, ch. 6 for *Ward* and ch. 7 for *Yorta Yorta*; and Tehan, "Hope Disillusioned," 558–63.

282. Kirby, "Judicial Dissent." http://www.hcourt.gov.au/assets/publications/speeches/former-justices/kirbyj/kirbyj_feb05.html.

283. The "Explanatory Memorandum to the Native Title Bill 1993," Part A at page 1 stated as follows:

> The Commonwealth's major purpose in enacting this legislation is to recognize and protect native title (see clauses 3 and 9). Native title is defined as the rights and interests that are possessed under the traditional laws and customs of Aboriginal peoples and Torres Strait Islanders in land and waters and that are recognized by the common law (clause 208). The Commonwealth has sought to adopt the common law definition.

284. E.g., *Ward* (n 266) 69 [25]:

> Yet again it must be emphasised that it is to the terms of the NTA that primary regard must be had, and not the decisions in *Mabo [No 2]* or *Wik*. The only present relevance of those decisions is for whatever light they cast on the *NTA*.

And *Yorta Yorta* (n 280) 453 [75]:

To speak of the "common law requirements" of native title is to invite fundamental error. Native title is not a creature of the common law, whether the Imperial common law as that existed at the time of sovereignty and first settlement, or the Australian common law as it exists today. Native title, for present purposes, is what is defined and described in s. 223(1) of the Native Title Act.

285. These two judgments are extremely technically complicated for the legal lay person, and so I am having to rely on secondary material for the discussion of these two cases.

286. Hepburn, *Principles of Property Law*, 143–45.

287. This is a summary of Bartlett, *Native Title*, 66–73.

288. *Yorta Yorta* (n 280) 461, 465, 466, 483, 485.

289. The case went in three phases, first heard in the Federal Court by Justice Olney, and then appeals were rejected first in the full Federal Court, and then in the High Court. The judgments are:

- *Members of the Yorta Yorta Aboriginal Community v Victoria* (1998) FCA 1606. http://www.austlii.edu.au/au/cases/cth/federal_ct/1998/1606.html;
- *Members of the Yorta Yorta Aboriginal Community v Victoria* (2001) 110 FCR 244; and
- *Members of the Yorta Yorta Aboriginal Community v Victoria and Others* (2002) 214 CLR 422. http://www.austlii.edu.au/au/cases/cth/high_ct/2002/58.html.

290. *Yorta Yorta Aboriginal Community v Victoria* (1998) FCA 1606, 17, quoted in Bartlett, *Native Title*, 75.

291. I am largely reliant on Richard Bartlett for highlighting the key points of the judgment. *Native Title*, 74–82.

292. *Delgamuukw v British Columbia* (1998) 1 CNLR 14. https://scc-csc.lexum.com/scc-csc/scc-csc/en/item/1569/index.do.

293. *Delgamuukw v British Columbia* (1998) 1 CNLR 14, 87.

294. The example comes from the writings of Edward Curr. He was one of the first squatters to occupy land in the claim area in the vicinity of Echuca, living there from 1841 to 1851. He wrote two books, published in 1883 and 1886, over three decades after he left the area. The particular example cited in the judgment by Olney J was that Curr had noticed that Yorta Yorta people had abandoned some fish by the river, but the Yorta Yorta people emphasized their conservation of the environment, so Olney J adjudged a change in tradition here: "It is said by a number of witnesses that consistent with traditional laws and customs it is their practice to take from the land and waters only such food as is necessary for immediate consumption. This practice, commendable as it is, is not one which, according to Curr's observations, was adopted by the Yorta Yorta people with whom he came into contact and cannot be regarded as the continuation of a traditional custom" (*Yorta Yorta Aboriginal Community v Victoria* (1998) FCA 1606, 123). There are several reasons why what was written by Curr should not simply

be taken as a matter of fact: he may have frightened the people away, leaving their catch at the water's edge; he may not have correctly observed, nor understood, nor remembered what happened; and he was making his observations through the prevailing cultural biases of the time, when he was personally involved in dispossessing the First Peoples. Atkinson, "Reflections on the Yorta Yorta," 6; Buchan, "'Tides of History,'" 10. Although the approach taken by Olney J may be legally defensible—he can only be expected to understand those things which are presented to him—there are problems that this was not properly resolved by the time that it was brought to the court system for the third time. Christine Choo and Margaret O'Connell write, "a historian could have assisted the court in the interpretation of particular historical documents the use of which became problematic for the applicants. It appears that the legal profession has much to learn about history as a profession and the value of the processes, methodologies and analysis of professional historians who are not simply 'gatherers of facts'" ("Historical Narrative," 18).

295. Tehan, "Hope Disillusioned," 563.

296. Bartlett, *Native Title*, 84.

297. Neate, "Turning Back the Tide?," 54–56; and Tehan, "Hope Disillusioned."

298. Burn, "Reconciliation and Land in Australia," sec. 5.4.

299. *Milirrpum* (n 133) 244.

300. For example, Wayne Atkinson states that $20 million of public money was spent opposing the Yorta Yorta claim. He writes, "non-indigenous professionals have become richer, while Indigenous claimants, on whose rights the [Native Title] industry is dependent, have had to sit it out impoverished on the periphery of the Native Title process" ("Reflections on the Yorta Yorta," 7).

301. French, "Moment of Change," 511–15; and R. Williams, "Native Title Mediation Practice."

302. Chaney, "Developments in Australia," 10; and Neate, "Turning Back the Tide?," 34.

303. Tehan, "Co-Existence of Interests in Land;" and Spindler, "Programme for Practical Reconciliation," 55.

304. E.g., Borrows, "Practical Reconciliation;" Patrick Dodson in Keefe, *Paddy's Road*, 313–14; and Milloo, "Native Title," 27.

305. Pearson, "Where We've Come From."

306. Neate, "'Tidal Wave' of Justice," 27.

307. Maddison, *Black Politics*, 65.

308. Nancy Williams, *Yolngu and Their Land*, xii.

309. Cowlishaw, "Helping Anthropologists," 19.

310. Atkinson, "Reflections on the Yorta Yorta," 8.

311. Bradley and Seton, "Self-Determination or 'Deep Colonising,'" 32.

312. Chaney, "Developments in Australia," 22–27, 31–33. Maureen Tehan

makes a similar point in "Hope Disillusioned," 569-70.

313. Langton et al., "Introduction," 21.

314. For example, see the papers in Baker et al., *Working on Country*; and Walsh and Mitchell, *Planning for Country*. David Foster reported on ten years of joint management of a national park: *Gurig National Park*.

315. Perhaps this too explains in part why non-Indigenous people are variously awed, don't know what to do with, and do not see the fecundity of large tracts of Australia. The following account by Diane Bell is worth pondering:

> When I first drove along he Stuart Highway north of Taylor Crossing to Warrabri, I heartily agreed with those who said it was the most barren stretch of country they had encountered. I couldn't cover the distance fast enough. Now I can drive barely a mile without seeing something worthy of comment. In what was once open spinifex plains broken only by the odd acacia stand, I now see highly differentiated foraging grounds, rich in small fruits and goanna; in burnt-out plains, I now see prime hunting grounds and I wonder, "Whose fire burnt through here?" Local people always know who has lit a fire because only persons in the correct relationship to a particular tract of land may do so. In the wide, dry creek beds, I now find the wild potato runners, I recognize the potential water sources, the places where frogs may be hidden deep in the cool, damp sand. I scan the horizon for smoke; I see a red tinge in the rock and I look for ochres.
>
> In the vast grandeur of the rolling sandhills I now recognize the body shape of certain ancestors, but in the finer details of clustering rocks, the overhanging wild figs and the patination on leave, I have also learnt to see signs of "intent towards man." At one point on the northward-bound track to Warrabri we crane our necks and look for a particular tree—its name would be called by somebody in our party and soft singing would accompany the telling of the story associated with the dreaming which that tree represented. At other points we would drive quietly, so as not to disturb the dreamings who had passed through this area. Women knew every inch of the country and always impressed upon me that I must travel with others, that there must be somebody with me who knew the country. It was their country, their yawulyu: I was never afraid we might lose our way and indeed we never did! (*Daughters of the Dreaming*, 23-24).

316. Recall the following, quoted near the end of the First Movement:

> Hobbles and other story tellers are concerned to show that invasion is not a process of the past which is now finished. Rather, they go to considerable effort to explain that the process is on-going and is continuing to destroy people and land. The other integral point, which is rarely stated explicitly, is that conquest is based on desire and on the illusion of winners and losers. One wins by disabling not only the opposition but the very life systems in which

the opposition is embedded. This is a fatal error, for there are no other life systems. As Riley Young said, "I know government say he can change him rule. But he'll never get out of this ground." (Rose, *Dingo Makes Us Human*, 191).

317. Many scholars believe that the books that we have preserved as 1 and 2 Corinthians are put together from a number of letters that Paul wrote to the church in Corinth and that some of his correspondence has been lost. See Thrall, *Commentary on Second Corinthians*, vol. 1:48–49 for a summary of some of the major theories. This has no impact on the work of this section.

318. Volf, *Exclusion and Embrace*.

319. Thompson and Martens, שׁוב, 56.

320. As a fictional exploration of this, consider Tyler, *Saint Maybe*. In outline, Ian's brother, Danny, committed suicide after Ian told Danny that his child was probably the result of a relationship his wife, Lucy, had had before they got married. (Danny and Lucy had got married very quickly after they first met.) Then Lucy went into depression, and died some months later from an overdose. Lucy's three children were then left without parents. Feeling a great weight of responsibility for the death of Danny and Lucy, Ian wanders into the "Church of the Second Chance," which met in a shop. During the worship he makes a public confession of his sin, and is prayed for by the church. Afterwards, he speaks with the minister, and explains what had happened. At the end of his explanation, he asks, "Don't you think that I'm forgiven?" The minister responds briskly, "Goodness no." He goes on to say, ". . . you can't just say 'I'm sorry, God.' Why anyone could do that much! You have to offer reparation—concrete, practical reparation, according to the rules of our church." For Ian, that meant dropping out of college and bringing up the three children.

321. Jonah is the prototypical example of the understanding of this dynamic, where Jonah refuses to go and pronounce God's judgment on Nineveh, the capital of the Assyrian Empire, the arch-enemies of Israel, because he knows that they will repent, and that God will withdraw the threat of destruction.

322. Moshe Weinfeld writes: "If we look for exactly what it was that the prophets opposed, we see that the main wrongdoing is not the perversion of the judicial process, but oppression perpetrated by the rich landowners and the ruling circles who control the socioeconomic order . . . [Isaiah 5:8] undoubtedly refers to those who foreclose the mortgages of the poor who cannot repay their debts, and turn their fields into their own personal property" (Weinfeld, "Justice and Righteousness," 239). Subverting justice is not the problem, but the enactment of unjust laws. Micah 2:5 looks forward to a future reallocation of land where landowners who have taken the land from others will not be allotted any land. Micah condemns those who take the land from women because their husbands are away at war (2:8–9). It is noteworthy that when a Shunamite women returns to her land after a seven-year absence due to famine to find that it has been taken by someone else, she petitions the king, and the land and its produce during her absence is returned to her (Weinfeld, "Justice and Righteousness," 238–41).

323. Fasting, sack cloth, and ashes (present together in Isaiah 58:5) were typical physical expressions of repentance (again, see Jonah 3:6–10). The logic of prayer and fasting seems to be this. An unbroken fast will lead to death. By fasting, the people are making explicit that they understand that their sin will lead to death. The prayer is prayer of repentance. They can only be saved from death caused by the fast if God causes them to break their fast by releasing them from their sin and its consequences.

324. Merklein, "μετανοέω, μετάνοια," 416.

325. Cf.: the central preoccupation of Matthew is "the revelation of the divine presence ('the kingdom of heaven') in the coming of Jesus as messiah, in fulfilment of scripture, to call Israel to repentance and through a renewed Israel, to bring God's blessing to the nations of the world" (Barton, "Gospel According to Matthew," 123–24).

326. Here he is assuming that Mark was written first, and that Matthew and Luke used Mark. His conclusion does not depend on this.

327. Ched Myers, *Binding the Strong Man*, 272–74. It is interesting to note that, where "in Matthew 19:21 the giving away of one's goods to the poor expresses how extremely serious a thing it is to follow Christ, in the *Gospel of the Nazaraeans* it is motivated by charity" (Schneemelcher and Wilson, *Gospels and Related Writings*, 158). An extract from Fragment 16 of the *Gospel of the Nazaraeans* reads:

> [Jesus] said to him: Go and sell all that thou possessest and distribute it among the poor, and then come and follow me. But the rich man then began to scratch his head and it [*the saying*] pleased him not. And the Lord said to him: How canst thou say, I have fulfilled the law and the prophets? For it stands written in the law: Love thy neighbour as thyself; and behold, many of thy brethren, sons of Abraham, are begrimed with dirt and die of hunger—and thy house is full of many good things and nothing at all comes forth from it to them!

(This fragment is quoted by Origen in his *Commentary on Matthew*, and this translation taken from Schneemelcher and Wilson, *Gospels and Related Writings*, 161.) The temptation to reduce the claims of justice to charity is an ever-present one.

328. This repentance is also perhaps seen in Acts 2:42–47, where the selling of goods and land could be seen as redistributing things accumulated through unjust economic practices. Richard Hays is right that a faithful response to this text is not to slavishly copy it, that the narrative "calls us to consider how in our own communities we might live analogously, how our own economic practices might powerfully bear witness to the resurrection, so that those who later write our story might say, 'And great grace was upon them all.' Such metaphorical mappings of the biblical stories onto our lives do not require us to imitate the narrated practices point for point or to reprisinate ancient economic conventions in detail . . . Rather, the metaphorical conjunction between the narrated church of Acts 2 and 4 and the church that we experience unsettles our 'commonsense'

view of economic reality and calls us to rethink our practices in radical ways" (*Moral Vision of the New Testament*, 302–3). He is surely correct when he writes that contemporary churches in the West have only practiced "modest forms of economic discipleship [which] fall far short of the New Testament Vision, and most of the churches I have known have been formed by the forces of market capitalism as least as much as by the teachings of Jesus" (*Moral Vision of the New Testament*, 468).

329. Cf. "After all, the cross is not forgiveness pure and simple, but God *setting aright the world of injustice and deception*" (Volf, *Exclusion and Embrace*, 298, author's italics).

330. Cf. Müller-Farenholz, *Art of Forgiveness*, 14–15.

331. This, then, is also meant to drive us to repentance. L. Gregory Jones writes, "the risen Christ—the Judge judged for us, the pure Victim sacrificed for us—returns to us his judges with a judgment that does not condemn but calls us to new life. By keeping our eyes steady on Christ, we can accept our responsibility for our own complicity in the universal disaster of sinful brokenness, and receive forgiveness and the re-establishment of communion. That is, forgiveness is done in such a way that it requires our repentance and turning away from our complicity in evil" (*Embodying Forgiveness*, 125).

332. I owe this observation to Judith Crane.

333. See, e.g., Dwyer, "Reconciliation for Realists," 81.

334. Cf., for example, the refusal of Native Americans to receive an apology from the General Council of the United Church in Canada, because words were not enough. Wink, *When the Powers Fall*, 58.

335. Müller-Farenholz, *Art of Forgiveness*, 25.

336. Tavauchis, *Mea Culpa*, 8.

337. Graham, *Sizzling Faith*, 82–88.

338. Graham, *Sizzling Faith*, 86, author's italics.

339. Graham, *Sizzling Faith*, 84.

340. Graham, *Sizzling Faith*, 86.

341. Graham, *Sizzling Faith*, 87.

342. Graham, *Sizzling Faith*, 88.

343. Mills and Mitchell, *Sins of the Fathers*. Mills and Pickering, *Fountains of Tears* give many more stories of people who have repented on behalf of others over incidents that happened in the past, and how this has brought restoration of relationships and healing in the present. See also Parker, *Healing Wounded History* on the possibility of the present generation bringing resolution of problems that remain from the past. It is beyond the scope of this book to investigate this phenomenon.

344. See note 95 for the derivation of this term.

345. Commonwealth of Australia, *Bringing Them Home*.

346. Recommendation 7 of the report.

347. My personal impression of the day in May 2005, when I took part in events in Canberra, and then scoured the media for coverage of events across Australia, is that it was not a big day in the consciousness of the majority of Australians. It seemed almost as if people felt that they had done their bit by saying sorry in the big events on the first "Sorry Day."

348. Commonwealth of Australia, *Bringing Them Home*, 249–50. The report also lists apologies already received from a number of churches and other bodies (250–53).

349. Ring, "Hardest Word."

350. Jon Howard's position was rather disingenuous, for he was a member of the House of Representatives from 1974, when the separation policy had only just ended; it was something his generation was partly responsible for.

351. It is also possible that John Howard was simply reflecting the opinion of many in Australia. For example, Mark Byrne wrote:

> Nevertheless, the government is motivated by popular opinion as well as ideology. Opinion polls have consistently shown that while the majority of Australians are willing to accept that Indigenous people were mistreated in the past, they are divided as to whether disadvantage today represents continuing mistreatment or is rather the fault of Indigenous people themselves. They are certainly not in favour of apologizing for the actions of people long dead, and do not see themselves as perpetuating racism and exploitation by their lifestyles and attitudes. In addition, the Howard government has done a sterling job of associating an apology to the Stolen Generation with personal and legal responsibility for their plight, rather than understanding "sorry" to be a simple expression of compassion. ("Reconciliation")

352. Phillip Coorey reports that "the State and Federal governments will pay for more than 100 members of the stolen generations to be in Canberra for the event. Among those invited will be the sporting stars Evonne Goolagong-Cawley, Matt Bowen, Greg Ingliss, David Peachey, Dean Widders, and Michael Long. Lady Wilson, the widow of Sir Ronald Wilson, who coauthored the 1997 *Bringing Them Home* report will be there, as will its coauthor, Mick Dodson. The activists Faith Bandler and Evelyn Scott, both of whom campaigned for voting rights for Aborigines before the 1967 referendum, will also be there" ("Rudd to Act").

353. The full text of his speech can be found in the Hansard of the House of Representatives for February 13, 2008, 167–73.

354. Hansard, February 13, 2008, 170.

355. Hansard, February 13, 2008, 170–71.

356. Hansard, February 13, 2008, 174.

357. Lederach, *Building Peace*, 78.

358. Writing of establishing peace in an armed conflict, John Paul Lederach says: "Crisis response tends to involve specific projects with short-term, measurable outcomes. In the interests of transforming the conflict, however, short-term efforts must be measured primarily by their long-term implications. For example, while achieving a cease-fire is an immediate necessity, this goal must not be mistaken for, or replace, the broader framework of peacebuilding activity. Rather, a sustainable transformative approach suggests that the key lies in the *relationship* of the involved parties, with all that term encompasses at the psychological, spiritual, social, economic, political, and military levels" (*Building Peace*, 75, author's italics).

359. For example, Pat McIntyre alerted me to this being expressed in interviews with people on Elcho Island about the Federal Government intervention in the Northern Territory (ABC 7.30 Report, July 18, 2007. http://www.abc.net.au/7.30/content/2007/s1981967.htm). Jack Horner, in the context of his work with Aboriginal and non-Aboriginal people over the decades, reflected that there "had been many decades, indeed generations, of oppression by whites on and off the Aboriginal reserves. Out of loyalty to their families and for self-respect, some Aboriginal and Islander people could never feel comfortable working with white people, however considerate they might be. It was a truth not to be dismissed, a legacy of past and present violence" (*Seeking Racial Justice*, 155).

360. See, for example, Helmick and Peterson, *Forgiveness and Reconciliation*; and Bethke Elshtain, "Politics and Forgiveness."

361. See, for example, Griswold, *Forgiveness*.

362. See, for example, Van Deusen Hunsinger, "Forgiving Abusive Parents." L. Gregory Jones rightly criticizes some therapeutic approaches to forgiveness which separate it out from its primary end, which is communion with God and with one another (*Embodying Forgiveness*, ch. 2).

363. Breytenbach, "God's Mercy," 3, in the prepublication manuscript.

364. See Balz and Schneider, *Exegetical Dictionary of the New Testament*, 181–83; and Danker, *Greek-English Lexicon*, 156–57.

365. Wink, *When the Powers Fall*, 16–17.

366. Choices made about translating the same word in different ways can have a dramatic effect on reading the text. For example, in a study of the translation of Paul's use of χάρις (charis), Kathy Ehrensperger shows that this word is usually translated as "grace" when used of God, but by a range of other words when the (grammatical) subject is not God. She then shows how this has a radical effect on the understanding of Paul's theology, or, perhaps, expresses the theological presuppositions of the translators, which then leads to a particular understanding of Paul's exercise of authority (*Paul and the Dynamics of Power*, ch. 4).

367. Of course, this is not unrelated to the quest of various liberation theologies. See also (Carter, *Matthew and Empire*, ch. 5) for an interesting study on what "he will save his people from their sins" (Matthew 1:21) might have meant in the context of the Roman Empire.

368. Shriver, *Ethic for Enemies*, 38–42.

369. E.g., Donald Shriver writes "... Jesus apparently went out of his way to affirm that forgiveness is the doorway through with a diversity of humans—many of them alienated by social custom from each other—can come together to form a new community" (*Ethic for Enemies*, 38).

370. It is usually assumed that Zacchaeus was extortionate in his taking of taxes, for this was common practice (see, for example, Carter, *Matthew and Empire*, ch. 8). The text, however, does not say that. It could be the case that the promise to give back four times any amount defrauded was in fact a claim of innocence regarding this assumed crime. Zacchaeus, however, was an agent of the oppressive Roman imperial regime, and so giving his money away was an important part of repenting of being part of the system.

371. The seeming exceptions to this are as follows:

- Acts 10:43 and 13:38, where forgiveness is associated with belief. In both cases, however, the statement about forgiveness comes as part of a narrative of the life of Jesus which begins with the baptism of John (Acts 10:37; 13:24) and Luke says that John's baptism was a baptism of repentance (Luke 3:3; Acts 13:24).

- Luke 1:77, in the song of Zechariah over his son John, but it has already been seen that John had a message which included a baptism of repentance for the forgiveness of sins (Luke 3:3).

- Luke 5:20, where Jesus forgives the sins of the paralyzed man. Here the focus of the pericope is the fact that Jesus can forgive sins; that is, it is making a christological point. Note also that sickness was often associated with sin in that culture. This can be read in the context of the next pericope, where Jesus says, "Those who are well have no need of a physician, but those who are sick. I have come to call not the righteous but sinners to repentance" (Luke 5:31–32), where sickness is being used at both a literal and spiritual level.

- Luke 7:36–50, where v. 47 is critical in understanding this story. The NRSV rightly translates this as: "Therefore, I tell you, her sins, which were many, have been forgiven; hence she has shown great love." Some commentators have argued that the woman is forgiven because she has loved much, but this is contrary to the force of the parable that Jesus tells in this instance, which says that love arises from being forgiven (Fiztmeyer, *Gospel According to Luke*, 686–87; and Marshall, *Luke*, 313–14). In this pericope, the forgiveness has been given offstage, and here the reader sees the loving response that results from truly receiving forgiveness. Jesus' words in v. 48 ("Your sins are forgiven") are simply a restatement of the reality of something that has already happened (Fiztmeyer, *Gospel According to Luke*, 692; and Marshall, *Luke*, 314). The reader is given no more details about how this happened. Further questions concerning the relationship between the forgiveness of Jesus and the forgiveness of God in Luke are raised by this story. Although the people at the meal understand Jesus as forgiving the sins of the woman (v. 49), Luke here uses the perfect passive form of the verb "to forgive" in vv. 47 and 48, just as he did in 5:20, unlike Mark and Matthew, who use the present passive. That is, in both incidents in Luke,

Jesus is proclaiming something which has already happened, even though his audience in both cases understand him as being the one who is conferring forgiveness on the person concerned, which is, in fact, what the Markan and Matthean narratives have Jesus doing. As yet, I have not been able to determine the significance of this observation.

372. Craddock, *Luke*; Evans, *Saint Luke*; Fitzmyer, *Gospel According to Luke*; and Marshall, *Gospel of Luke*; to which must be added: Volf, *Exclusion and Embrace* 122, 125; and L. G. Jones, *Embodying Forgiveness*, 101–3.

373. Troy Martin sees this as critical in dealing with people who refuse to repent: "When a victim has exhausted every means of holding a perpetrator accountable, this victim should transfer responsibility for the recalcitrant perpetrator to God. This transference provides emotional, psychological, and spiritual freedom to the offended even while the unresolved relationship with the offender remains ... By transferring the responsibility of forgiveness to God, the injured party is able to recognize the continued injustice of the situation without being chained to the perpetrator" ("Christian's Obligation Not to Forgive," 362).

374. Pokrifa-Joe, "Probing the Relationship." Stanley Saunders is instructive:

Matthew also frames the gospel with the identification of Jesus as "Emmanuel, God with us" (1:23; 28:20), which renders everything in between an extended illustration of what it means for Jesus to be "God with us." In other words, the gospel is showing those who follow Jesus what it is like to live in the presence of God, thereby turning the whole story into a manual for "spiritual formation." The presence of God in Jesus fundamentally alters the human experience of space, both physical and relational. In the "reign of heaven" depicted by Matthew, both Jesus and his disciples possess the power to heal and to exorcise demons (10:1). In this reconstruction of space in the presence of God, new social relationships that would be unthinkable in the old time and space are now made possible, including reconciliation with enemies (5:38–48), the restoration of the lost sheep of the house of Israel (9:35–38; 10:6), and limitless forgiveness (18:21–22). In a world where God supplies each day what is needed (6:25–33), there is no need for social and economic practices based on the assumption of scarcity (14:13–21; 15:32–39; 19:16–30). Where God is present, there is no need to continue the practices of domination (20:24–28; 23:1–12). God is present, in fact, among the "least ones" of the world (25:31–46). In God's presence, the world is no longer held captive by the politics of violence and fear (2:1–23). By the story's end, even the Empire's use of crucifixion to intimidate and control has been robbed of its power. ("Learning," 160–61).

375. cf. Ephesians 4:32: "Be kind to one another, tender-hearted, forgiving one another, as God in Christ forgave you." L. Gregory Jones writes that "Christians seek to provide a faithful witness to God's Kingdom by embodying the forgiveness wrought by Jesus in the power of the Holy Spirit" (*Embodying Forgiveness*, 103). Note that in this parable forgiveness follows repentance. It remains true

that God's offer of forgiveness can only be appropriated by repentance and, Matthew adds, by also forgiving others.

376. David Garland contrasts this with a similar process in the Qumran literature (1QS 5:25—6:1; CD 7:2–3; CD 9:2–8, 16–22), where the process is judicial, rather than reconciliatory (Garland, *Reading Matthew*, 191–92).

377. In Luke 15:3-7 the sheep is lost, whilst in Matthew it goes astray, and the other ninety-nine in Luke are the righteous, but in Matthew they are the ones who did not go astray. In Matthew there is the hint that erring members may not be recovered. Matthew is concerned that the church should not let the "little ones" drift away because they are superfluous. That is, the thrust of the parable is about relationships within the community, rather than adding people to the community. Garland, *Reading Matthew*, 189–90.

378. A person who does not wish to repent and be reconciled is to be treated as a "Gentile and a tax collector" (Matthew 18:17). In Matthew, there are Gentiles who display significant faith (e.g., the magi, the centurion, the Canaanite woman, and Pilate's wife). Jesus eats with tax collectors (Matthew 9:10–11), is reprimanded for eating with tax collectors (Matthew 11:19), and says that tax collectors will enter the kingdom of God ahead of the temple authorities (21:31–32). See Garland, *Reading Matthew*, 192.

379. L. G. Jones, *Embodying Forgiveness*, 37–39. Christopher Jones writes, ". . . the Lord's prayer, the whole direction of Jesus' teaching and life which the prayer sums up, and the narratives of Jesus' death all make clear that being forgiven and forgiving others are inseparable. Therefore the mediation of forgiveness is not a private transaction between God and the individual but the ordering of the life of the Christian *community* by the dynamic of forgiveness—divine and human, received and offered" ("Loosing and Binding," 31, author's italics).

380. Martin, "Christian's Obligation Not to Forgive"; and Schreiter, *Ministry of Reconciliation*, 66–68. But Miroslav Volf argues that "a certain sort of forgetting" is essential, the eschatological forgetting that "assumes that the matters of 'truth' and 'justice' have been taken care of . . . that perpetrators have been named, judged, and (hopefully) transformed . . . that victims are safe and their wounds healed . . . a forgetting that can therefore ultimately take place *only together with* the creation of 'all things new.' . . . The alternative is the eternal suffering caused by memory" (*Exclusion and Embrace*, 131, author's italics).

381. E.g., Christopher Jones writes: "Rowan Williams has shown how in the resurrection narratives the risen Jesus generates hope by resolving the ambivalence of the disciples' memories: they are confronted by their victim as their judge, but his judgment is merciful and healing, the source of repentance and newness of life" ("Loosing and Binding," 42). He goes on to quote from Rowan Williams: "If forgiveness is liberation, it is also a recovery of the past in hope, a return of memory, in which what is potentially threatening, destructive, despair-inducing, in the past is transfigured into the ground of hope" (*Resurrection*, 32).

382. L. Gregory Jones discusses Flannery O'Connor's story "Revelation," where a woman, Ruby, learns to see differently through an encounter with the purifying fire of God's judgment of grace, a fire that forces her to acknowledge her own sin and need of grace (*Embodying Forgiveness*, 53–59). He concludes

that "the revelation of the judgment of grace that comes to Ruby, like the revelations that the two sons receive in Jesus' parable, suggests that forgiveness is a free gift and that its purpose is the restoration of communion with God and with others in Christian community and the re-creation of human life with holiness as its destiny. But this forgiveness is inseparable both from the judgment that challenges human self-deception and from the repentance that becomes possible as we learn to see ourselves more clearly" (*Embodying Forgiveness*, 59). See also his *Embodying Forgiveness*, ch. 5.

383. For example, Robert Schreiter writes: "Human forgiveness, that is, human beings forgiving one another, . . . is about not being controlled by the past. It is the possibility of having a future different from the one that appears to be dictated by past wrongdoing. Forgiveness is an act of freedom" (*Ministry of Reconciliation*, 57–58).

384. Volf, "Forgiveness, Reconciliation and Justice," 45–46n30. Cf. Schreiter, *Ministry of Reconciliation*, 57. Recall that only God can forgive sin (Luke 5:21).

385. Volf, *Exclusion and Embrace*, 115–19. Olga Botcharova observed over her six years of being involved in conflict resolution training for religious people and community leaders in the former Yugoslavia that "no skill training for problem solving was possible until the feelings of trauma were addressed and some basic healing from victimhood was achieved. Achieving forgiveness, as the culmination of the healing process, made it possible for the parties to move forward to reconciliation." She further notes that the "first steps in healing require restoring love to oneself. Forgiveness begins for the victims when they make themselves look at the "ugly gaping wound" caused by loss and confront the secret shame and guilt that accompany the damage done to their sense of self-identity. The process of attending and overcoming the shame is as painful as the process of opening and cleansing the wound, which is needed in order to give it a chance to heal. Confronting the fears of their new reality requires identifying and naming each fear, recognizing them one by one. Only by pulling them out of the darkness, admitting them, sorting them out, do we deprive them of the power that they have over us" ("Implementation of Track Two Diplomacy," 288–89).

386. Volf, *Exclusion and Embrace*, 124.

387. Wink, *When the Powers Fall*, 23–24. Cf. the following from Sheila Cassidy:

> I know what it is like to be powerless to forgive. That is why I would never say to someone, "You must forgive." I would not dare. Who am I to tell a woman whose father abused her or a mother whose daughter has been raped that she must forgive? I can only say: however much we have been wronged, however justified our hatred, if we cherish it, it will poison us. Hatred is a devil to be cast out, and we must pray for the power to forgive, for it is in forgiving our enemies that we are healed. (quoted in Wink, *When the Powers Fall*, 24)

388. L. G. Jones, *Embodying Forgiveness*, 230.

389. L. G. Jones, *Embodying Forgiveness*, 231. See also Linn et al., *Don't*

Forgive Too Soon.

390. Volf, *Exclusion and Embrace*, 125. Geiko Müller-Fahrenholz reminds us that it is easier for the victim to "hide behind barricades of repression, anger, and self-righteousness ... There is a moment of *Entblössung* [literally, 'denuding oneself'] and disarmament on the victims' side which must be taken very seriously indeed" (*Art of Forgiveness*, 26).

391. Miroslav Volf writes, "As Dietrich Bonhoeffer saw clearly, forgiveness is a form of suffering (Bonhoffer, *Cost*, 100); when I forgive I have not only suffered a violation but also suppressed the rightful claims of strict restitutive justice. Under the foot of the cross we learn, however, that in a world of irreversible deeds and partisan judgments redemption from the passive suffering of victimization cannot happen without the active suffering of forgiveness" (*Exclusion and Embrace*, 125).

392. Volf, "Forgiveness, Reconciliation and Justice," 38.

393. Robert Schreiter argues that in problems between individuals, the first step is God's healing of the person who has been wronged, who then must forgive the perpetrator, which then leads the wrongdoer to repentance. Interestingly, for problems between communities of people, he says that repentance must come first, then forgiveness, then reconciliation (*Ministry of Reconciliation*, 63–66).

394. See, e.g., Lin et al., *Don't Forgive Too Soon*; Botcharova, "Implementation of Track Two Diplomacy"; and Schreiter, *Ministry of Reconciliation*, 58.

395. L. G. Jones, *Embodying Forgiveness*, 4.

396. Shriver, *Ethic for Enemies*, 178.

397. Shriver, *Ethic for Enemies*, 173. Strangely, whilst in his inaugural presidential address Barack Obama made extensive reference to the history and future of relationships between black and white Americans, he said nothing about the prior, gaping wound of the relationship between the native Americans and the incomers.

398. Tutu, *No Future Without Forgiveness*, 226–27.

399. Strabo *Geogr.* 8.6.23. Welborn notes this passage, but does not make the inferences that will be drawn here ("Discord in Corinth," 41). The translation is taken from the webpage: http://www.perseus.tufts.edu/hopper/text?doc=Strab.+8.6.23&fromdoc=Perseus%3Atext%3A1999.01.0198.

400. Chow, "Patronage in Roman Corinth," 106. Chow further notes that "The voting tribes or local political divisions would also remind people of the imperial presence in Corinth. Some of the voting names are Agrippia, Atia, Aurelia, Calpurnia, Claudia, Dommitia, Hostilia, Livia, Maneia, Vatinia and Vinicia" ("Patronage in Roman Corinth," 106).

401. Horsley, "1 Corinthians," 242.

402. Further information about patronage systems can be found in: Chow, "Patronage in Roman Corinth"; Danker, *Benefactor*; Lampe, "Paul, Patrons, and Clients"; Thiselton, *1 Corinthians*, 6–9; Garnsey and Saller, "Patronal Power Relations"; Gordon, "Veil of Power"; and Witherington, *Conflict and Community in*

Corinth, 22–24.

403. Nevertheless, some very fascinating insights can be had into the lives of ordinary people by a careful study of archaeological and other materials. See for example Lampe, *From Paul to Valentinus*; and Oakes, *From People to Letter*.

404. Chow, "Patronage in Roman Corinth," 104. See his footnote for the source and translation history of this.

405. Further information about the all-pervasive imperial cult can be found in Price, *Rituals*, and essays in Horsley, *Paul and the Roman Imperial Order*.

406. Welborn, "Discord in Corinth," 41.

407. Mitchell, *Paul and the Rhetoric of Reconciliation*, 192–94.

408. Mitchell, *Paul and the Rhetoric of Reconciliation*, 1, 303.

409. This is Margaret Mitchell's own translation (*Paul and the Rhetoric of Reconciliation*, 1). See also Witherington, *Conflict and Community in Corinth*, 94–95, which is largely derivative of Margaret Mitchell's work.

410. Margaret Mitchell makes a sound case for translating κατηρτισμένοι (katērtismenoi) as "to be reconciled." Part of her argument is to show that καταρτίζειν (katartizein) is often used to mean bringing warring factions back together, and it is used as an antidote for factions well into the Graeco-Roman period (*Paul and the Rhetoric of Reconciliation*, 74–75). See also Lightfoot, *Notes on the Epistles of St Paul*, 157, 47. Later, it will be seen that Paul uses the verb καταλλάσσω (katallassō), translated as "reconcile," in 2 Corinthians 5:18–20. Margaret Mitchell does not notice that, significantly, both καταρτίζειν and καταλλάσσω are brought together in Herodotus:

> (5.28.1) . . . but for two generations before this she had been very greatly troubled by faction, till the Parians made peace [καταρτίζειν] among them, being chosen out of all Greeks by the Milesians to be peace-makers [καταρτιστῆρες (katartistēres)].
> (5.29.1) The Parians reconciled [κατατήλλαξαν (katatēllaxan)] them in the following manner . . .

The translation of 5.28.1 is from Mitchell, *Paul and the Rhetoric of Reconciliation*, 75; that of 5.29.1 is from the Perseus database: http://www.perseus.tufts.edu/hopper/text?doc=Hdt.+5.29.1&redirect=true.

411. Mitchell, *Paul and the Rhetoric of Reconciliation*, 19.

412. Welbourn, "Discord in Corinth," 7.

413. Welborn, "Discord in Corinth," 6–7.

414. Thiselton, *First Epistle to the Corinthians*, 33. Cf. Mitchell, *Paul and the Rhetoric of Reconciliation*, 17–19.

415. Thiselton, *First Epistle to the Corinthians*, 33–34, author's italics.

416. Many scholars believe that the canonical 2 Corinthians was formed from a number of different letters. The main theories are summarized in Thrall, *Commentary on Second Corinthians*, 1:48–49. The argument of this book does not depend on the unity or otherwise of the canonical 2 Corinthians.

417. Georgi, *Opponents of Paul*, 237. Cf.: "To the degree to which Corinthian Christians imbibed secular Corinthian culture with an emphasis on peer groups and *local* value systems, the church had indeed become embroiled in what we have termed a *postmodern pragmatism of the market* with its related *devaluation of truth, tradition, rationality, and universals*" (Thiselton, *First Epistle to the Corinthians*, 33, author's italics).

418. Georgi, *Opponents of Paul*, 237.

419. Mitchell, *Paul and the Rhetoric of Reconciliation* 17.

420. The only thing that can be known with relative certainty is that these people have come to Corinth from elsewhere, Thrall, *Commentary on Second Corinthians*, 2:664–65. The term "incomer" will be used here as a translation of ὁ ἐρχόμενος (ho erchomenos) (2 Corinthians 11:4) to describe these people. The frisson in the term "incomer" is supposed to capture Paul's feeling that these people should not be trespassing on his territory (2 Corinthians 10:13–16) and to make a link with the situation in Australia, where the First Fleet were the first incomers for thousands of years.

421. Thrall, *Commentary on Second Corinthians*, 2:926.

422. Thanks to David Horrell for reminding me of this.

423. Thanks to David Horrell for reminding me of this.

424. Thrall, *Commentary on Second Corinthians*, 2:926–45.

425. Cf. Galatians 2:1–10; 2 Corinthians 10:13–16.

426. Thrall, *Commentary on Second Corinthians*, 2:940–41.

427. Barclay, "Thessalonica and Corinth," 185.

428. Barclay, "Thessalonica and Corinth," 185–87.

429. Barclay, "Thessalonica and Corinth," 186.

430. Barclay, "Thessalonica and Corinth," 195.

431. Chow, "Patronage in Roman Corinth," 122–23.

432. Perhaps it is significant that Paul says to the Corinthians that they "proclaim the Lord's death" in eating the bread and drinking the wine (1 Corinthians 11:26), which refers back to Paul's earlier discussion of the cross, and so emphasizing a cruciform lifestyle as against the patronage system. That is, this is not a definitive statement of what is happening in the Eucharist, but part of the significance of this meal that is being highlighted as being important in the political context of the patronage system. Reflecting on this in the contemporary world, William Cavanaugh writes,

> . . . the Eucharist does not simply tell the story of a united human race, but brings to light barriers where they actually exist. When Paul discovers that the Corinthians are unworthily partaking of the Lord's supper because of the humiliation of the poor by the rich, Paul tells them, "Indeed, there have been faction among you, for only so will it become clear who among you are genuine" (1 Corinthians 11.9). This verse is puzzling unless we consider that

the Eucharist can falsely be told as that which unites Christians around the globe while in fact some live off the hunger of others. Theologians of the Southern hemisphere remind us that the imperative of "church unity" is often a cover for exploitation of the worst kind. In the North American context, many of our Eucharistic celebrations too have been colonized by a banal consumerism and sentimentality. The logic of globalization infects the liturgical life of the church itself; Christ is betrayed again at every Eucharist. Where the body is not discerned, Paul reminds the Corinthians, consumption of the Eucharist can make you sick or kill you (1 Corinthians 11:30). This might explain the condition of some of our churches. (Cavanaugh, "World in a Wafer," 193)

433. Lampe, "Paul, Patrons and Clients," 495–98.

434. Peter Marshall has interpreted 2 Corinthians according to the conventions of friendship and enmity. Whilst Paul had every right to refuse aid from (a faction of) the Corinthian church within the conventions of friendship, Peter Marshall argues that Paul's refusal to do so was interpreted by the Corinthian church as a breach of friendship, and was thus the cause of their hostility towards him. The fact that the rival apostles became friends with the Corinthian Christians meant that they became, according to the conventions of friendship, joint enemies of Paul, which would perhaps explain why Paul found it so hard to re-establish his relationship with the Corinthians (*Enmity in Corinth*, ch. 6 and 396–98). Cf. David Horrell, who writes that "the issue of Paul's rejection of material support emerges, then, at crucial points in 2 Corinthians 10–13. In the main body of the letter it is both the opening and the closing issue on which Paul makes a defence. It must be seen as a major cause of conflict between Paul and the Corinthians. This issue plays a fundamental role in the process whereby a significant number of the congregation rebel against Paul" (*Social Ethos of the Corinthian Correspondence*, 225).

435. See 1 Corinthians 16:1–4; 2 Corinthians 8 and 9. Dieter Georgi suggests that the Corinthians had understood "Paul's request as an indirect demand for acknowledgement. What he did not dare to request directly he tried to get indirectly" (*Opponents of Paul*, 242). Cf. 2 Corinthians 12:16.

436. Cf. Stagg, "Text," which argues that reconciliation, or the ministry of reconciliation, is the purpose of the collection.

437. Not only did they give to Paul, but they gave generously, beyond their means, to the collection for Jerusalem (2 Corinthians 8:1–4).

438. E.g., Lampe, "Paul, Patrons and Clients," 497.

439. Cf. Lampe, "Paul, Patrons and Clients," 503–4; Witherington, *Conflict and Community in Corinth*, 341–43.

440. Bieringer, "Paul's Divine Jealousy," 238. Peter Oakes argues that the suffering of the Philippian Christians was primarily economic and the scenario that he describes, demonstrating how allegiance to Christ causes an economic crisis for a Christian family, is only too plausible (*From People to Letter*, 89–91).

441. Bieringer, "Paul's Divine Jealousy," 238.

442. E.g., Danker, *Benefactor*, 322, 437–38; and Witherington, *Conflict and Community in Corinth*, 341–43. For a discussion of the metaphor of parent, see e.g., Burke, "Pauls' Role as 'Father.'"

443. Lampe is probably overstating the case when he says that Paul has equality in mind ("Paul, Patrons and Clients," 504).

444. Strangely Paul wrote recommendations for people in his own letters. Efrain, "Paul and Commendation," 101.

445. Note that Paul addresses key aspects of the patronage system both in 2:14—6:13 + 7:2-4 and in chapters 10–13, and he mentions his weakness and suffering several times (e.g., 2:14; 4:7-11; 6:4-10), which contrasts with a patronage system that was comprehensible to the Corinthians. Thus, Paul was already concerned about the patronage system operating in Corinth when he wrote 2:14—6.13 + 7:2-4, even if he did not write chapters 10–13 until later.

446. See the introduction to the extract of Nils Dahl's essay that is published in Dahl, "Paul and the Church at Corinth," 86.

447. Mitchell, *Paul and the Rhetoric of Reconciliation*, 86. Cf. her comment, "Paul compares the factionalists to silly children whose cries for superiority actually demonstrate their infantile dependence on their leaders" (*Paul and the Rhetoric of Reconciliation*, 96).

448. This is a common *topos* in talking about factions: see Welbourn, "Conciliatory Principle in 1 Corinthians 4:6," 61; and Mitchell, *Paul and the Rhetoric of Reconciliation*, 96.

449. Bieringer, "Paul's Divine Jealousy," 246.

450. Victor Furnish notes that while "alteration between the first person singular and plural is common in Paul's letters—and notoriously difficult to assess . . .—the kind of shift apparent here in 2 Corinthians appears in no other letter" (*II Corinthians*, 32). The point being made in this paragraph does not depend on whether Paul is using an epistolary plural, or if he is including others from his team in some of the points he is making.

451. The same verb, συνεργέω (synergeō), is found in 2 Corinthians 6:1, but the text does not specify who is being worked with. Margaret Thrall concludes quite reasonably, with many other scholars and biblical translations, that Paul has his working with God in mind in this verse (Thrall, *Commentary on Second Corinthians*, 1:451).

452. Margaret Thrall notes that this is rare compared with 1 Corinthians, and suggests a number of ideas why this might be the case, including that Paul was unable to do this in 2 Corinthians because he felt that his pastoral authority was under threat, and so he could not use this term of equality with the Corinthians. But at the end of the letter (she sees 2 Corinthians 10–13 as a separate letter), "Paul reverts to his original form of address, as a gesture of conciliation and in the hope that he may now be understood" (*Commentary on Second Corinthians*, 2:905–6).

453. Bieringer, "Paul's Divine Jealousy," 247. There are other possible explanations for speaking to the Corinthians as a group. Another striking feature

of 2 Corinthians is that Paul does not mention any Corinthian individuals by name. Whilst he does not always do this, it is unusual, especially as he does so in 1 Corinthians. Perhaps he is stressing their common identity as the church in Corinth, not a group of factions, or, even more, perhaps he is holding them jointly responsible for their falling out with him, even if some may have thought themselves innocent.

454. Davies, *Gospel of the Land*, 209.

455. Fitzgerald, "Paul and Paradigm Shifts," 257. Similar views are expressed in Beale, "Old Testament Background of Reconciliation," 552, 557, 565; Crafton, *Agency of the Apostle*, 98; Furnish, *II Corinthians*, 353; Gloer, *Exegetical and Theological Study*, 5, 84; De Gruchy, *Reconciliation*, 53; I. H. Marshall, "Meaning of Reconciliation," 119; Mead, "Exegesis," 160; and Turner, "Paul and the Ministry of Reconciliation," 79, 86. There are some dissenting voices, including Thrall, *Commentary on Second Corinthians*, 1:438–39; and Abernathy, "Paul's Ministry of Reconciliation," 58. The logic of Paul's argument, however, seems to be well summarized by the quotation from Fitzgerald.

456. In his study of epigraphic material, Anthony Bash notes that both the sender and the receiver of an embassy knew that the supplicant was making the request from a position of weakness (*Ambassadors for Christ*, 48–51).

457. Cf. "He came to accept his limitations; and 2 Corinthians 1–9 reveals a chastened Paul. He apologises for his previous letter, pleads for affection, and reveals an acceptance of life, a reconciliation to experience" (Davies, *Gospel and the Land*, 209–10).

458. Whilst these words do not come from the pen of Paul, they are not inconsistent with his own accounts of the incident (e.g., Galatians 1:13–16), and in Romans 5:10 he writes, "for if while we were enemies, we were reconciled to God."

459. If 1 Timothy was not written by Paul, then the author has certainly got to the heart of the matter when Paul describes himself as the foremost of sinners because he "was a blasphemer, a persecutor, and a man of violence" (1 Timothy 1:12–16). To strike at the church was to attack Christ and so be alienated from God.

460. Cf. Galatians 1:12–16, where the persecution of the church of God is linked with Paul's zeal. Perhaps Paul saw that the Corinthians suffered from the same problem, that their zeal was not properly focused (cf. 2 Corinthians 7:7, 11).

461. There are some interpretations of the Christian worship—variously entitled "Eucharist," "Holy Communion," and "Mass"—which see it only as a proclamation of Christ's death until he comes again in glory. This, however, is to miss the point of what Paul is writing: in the context of the patronage system, it is this aspect of celebration of the Eucharist, namely, the proclamation of the death of Christ, which is brought to the fore because it challenges and undermines a church that is built on the patronage system.

462. Dwyer, "Reconciliation for Realists," 82.

463. Porter, Καταλλάσσω, 13.

464. Vorländer and Brown, "Reconciliation," 166.

465. Merkel, "καταλλάσσω," 261.

466. Porter, Καταλλάσσω, 16.

467. Merkel, "καταλλάσσω," 261.

468. David Williams demonstrates the diverse contexts from which Paul draws his metaphors, as well as the extraordinary range of metaphors that he uses (*Paul's Metaphors*).

469. Breytenbach, "On Reconciliation", 65–66. Paul brings them together in Romans 5:9–10, written after he had introduced the reconciliation terminology in 2 Corinthians.

470. For example, Ralph Martin argues that the term reconciliation is "a suitable umbrella under which the main features of Paul's *kerygma* and its practical outworking may be set" (*Reconciliation*, 239). Peter Stuhlmacher is even bolder in arguing that the thrust of the whole of the New Testament can be placed "under the heading: *The Gospel of Reconciliation in Christ*" ("Gospel of Reconciliation," 164, author's italics).

471. This is established in Burn, "Reconciliation and Land in Australia," section 2.3.

472. Amongst recent authors, Seyoon Kim is the one who presents the most thoroughgoing argument that Paul's use of the metaphor of reconciliation originated from his personal experience of God's reconciliation of Paul to himself on the road to Damascus. See Burn, "Reconciliation and Land in Australia," 101–2n111. Whilst Kim goes too far in arguing that Paul's experience is also the source of his terminology, it must be true that Paul's experience on the road to Damascus was a decisive catalyst for his theological development of the idea; cf. Ralph Martin, *Reconciliation*, 46–47. Chris Budden writes that when Paul recognizes who it is who is speaking to him in Acts. 9:4, the question is: "Will Paul be punished or destroyed, or simply allowed to move on? The answer is neither. God names the injustice, challenges Saul to tell God why he would do this thing, and confronts Paul with a new future in the very act of offering reconciliation and a new beginning. The putting right that was demanded of Saul, as he became Paul, was that he would now build, and defend, the very church that he had set out to destroy" (*Following Jesus in Invaded Space*, 161).

473. P. Marshall, *Enmity in Corinth*, 35.

474. Aristotle, *Rhet.* 1.9.24, quoted in P. Marshall, *Enmity in Corinth*, 38.

475. Xenophon, *Mem.* 2.6.35, available on the webpage: http://perseus.uchicago.edu/perseus-cgi/citequery3.pl?dbname=GreekTexts&query=Xen.%20Mem.%202.6.35&getid=1. I was alerted to this saying by P. Marshall, *Enmity in Corinth*, 36.

476. P. Marshall, *Enmity in Corinth*, 37.

477. P. Marshall, *Enmity in Corinth*, 43–44.

478. Fitzgerald, "Paul and Paradigm Shifts," 248–52.

479. The Greek words include παρακαλέω (parakaleō, "to appeal") and δέομαι (deomai, "to beseech"). Significantly, both these words are used in 2 Corinthians 5:20: "So we are ambassadors for Christ, since God is making his *appeal* through us; we *entreat* you on behalf of Christ, be reconciled to God."

480. Bash, *Ambassadors for Christ*, 48–52.

481. See above, point 4 of the standard paradigm of reconciliation.

482. Cf. Breytenbach, who writes: "There are various examples in the Corpus Hellenisticum where the stronger party ends the war by imposing the conditions of the peace treaty on the weaker side. *Katallasso* refers to the termination of the hostilities, *katallagai* to the new peace relation between the former enemies. The relation between the parties has been changed, not the parties themselves. Usually *katallage* 'reconciliation' meant that the fighting parties forgive each other and that amnesty is granted" ("On Reconciliation," 67).

483. Note that this is different from Paul's use of it in 1 Corinthians 7:11, where Paul's advice to a woman who has divorced her husband is to remain single or to be reconciled with her husband. Cf. I. H. Marshall, "Meaning of Reconciliation," 121, 127.

484. I. H. Marshall documents four different ways that καταλλάσσω and διαλλάσσω (diallassō) are used in the literature:

1. X persuades Y and Z to give up their mutual anger (active).

2. X persuades Y to give up Y's anger against X (active).

3. X persuades Y to give up Y's anger against X (passive/deponent).

4. X gives up his own anger against Y (passive).

Paul's use does not fit this pattern, and he conjectured that Paul was the first person to use the following grammatical structure:

5. X removes the cause of his own anger against Y, namely, Y's sin (active)). ("Meaning of Reconciliation," 127–28)

Stanley Porter divides the first case into two (one where goods are exchanged, and one where reconciliation is enabled) and notes that some other categories could have been added, but that this would only cloud the main hypothesis (*Καταλλάσσω*, 16–18).

485. Porter, *Καταλλάσσω*, 15–16. Recall that Paul's usage caused an explosion of the use of καταλλάσσω in Greek literature (Porter, *Καταλλάσσω*, 16).

486. Cf. Fitzgerald, "Paul and Paradigm Shifts," 253.

487. Fitzgerald, "Paul and Paradigm Shifts," 259.

488. Fitzgerald, "Paul and Paradigm Shifts," 254; and Bash, *Ambassadors for Christ*, 155.

489. Bash, *Ambassadors for Christ*, 98–99.

490. Fitzgerald, "Paul and Paradigm Shifts," 255–56.

491. Cf. Fitzgerald, "Paul and Paradigm Shifts," 325.

492. Commentators often make the mistake of finding in this a condensed, and not quite comprehensible, statement of "substitutionary atonement"; e.g., Gunton, "Towards a Theology of Reconciliation," 170. As has already been shown earlier in this chapter, however, there is no atonement language in the immediate vicinity of 2 Corinthians 5:21. The problem of interpreting these verses is removed if it is realized that there is no interest in the mechanism of the exchange at this point, only in the fact of the exchange itself.

493. Cf. Joseph Fitzmyer, who writes that the righteousness of God is an objective genitive here, the righteousness that God gives to human beings as a gift. (*Romans*, 258.)

494. Dunn, *Theology of Paul*, 433. He further argues that in Greek thought righteousness is the ideal against which individual action can be measured, but in Hebrew thought it is more relational, the meeting of obligations laid upon the individual by the relationship of which he or she is part (Dunn, *Theology of Paul*, 340–46). Cf. C. Marshall, *Beyond Retribution*, 20, 47–48.

495. If you have not come across restorative justice, I encourage to begin the journey by watching "The Woolf Within": https://restorativejustice.org.uk/resources/woolf-within-peter-wills-story.

496. Commonwealth of Australia, "Final Report on the Referendum Council."

497. This reflection is, in part, due to Wink, *Unmasking the Powers*, 43–52.

498. Moran, *Serious Whitefella Stuff*, 182. See also section III of the First Movement.

499. Yunupingu, "Foreword."

500. Freeman and Hunter, "When Two Rivers Become One."

501. Morris, "False Equality," 235–36.

502. Remnick, "Going the Distance."

503. Braaten, *Christ and Counter-Christ*, 11.

504. Ó Tuama, *In the Shelter*, 89.

505. Commonwealth of Australia, *Final Report of the Referendum Council*, 1.

506. https://www.youtube.com/watch?v=5iOMy9Tg9Bg.

507. Keeting, "Redfern Speech," quoted in Commonwealth of Australia, *Final Report of the Referendum Council*, iii.

508. Huggins and Little, "Rightful Place," 160.

509. Yunupingu, "Tradition, Truth and Tomorrow."

510. Noel Pearson has listed these four elements as being common grievances of indigenous peoples around the world ("Rightful Place," 17, 109).

511. See, for example, how nonlocal knowledge was necessary to understand what had been happening to the warru (black-footed rock-wallaby) in Nesbitt et al., "Co-Operative Cross-Cultural Biological Surveys," 190.

512. Sarah Maddison is very strong on her analysis of how those in power have an investment in this way of defining Australia, which then leads to confusion about national identity and what can or must be done about the past, making it difficult to understand and resolve our guilt (*Beyond White Guilt*).

513. Pearson, "Rightful Place," 17, 109.

514. Colermajer, "Is Speed Worth the Moral Cost?," quoted in Davis, "Self-Determination," 133.

515. Colermajer, "Is Speed Worth the Moral Cost?," quoted in Davis, "Self-Determination," 133.

516. Braaten, *Christ and Counter-Christ*, 11.

Bibliography

THE WORKS HERE ARE those which are referred to in the text of the book. A longer bibliography of the literature that has formed the thinking of this book can be found in Burn, "Reconciliation and Land in Australia."

Abernathy, David. "Paul's Ministry of Reconciliation: Exegeting and Translating 2 Corinthians 5:11—6.2." *Notes on Translation* (Summer Institute of Linguistics) 15/4 (2000) 48–64.

Adams, Michael, and Anthony English. "'Biodiversity Is a Whitefellas Word': Changing Relationships between Aborigines and the New South Wales National Parks and Wildlife Service." In *The Power of Knowledge: The Resonance of Tradition*, edited by Luke Taylor et al., 86–97. Canberra: Aboriginal Studies, 2005.

Altman, Jon. "Economic Development of the Indigenous Economy and the Potential Leverage of Native Title." In *Native Title in the New Millennium*, edited by Bryan Keon-Cohen, 105–15. Canberra: Aboriginal Studies, 2001.

Atkinson, Wayne. "Reflections on the Yorta Yorta Native Title Claim, 1994–2003." *Journal of Australian Indigenous Issues* 6/1 (2003) 3–11.

Attwood, Bain. "'Learning About the Truth': Stolen Generations Narrative." In *Telling Stories: Indigenous History and Memory in Australia and New Zealand*, edited by Bain Attwood and Fiona Magowan, 183–212, 241–60. Crows Nest: Allen & Unwin, 2001.

Baker, Richard, Elspeth Young, and Jocelyn Davies. *Working on Country: Contemporary Indigenous Management of Australia's Lands and Coastal Regions*. Melbourne: Oxford University Press, 2001.

Baldwin, James. "White Man's Guilt." Reprinted in his *Dark Days*, 41–50. London: Penguin, 2018. Also available at http://kaz2.docdat.com/docs/index-145920.html.

Balz, Horst, and Gerhard Schneider. *Exegetical Dictionary of the New Testament*. Vol. 1. Grand Rapids: Eerdmans, 1990.

Barclay, John M. G. "Thessalonica and Corinth: Social Contrasts in Pauline Christianity." In *Christianity in Corinth: The Quest for the Pauline Church*, edited by Edward Adams and David G Horrell, 183–96. Louisville: Westminster John Knox, 2004.

Bartlett, Richard H. "Canada: Indigenous Land Claims and Settlements." In *Native Title in the New Millennium*, edited by Bryan Keon-Cohn, 355–66. Canberra: Aboriginal Studies, 2001.

———. *Native Title in Australia*. 2nd ed. Sydney: LexisNexis Butterworths, 2004.

Barton, Stephen. "The Gospel According to Matthew." In *The Cambridge Companion to the Gospels*, edited by Stephen Barton, 121–38. Cambridge: Cambridge University Press, 2006.

Bash, Anthony. *Ambassadors for Christ: An Exploration of Ambassadorial Language in the New Testament*. Tübingen: Mohr, 1997.

Bauer, W., F. W. Danker, W. F. Arndt, and F. W. Gingrich. *A Greek-English Lexicon of the New Testament and Other Early Christian Literature*. 3rd ed. Chicago: University of Chicago Press, 2000.

Bauman, Zygmunt. *Modernity and the Holocaust*. Cambridge: Polity, 2000.

Beale, G. K. "The Old Testament Background of Reconciliation in 2 Corinthians 5–7 and Its Bearing on the Literary Problem of 2 Corinthians 6:14—7:1." *New Testament Studies* 35 (1989) 550–81.

Beckett, Jeremy. *Torres Strait Islanders: Custom and Colonialism*. Cambridge: Cambridge University Press, 1987.

Belgrave, Michael, et al., eds. *Waitangi Revisited: Perspectives on the Treaty of Waitangi*. Melbourne: Oxford University Press, 2005.

Bell, Diane. "Aboriginal Women and the Religious Experience (1980)." In *Religious Business: Essays on Australian Aboriginal Spirituality*, edited by Max Charlesworth, 46–71. Cambridge: Cambridge University Press, 1998.

———. *Daughters of the Dreaming*. 3rd ed. Melbourne: Spinifex, 2002.

———. *Ngarrindjeri Wurruwarrin: A World That Is, Was and Will Be*. Melbourne: Spinifex, 1998.

———. "The Word of a Woman: Ngarrindjeri Stories and a Bridge to Hindmarsh Island." In *Words and Silences: Aboriginal Women, Politics and Land*, edited by Peggy Brock, 117–38, 181–83. Crows Nest: Allen & Unwin, 2001.

Benion, Tom. "New Zealand: Indigenous Land Claims and Settlements." In *Native Title in the New Millennium*, edited by Brian Keon-Cohn, 367–76. Canberra: Aboriginal Studies, 2001.

Bethke Elshtain, Jean. "Politics and Forgiveness." In *Burying the Past: Making Peace and Doing Justice after Civil Conflict*, edited by Nigel Biggar, 40–56. Washington, DC: Georgetown University Press, 2001.

Bieringer, R. "Paul's Divine Jealousy: The Apostle and His Communities in Relationship." Reprinted in *Studies in 2 Corinthians*, edited by R. Bieringer and J. Lambrecht, 223–53. Leuven: Leuven University Press, 1994.

Bonhoeffer, Dietrich. *The Cost of Discipleship*. Translated by Reginald Horace Fuller. New York: McMillan, 1963.

Borrows, John. "Practical Reconciliation, Practical Re-Colonisation?" *Land, Rights, Laws: Issues of Native Title* 2/27 (2004).

Botcharova, Olga. "Implementation of Track Two Diplomacy: Developing a Model of Forgiveness." In *Forgiveness and Reconciliation: Religion, Public Policy, and Conflict*, edited by Raymond G. Helmick and Rodney L. Peterson, 269–94. Philadelphia: Templeton Foundation, 2001.

Braaten, Carl. *Christ and Counter-Christ: Apocalyptic Themes in Theology and Culture*. Philadelphia: Westminster, 1972.

Bradley, John, and Kathryn Seton. "Self-Determination or 'Deep Colonising': Land Claims, Colonial Authority and Indigenous Representation." In *Unfinished Constitutional Business?: Rethinking Indigenous Self-Determination*, edited by Barbara A. Hocking, 32–46. Canberra: Aboriginal Studies, 2005.

Bibliography

Brearly, David, and David Nason. "The Long Division, When Can Black and White Australia Expect to Be Reconciled?" *Weekend Australian*, 24–25 October, 1998, 25.

Brennan, Frank. *The Wik Debate: Its Impact on Aborigines, Pastoralists and Miners.* Sydney: University of New South Wales Press, 1998.

Brennan, Sean, et al. *Treaty*. Sydney: Federation, 2005.

Breytenbach, Cilliers. "God's Mercy and Our Forgiveness. Reflections on the Synoptic Tradition." In *Friendship and Love Where There Were None*, edited by J. G. van der Watt et al., 84–95. Pretoria: University of Pretoria, Institute for Missiological and Ecumenical Research, 2005.

———. "On Reconciliation: An Exegetical Response." *Journal of Theology for Southern Africa* 70 (1990) 64–68.

Broome, Richard. *Aboriginal Australians: Black Responses to White Dominance, 1788–2001*. 3rd ed. Sydney: Allen & Unwin, 2002.

Buchan, Bruce. "The 'Tides of History': The Yorta Yorta, Native Title, and Colonial Attitudes to Indigenous Sovereignty." *Journal of Australian Indigenous Issues* 7/2 (2004) 3–23.

Budden, Chris. *Following Jesus in Invaded Space: Doing Theology on Aboriginal Land.* Eugene, OR: Pickwick, 2009.

Buick-Constable, John. "Indigenous State Relations in Aotearoa/New Zealand: A Contractual Approach to Self-determination". In *Unfinished Constitutional Business?: Rethinking Indigenous Self-Determination*, edited by Barbara A. Hocking, 118–32. Canberra: Aboriginal Studies, 2005.

Burke, Trevor J. 2003. "Pauls' Role as 'Father' to His Corinthian 'Children' in Socio-Historical Context (1 Corinthians 4:14–21)." In *Paul and the Corinthians: Studies on a Community in Conflict. Essays in Honour of Margaret Thrall*, edited by Trevor J. Burke and J. Keith Elliott, 95–113. Leiden: Brill, 2003.

Burn, Geoffrey. "Reconciliation and Land in Australia: A Theological Approach." PhD diss., University of Exeter, 2010. http://hdl.handle.net/10036/117230.

Butt, Peter, and Robert Eagleson. *Mabo Wik & Native Title*. 4th ed. Sydney: Federation, 2001.

Byrne, David. "Sharing Country." In *Sharing Country: Land Rights, Human Rights, and Reconciliation after Wik: Proceedings of a Public Forum Held at the University of Sydney on February 28, 1997*, 111–14. Sydney: Research Institute for Humanities and Social Sciences, University of Sydney.

Cape York Institute for Policy and Leadership. "From Hand Out to Hand Up: Cape York Welfare Reform Project: Aurukun, Coen, Hope Vale, Mossman Gorge." May 2007. https://capeyorkpartnership.org.au/wp-content/uploads/2014/07/from-handout-to-hand-up-welfare-reform-report.pdf.

Cape York Partnership. https://capeyorkpartnership.org.au.

Carter, Warren. *Matthew and Empire: Initial Explorations*. Harrisburg, PA: Trinity, 2001.

Cavanaugh, William T. *Torture and Eucharist: Theology, Politics, and the Body of Christ.* Oxford: Blackwell, 1998.

———. "The World in a Wafer: A Geography of the Eucharist as Resistance to Globalization." *Modern Theology* 15 (1999) 181–96.

Chaney, Fred. "Developments in Australia: Native Title and Reconciliation." *Canadian Aboriginal Minerals Association Conference: Certainty Through Partnership: Aboriginal Community and Resources Sector Development*. Yellowknife, Canada: 2004.

Chartrand, Paul. "Aboriginal Peoples in Canada: Aspirations for Distributive Justice as Distinct Peoples." In *Indigenous Peoples' Rights in Australia, Canada and New Zealand*, edited by Paul Havemann, 88–107. Melbourne: Oxford University Press, 1999.

Childs, Brevard. *The New Testament as Canon: An Introduction*. London: SCM, 1984.

Choo, Christine, and Margaret O'Connell. "Historical Narrative and Proof of Native Title." In *Through a Smoky Mirror: History and Native Title*, edited by Geoffrey Gray and Paul Mandy, 11–21. Canberra: AIATSIS, 2002.

Chow, John K. "Patronage in Roman Corinth." In *Paul and Empire: Religion and Power in Roman Imperial Society*, edited by Richard Horsley, 104–25. Harrisburg: Trinity, 1997.

Clément, Olivier. *On Being Human: A Spiritual Anthropology*. New York: New City, 2000.

Colermajer, Danielle. "Is Speed Worth the Moral Cost?" *The Minefield*, ABC Radio National, 14 June 2017.

Commonwealth of Australia. *Bringing Them Home: Report of the National Inquiry into the Separation of Aboriginal and Torres Strait Islander Children from Their Families*. 1997. https://www.humanrights.gov.au/our-work/aboriginal-and-torres-strait-islander-social-justice/publications/bringing-them-home-stolen.

———. *Final Report of the Referendum Council*. 30 June 2017. https://www.referendumcouncil.org.au/sites/default/files/report_attachments/Referendum_Council_Final_Report.pdf.

Coorey, Phillip. "Rudd to act on 'blight on the nation's soul.'" *Sydney Morning Herald*, 11 February 2008.

Cowlishaw, Gillian K. "Helping Anthropologists: Cultural Continuity in the Constructions of Aborigines." *Canberra Anthropology* 13/2 (1990) 1–8.

———. "Studying Aborigines: Changing Canons in Anthropology and History." In *Power, Knowledge and Aborigines*, edited by Brian Attwood and John Arnold, 20–31. Victoria: La Trobe University Press, 1992.

Craddock, Fred B. *Luke*. Interpretation. Louisville: John Knox, 1990.

Crafton, Jeffrey A. *The Agency of the Apostle: A Dramatic Analysis of Paul's Responses to Conflict in 2 Corinthians*. Sheffield: Sheffield Academic, 1991.

Curthoys, Ann. "Mythologies." In *The Australian Legend and Its Discontents*, edited by Richard Nile, 11–41. Brisbane: University of Queensland Press, 2000.

Dahl, Nils Alstrup. "Paul and the Church at Corinth According to 1 Corinthians 1:10—4:21." In *Christianity at Corinth: The Quest for the Pauline Church*, edited by Edward Adams and David Horrell, 85–95. Louisville: Westminster John Knox, 2004.

Danker, Frederick W. *Benefactor: Epigraphic Study of a Graeco-Roman and New Testament Semantic Field*. St. Louis: Clayton, 1982.

Davies, W. D. *The Gospel and the Land: Early Christianity and Jewish Territorial Doctrine*. Sheffield: Sheffield Academic, 1994.

Davis, Megan. "Self-Determination and the Right to Be Heard." In *A Rightful Place: A Road Map to Recognition*, edited by Shireen Morris, 119–46. Carlton: Black, 2017.

De Costa, Ravi. "Treaties in British Columbia: Comprehensive Agreement Making in a Democratic Context." In *Honour Among Nations?: Treaties and Agreements with Indigenous People*, edited by Marcia Langton et al., 133–46. Melbourne: Melbourne University Press, 2004.

De Gruchy, John W. *Reconciliation: Restoring Justice*. Minneapolis: Fortress, 2002.
Dodson, Patrick. "Unfinished Business: A Shadow Across Our Relationships." In *Treaty: Let's Get It Right! A Collection of Essays from ATSIC's Treaty Think Tank and Authors Commissioned by AIATSIS on Treaty Issues*, edited by Hannah McGlade, 30–40, 200–216. Canberra: Aboriginal Studies, 2003.
Donovan, Vincent J. *Christianity Rediscovered: An Epistle from the Masai*. London: SCM, 1978.
Dorsett, Shaunnagh, and Lee Godden. *A Guide to Overseas Precedents of Relevance to Native Title*. Canberra: AIATSIS, 1998.
Duchrow, Ulrich, and Franz Hinkelammert. *Property for People, Not for Profit: Alternatives to the Global Tyranny of Capital*. Geneva: World Council of Churches, 2004.
Dunn, James D. G. *The Theology of Paul the Apostle*. Edinburgh: T. & T. Clark, 1998.
Dwyer, Susan. "Reconciliation for Realists." *Ethics and International Affairs* (Carnegie Council on Ethics and International Affairs) 13/1 (1999) 81–98.
Edmunds, Mary. "Conflict in Native Title Claims." Land, Rights, Laws: Issues of Native Title 1, Issues Paper No. 7. Canberra: AIATSIS, February 1995.
Efrain, Augosto. "Paul and Commendation." In *Paul in the Greco-Roman World: A Handbook*, edited by J. P. Sampley, 101–33. Harrisburg, PA: Trinity, 2003.
Ehrensperger, Kathy. *Paul and the Dynamics of Power: Communication and Interaction in the Early Christ-Movement*. Edinburgh: T. & T. Clark, 2009.
Evans, Christopher F. *Saint Luke*. TPI New Testament Commentaries. London: SCM, 1990.
Feary, Sue. "Moving Towards Joint Management in New South Wales: A Jervis Bay Case Study." In *Working on Country: Contemporary Indigenous Management of Australia's Lands and Coastal Regions*, edited by Richard Baker et al., 276–94. Melbourne: Oxford University Press, 2001.
Fischer, Tim. "Interview with Tim Fischer by John Highfield on Native Title Act Amendments." *World at Noon*, ABC TV, 4 September 1997.
Fitzgerald, John T. "Paul and Paradigm Shifts: Reconciliation and Its Linkage Group." In *Paul Beyond the Judaism/Hellenism Divide*, edited by Troels Engberg-Pederson, 241–62, 316–25. Louisville: Westminster John Knox, 2001.
Fitzmyer, Joseph A. *The Gospel According to Luke X–XXIV*. Anchor Bible 28a. New York: Doubleday, 1985.
———. *Romans*. Anchor Bible 33. London: Geoffrey Chapman, 1993.
Foley, Charmaine, and Ian Watson. *A People's Movement: Reconciliation in Queensland*. Southport: Keeaira, 2001.
Foster, David. *Gurig National Park: The First Ten Years of Joint Management*. Canberra: AIATSIS, 1997.
Freeman, Damien, and Nolan Hunter. "When Two Rivers Become One." In *A Rightful Place: A Roadmap to Recognition*, edited by Shireen Morris, 173–94. Carlton: Black, 2017.
French, Robert S. "A Moment of Change—Personal Reflections on the National Native Title Tribunal 1994–98." *Melbourne University Law Review* 27/2 (2003) 488–522.
Fulcher, James. "Sui Generis History?: The Use of History in Wik." In *The Wik Case and Its Implications*, edited by Graham Hiley, 51–56. Sydney: Butterworths, 1997.
Furnish, Victor Paul. *II Corinthians: A New Translation with Introduction and Commentary*. Anchor Bible 32a. New York: Doubleday, 1984.

Gambold, Nic. "The Role of Traditional Ecological Knowledge and Skills in 'Modern' Aboriginal Land Management and Education." In *Planning for Country: Cross-Cultural Approaches to Decision-Making on Aboriginal Lands*, edited by Fiona Walsh and Paul Mitchell, 142–47. Alice Springs: Jukurrpa, 2002.

Gammage, Bill. *The Biggest Estate on Earth: How Aborigines Made Australia*. Sydney: Allen & Unwin, 2012.

Garland, David E. *Reading Matthew: A Literary and Theological Commentary on the First Gospel*. New York: Crossroad, 1995.

Garnsey, Peter, and Richard Saller. "Patronal Power Relations." In *Paul and Empire: Religion and Power in Roman Imperial Society*, edited by Richard A. Horsley, 96–103. Harrisburg, PA: Trinity, 1997.

Georgi, Dieter. *The Opponents of Paul in Second Corinthians*. Philadelphia: Fortress, 1986.

Gibbs, Harry. "Foreword." In *Mabo: A Judicial Review*, edited by M A Stephenson and Suri Ratnapala, i–xvii. St Lucia: University of Queensland Press, 1993.

Gloer, W. Hulitt. *An Exegetical and Theological Study of Paul's Understanding of New Creation and Reconciliation in 2 Cor. 5:14–21*. Mellen Biblical Press Series 42. Lewiston, NY: Edwin Mellen, 1996.

Gordon, Richard. "The Veil of Power." In *Paul and Empire: Religion and Power in Roman Imperial Society*, by Richard A. Horsley, 126–37. Harrisburg, PA: Trinity, 1997.

Gould, Richard A. "To Have and Have Not: The Ecology of Sharing Among Hunter-Gatherers." In *Resource Managers: North American and Australian Hunter-Gatherers*, edited by Nancy M. Williams and Eugene S. Hunn, 69–91. American Association for the Advancement of Science Selected Symposium 67. Boulder, CO: Westview, 1982.

Graham, Martin. *Sizzling Faith: The Dream That Got the Church on the Move!* Eastbourne: Kingsway, 2006.

Grant, Stan. *Talking to My Country*. Sydney: HarperCollins, 2016.

Griswold, Charles L. *Forgiveness: A Philosophical Exploration*. New York: Cambridge University Press, 2007.

Gumbert, M. *Neither Justice nor Reason: A Legal and Anthropological Analysis of Aboriginal Land Rights*. St. Lucia: University of Queensland Press, 1984.

Gunstone, Andrew. "The Responses of Australian Governments to Indigenous Challenges to the Australian State: 1967–2003." *Journal of Australian Indigenous Issues* 6/2 (2003) 3–25.

Gunton, Colin E. "Towards a Theology of Reconciliation." In T*he Theology of Reconciliation*, edited by Colin E. Gunton, 167–74. Edinburgh: T. & T. Clark, 2003

Hardy, Daniel W. "Created and Redeemed Sociality." In *On Being the Church: Essays on the Christian Community*, edited by Colin E. Gunton and Daniel W. Hardy, 21–47. Edinburgh: T. & T. Clark, 1989.

Harris, John. *One Blood: Two Hundred Years of Aboriginal Encounter with Christianity: A Story of Hope*. Sutherfield: Albatross, 1990.

Hays, Richard. *The Moral Vision of the New Testament: A Contemporary Introduction to New Testament Ethics*. Edinburgh: T. & T. Clark, 1996.

Heiss, Anita, ed. *Growing Up Aboriginal in Australia*. Carlton: Black, 2018.

Helmick, Raymond G., and Rodney L. Peterson. *Forgiveness and Reconciliation: Religion, Public Policy, and Conflict Transformation*. Philadelphia: Templeton Foundation, 2001.

Hepburn, Samantha. *Principles of Property Law*. 3rd ed. Coogee: Routledge Cavendish, 2006.
Herbert, Eileen. "Reconciliation in Cape York Peninsula." *Chain Reaction* (75) (1996) 34–36.
Hewson, Alex, with Emily Knight. *Bromley Briefings Prison Factfile*. Prison Reform Trust, Autumn 2018. http://www.prisonreformtrust.org.uk/Portals/0/Documents/Bromley%20Briefings/Autumn%202018%20Factfile.pdf.
Hiley, Graham. "Introduction." In *The Wik Case: Issues and Implications*, edited by Graham Hiley, 1–5. Sydney: Butterworths, 1997.
———. *The Wik Case: Issues and Implications*. Sydney: Butterworths, 1997.
Hinkson, Melinda. "Exploring 'Aboriginal' Sites in Sydney: A Shifting Politics of Place?" *Aboriginal History* 26 (2002) 62–77.
Horner, Jack. *Seeking Racial Justice: An Insider's Memoir of the Movement for Aboriginal Advancement, 1938–1978*. Canberra: Aboriginal Studies, 2004.
Horrell, David. *The Social Ethos of the Corinthian Correspondence: Interests and Ideology from 1 Corinthians to 1 Clement*. Edinburgh: T. & T. Clark, 1996.
Horsley, Richard A. "1 Corinthians: A Case Study of Paul's Assembly as an Alternative Society." In *Paul and Empire: Religion and Power in Roman Imperial Society*, edited by Richard A Horsley, 242–52. Harrisburg, PA: Trinity, 1997.
———, ed. *Paul and the Roman Imperial Order*. Harrisburg, PA: Trinity, 2004.
Horstman, Mark. "Black Shadows, White Shadows, Grey Shadows: Does the Cape York Regional Agreement Provide a Model for the Reconciliation Process?" *Arena Magazine*, April–May 1997, 26–31.
Howley, Pat. *Breaking Spears and Mending Hearts: Peacemakers and Restorative Justice in Bouganville*. London: Zed, 2002.
Huggins, Jackie, and Rod Little. "A Rightful Place at the Table." In *A Rightful Place: A Road Map to Recognition*, edited by Shireen Morris, 147–72. Carlton: Black, 2017.
Jennett, Christine. "Aboriginal Affairs Policy." In *Hawke and Australian Public Policy: Consensus and Restructuring*, edited by Christine Jennett and Stewart Randall, 245–83. Melbourne: MacMillan, 1990.
Johnson, Louise, Jackie Huggins, and Jane Jacobs. *Placebound: Australian Feminist Geographies*. Melbourne: Oxford University Press, 2000.
Jones, Christopher. "Loosing and Binding: The Liturgical Mediation of Forgiveness." In *Forgiveness and Truth*, edited by Alistair McFadyen and Marcel Sarot, 31–52. Edinburgh: T. & T. Clark, 2001.
Jones, Jilpia Nappaljari. "We May Have the Spirit, but Do Men Have All The Land? Women and Native Title." Paper presented at the Native Title Conference, Coffs Harbour, 2005.
Jones, L. Gregory. *Embodying Forgiveness: A Theological Analysis*. Grand Rapids: Eerdmans, 1995.
Jones, R. "Fire Stick Farming." *Australian Natural History* 16 (1969) 224–28.
Joyce, Paul. *Divine Initiative and Human Response in Ezekiel*. Sheffield: Sheffield Academic, 1989.
Kaberry, Phyllis. "The Life and Secret Ritual of Aboriginal Women in the Kimberleys." *Mankind* 2/7 (1939).
Kaminsky, Joel S. *Corporate Responsibility in the Hebrew Bible*. Sheffield: Sheffield Academic, 1995.

———. "The Sins of the Fathers: A Theological Investigation of the Biblical Tension Between Corporate and Individualized Retribution." *Judaism* 46/3 (1997).

Kawharu, I. H. *Waitangi: Maori and Pakeha Perspectives of the Treaty of Waitangi*. Auckland: Oxford University Press, 1989.

Keating, Paul. "The Redfern Park Speech." In *Essays on Australian Reconciliation*, edited by Michelle Grattan, 60–64. Melbourne: Black, 2000.

Keefe, Kevin. *Paddy's Road: Life Stories of Patrick Dodson*. Canberra: Aboriginal Studies, 2003.

Keeley, A. "Women and the Land: The Problems Aboriginal Women Face in Providing Gender Restricted Evidence." *Aboriginal Law Bulletin* 87 (1996) 4–7.

Keon-Cohen, B. A. "Some Problems of Proof: The Admissibility of Traditional Evidence." In *Mabo: A Judicial Revolution*, edited by M. A. Stephenson and Suri Ratnapala, 185–205. St. Lucia: University of Queensland Press, 1993.

Kim, Seyoon. *The Origins of Paul's Gospel*. 2nd ed. Tübingen: Mohr-Siebeck, 1984.

———. "2 Cor. 5.11–21 and the Origin of Paul's Concept of 'Reconciliation.'" *Novum Testamentum* 39/4 (1997) 360–84.

Kimber, Richard. "Diane Bell, the Ngarrindjeri and the Hindmarsh Island Affair: 'Value-free' Ethnography." *Aboriginal History* 21 (1997) 202–32.

Kirby, Michael. "Judicial Dissent Is an Appeal to the Future." Speech to the Law Students' Society, James Cook University, Cairns, 2005.

Lampe, Peter. *From Paul to Valentinus: Christians at Rome in the First Two Centuries*. Minneapolis: Fortress, 2003.

———. "Paul, Patrons, and Clients." In *Paul in the Greco-Roman World: A Handbook*, edited by J. Paul Sampley, 488–523. Harrisburg, PA: Trinity, 2003.

Langton, Marcia. "Finding a Resolution to Constitutional Recognition of Indigenous Australians." In *It's Our Country: Indigenous Arguments for Meaningful Constitutional Recognition and Reform*, edited by Megan Davis and Marcia Langton, 27–41. Melbourne: Melbourne University Press, 2016.

———. "Grandmothers' Law, Company Business and Succession in Changing Aboriginal Land Tenure Systems." In *Our Land Is Our Life: Land Rights—Past, Present and Future*, edited by Galarrwuy Yunupingu, 84–116. St. Lucia: University of Queensland Press, 1997.

———. "Medicine Square." In *Being Black: Aboriginal Cultures in 'Settled' Australia*, edited by Ian Keen, 201–25. Canberra: Aboriginal Studies, 1988.

Langton, Marcia, et al. "Introduction." In *Honour Among Nations?: Treaties and Agreements with Indigenous People*, edited by Marcia Langton et al., 1–26. Melbourne: Melbourne University Press, 2004.

Layton, Robert. "Ambilineal Descent and Traditional Pitjantjatjara Rights to Land." In *Aborigines, Land and Land Rights*, edited by Nicolas Peterson and Marcia Langton, 1–32. Canberra: Australian Institute of Aboriginal Studies, 1983.

———. "Pitjantjatjara Processes and the Structure of the Land Rights Act." In *Aborigines, Land and Land Rights*, edited by Nicolas Peterson and Marcia Langton, 226–37. Canberra: Australian Institute of Aboriginal Studies, 1983.

Lederach, John Paul. *Building Peace: Sustainable Reconciliation in Divided Societies*. Washington, DC: United States Institute of Peace, 1997.

Lewis, Henry T. "Fire Technology and Resource Management in Aboriginal North America and Australia." In *Resource Managers: North American and Australian Hunter-Gatherers*, by edited by Nancy M. Williams and Eugene S. Hunn, 45–67. Boulder, CO: Westview, 1987.

Lightfoot, J. B. *Notes on the Epistles of St. Paul from Unpublished Commentaries*. London: MacMillan, 1904.
Linn, Dennis, Sheila Fabricant Linn, and Matthew Linn. *Don't Forgive Too Soon: Extending the Two Hands that Heal*. New York: Paulist, 1997.
MacIntyre, Alisdair. *After Virtue: A Study in Moral Theology*. 3rd ed. London: Duckworth, 2007.
Maddison, Sarah. *Beyond White Guilt: The Real Challenge for Black-White Relations in Australia*. Sydney: Allen & Unwin, 2011.
———. *Black Politics: Inside the Complexity of Aboriginal Political Culture*. Crows Nest: Allen & Unwin, 2009.
Marshall, Christopher D. *Beyond Retribution: A New Testament Vision for Justice, Crime, and Punishment*. Grand Rapids: Eerdmans, 2001.
Marshall, I. Howard. *The Gospel of Luke: A Commentary on the Greek Text*. Grand Rapids: Eerdmans, 1978.
———. "The Meaning of Reconciliation." In *Unity and Diversity in New Testament Theology*, edited by R. Guelich, 117–32. Grand Rapids: Eerdmans, 1978.
Marshall, Peter. *Enmity in Corinth: Social Conventions in Paul's Relations with the Corinthians*. Tübingen: Mohr, 1987.
Martin, Ralph P. *Reconciliation: A Study of Paul's Theology*. 2nd ed. Eugene, OR: Wipf and Stock, 1989.
Martin, Troy B. "The Christian's Obligation Not to Forgive." *Expository Times* 108/12 (1996) 360–62.
Mbiti, John S. *African Religions and Philosophy*. New York: Doubleday, 1970.
McFadyen, Alistair. *Bound to Sin: Abuse, Holocaust and the Christian Doctrine of Sin*. Cambridge: Cambridge University Press, 2000.
———. *The Call to Personhood: A Christian Theory of the Individual in Social Relationships*. Cambridge: Cambridge University Press, 1990.
McGlade, Hannah. "'Not Invited to the Negotiating Table': The Native Title Amendment Act 1998 (Cth) and Indigenous Peoples Right to Political Participation and Self-Determination Under International Law." *Balayi: Culture, Law and Colonialism* 1/1 (2000) 97–113.
McGrath, Ann. *Born in the Cattle: Aborigines in Cattle Country*. Sydney: Allen & Unwin, 1987.
McIntosh, Ian S. *Aboriginal Reconciliation and the Dreaming: Warramiri Yolngu and the Quest for Equality*. Needham Heights: Allyn & Bacon, 2000.
McKenna, Mark. *Looking for Blackfellas' Point: An Australian History of Place*. Sydney: University of New South Wales Press, 2002.
Mead, Richard T. "Exegesis." In *Interpreting 2 Corinthians 5:14–21: An Exercise in Hermeneutics*, edited by Jack P. Lewis, 143–62. Lewiston, NY: Edwin Mellen, 1989.
Memmot, Peter. "Social Structure and Use of Space Amongst the Lardil." In *Aborigines, Land and Land Rights*, edited by Nicolas Peterson and Marcia Langton, 33–65. Canberra: Australian Institute of Aboriginal Studies, 1983.
Merkel, H. "καταλλάσσω, ἀποκαταλλάσσω, καταλλαγή". *Exegetical Dictionary of the New Testament*, edited by Horst Balz and Gerhard Schneider, 2:261–63. Grand Rapids: Eerdmans, 1991.
Merklein, H. "μετανοέω, μετάνοια". *Exegetical Dictionary of the New Testament*, edited by Horst Balz and Gerhard Schneider, 2:415–19. Grand Rapids: Eerdmans, 1991.

Merlan, Francesca. "The Regimentation of Customary Practice: From Northern Territory Land Claims to Mabo." *Australian Journal of Anthropology* 6/1–2 (1995) 64–82.

Milloo, Wryker. "Native Title Is Not Land Rights: An Alternative Indigenous Perspective." *Journal of Australian Indigenous Issues* 1/1 (1998) 25–34.

Mills, Brian, and Roger Mitchell. *Sins of the Fathers: How National Repentance Removes Obstacles for Revival*. Tonbridge: Sovereign World, 1999.

Mills, Brian, and Brian Pickering. *Fountains of Tears: Changing Nations Through the Power of Repentance and Forgiveness*. Tonbridge: Sovereign World, 2004.

Mitchell, Margaret. *Paul and the Rhetoric of Reconciliation: An Exegetical Investigation of the Language and Composition of 1 Corinthians*. Louisville: Westminster John Knox, 1991.

Moran, Mark. *Serious Whitefella Stuff: When Solutions Became Problems in Indigenous Affairs*. Melbourne: Melbourne University Press, 2016.

Morphy, Howard. *Aboriginal Art*. London: Phaidon, 1988.

———. "'Now You Understand': An Analysis of the Way Yolngu Have Used Sacred Knowledge to Retain Their Autonomy." In *Aborigines, Land and Land Rights*, edited by Nicolas Peterson and Marcia Langton, 110–33. Canberra: Australian Institute of Aboriginal Studies, 1983.

Morris, Shireen. "False Equality." In *A Rightful Place: A Roadmap to Recognition*, edited by Shireen Morris, 209–38. Carlton: Black, 2017.

Morse, Bradford W. "Indigenous-Settler Treaty Making in Canada." In *Honour Among Nations?: Treaties and Agreements with Indigenous Peoples*, edited by Marcia Langton et al., 50–68. Melbourne: Melbourne University Press, 2004.

Moyle, Richard. "Songs, Ceremonies and Sites: The Agharringa Case." In *Aborigines, Land and Land Rights*, edited by Nicolas Peterson and Marcia Langton, 66–93. Canberra: Australian Institute for Aboriginal Studies, 1983.

Müller-Farenholz, Geiko. *The Art of Forgiveness: Theological Reflections on Healing and Reconciliation*. Geneva: World Council of Churches, 1997.

Myers, Ched. *Binding the Strong Man: A Political Reading of Mark's Story of Jesus*. Maryknoll, NY: Orbis, 1988.

Myers, Fred. "Always Ask: Resource Use and Land Ownership Among Pintupi Aborigines of the Australian Western Desert." In *Resource Managers: North American and Australian Hunter-Gatherers*, edited by Nancy M Williams and Eugene S Hunn, 173–95. Boulder, CO: Westview, 1982.

National Native Title Tribunal. *Mediating Native Title Applications: A Guide to National Native Title Tribunal Practice*. Canberra: Commonwealth of Australia, 2003.

Neate, Graeme. *Aboriginal Land Rights Law in the Northern Territory*. Vol. 1. Chippendale: Alternative Publishing Co-Operative, 1989.

———. "Review of the Northern Territory Land Rights Act." *Indigenous Law Bulletin* 4/15 (1988). http://www.austlii.edu.au/au/journals/ILB/1998/71.html.

———. "The 'Tidal Wave' of Justice and the 'Tide of History.'" Presented at the Fifth World Summit of Nobel Peace Laureates, Rome, 2004.

———. "Turning Back the Tide? Issues in the Legal Recognition of Continuity and Change in Traditional Laws and Customs." Paper presented at the AIATSIS Native Title Conference, 2002.

Nesbitt, Brad, et al. "Cooperative Cross-cultural Biological Surveys in Resource Management: Experiences in the Anangu Pitjantjatjara Lands." In *Working on Country: Contemporary Indigenous Management of Australia's Lands and Coastal Regions*, edited by Richard Baker et al., 187–98. Melbourne: Oxford University Press, 2001.

Norman, Heidi. "An Examination of the Limitations of Reconciliation as a Framework for Aboriginal Policy Development," *Journal of Australian Indigenous Issues* 5/2 (June 2002) 10–17.

Ó Tuama, Pádraig. *In the Shelter: Finding a Home in the World*. London: Hodder, 2015.

Oakes, Peter. *Philippians: From People to Letter*. Cambridge: Cambridge University Press, 2001.

Olive, Noel. *Karijini Mirlimirli: Aboriginal Histories from the Pilbara*. Freemantle: Freemantle Arts Centre, 1997.

Parker, Russ. *Healing Wounded History: Reconciling Peoples and Places*. Cleveland: Pilgrim, 2001.

Pascoe, Bruce. *Dark Emu*. Broome: Magabala, 2018.

———. *The Little Red Yellow Black Book: An Introduction to Indigenous Australia*. Canberra: Australian Institute of Aboriginal and Torres Strait Islander Studies, 2012.

Pearson, Noel. "Aboriginal Disadvantage." In *Essays on Australian Reconciliation*, edited by Michelle Grattan, 165–75. Melbourne: Black, 2000.

———. "The Fifth Annual Bob Hawke Lecture." Bob Hawke Prime Ministerial Centre, University of South Australia, 2002.

———. "The High Court's Abandonment of 'the Time-Honoured Methodology of the Common Law' in Its Interpretation of Native Title in Mirriuwung Gajerrong and Yorta Yorta." Sir Ninian Stephen Annual Lecture, University of Newcastle Law School, 2003.

———. "Land Is Susceptible of Ownership." In *Honour Among Nations?: Treaties and Agreements with Indigenous People*, edited by Marcia Langton et al., 83–100. Melbourne: Melbourne University Press, 2004.

———. "A Rightful Place." In *A Rightful Place: A Road Map to Recognition*, edited by Shireen Morris, 1–117. Carlton: Black, 2017.

———. "Where We've Come from and Where We're at with the Opportunity That Is Koiki Mabo's Legacy to Australia." Paper presented at the AIATSIS Native Title Conference, 2003.

Perkins, Rachel, and Marcia Langton. *First Australians: An Illustrated History*. Carlton: Miegunyah, 2008

Peterson, Nicolas, and Marcia Langton, eds. *Aborigines, Land and Land Rights*. Canberra: Australian Institute of Aboriginal Studies, 1983.

Pink, Olive. "Land Ownership among the Aborigines." *Mankind* 1/11 (1935).

Pokrifka-Joe, Todd. "Probing the Relationship between Divine and Human Forgiveness in Matthew: Hearing a Neglected Voice in the Canon." In *Forgiveness and Truth*, edited by Alistair McFadyen and Marcel Sarot, 165–72. Edinburgh: T. & T. Clark, 2001.

Porter, Stanley E. *Καταλλάσσω in Ancient Greek Literature, with Reference to the Pauline Writings*. Cordoba: Edicions El Almendro de Cordoba, 1994.

Price, S. R. F. *Rituals and Power: The Roman Imperial Cult in Asia Minor*. Cambridge: Cambridge University Press, 1984.

Read, Peter. *Belonging: Australians, Place and Aboriginal Ownership.* Cambridge: Cambridge University Press, 2000.

———. "The Stolen Generations: The Removal of Aboriginal Children in New South Wales 1883 to 1969." New South Wales Ministry of Aboriginal Affairs Occasional Paper No. 1.

Reeves, J. "Building on Land Rights for the Next Generation: Report of the Review of the Aboriginal Land Rights (Northern Territory) Act 1976." Canberra: Australian Government Publishing Service, 1998.

Remnick, David. "Going the Distance: On and Off the Road with Barack Obama." *The New Yorker*, 27 January 2014. https://www.newyorker.com/magazine/2014/01/27/going-the-distance-david-remnick.

Reynolds, Henry. *Fate of a Free People.* 2nd ed. Ringwood: Penguin, 2004.

———. *Frontier: Aborigines, Settlers and Land.* Sydney: Allen & Unwin, 1987.

———. *The Law of the Land.* Ringwood: Penguin, 1992.

———. *Why Weren't We Told? A Personal Search for the Truth About Our History.* Ringwood: Viking, 1999.

Reynolds, Henry, and Jamie Dalziel. "Aborigines and Pastoral Leases—Imperial and Colonial Policy 1826–1855." *University of New South Wales Law Journal* 19/2 (1996) 315–77.

Ridgeway, Aden. "Mabo Ten Years On—Small Steps or Giant Leap?" In *Let's Get It Right! A Collection of Essays from ATSIC's Treaty Think Tank and Authors Commissioned by AIATSIS on Treaty Issues*, edited by Hannah McGlade, 185–97, 200–216. Canberra: Aboriginal Studies, 2003.

Ring, Graham. "The Hardest Word Has Just Been Uttered." *New Mathilda*, 13 February 2008.

Ritter, David. "The Rejection of Terra Nullius." *Sydney Law Review* 18/1 (1996) 5–33.

Rose, Deborah Bird. *Dingo Makes Us Human: Life and Land in an Aboriginal Australian Culture.* Cambridge: Cambridge University Press, 1992.

———. "Histories and Rituals." In *In the Age of Mabo*, edited by Bain Attwood, 33–53. St. Leonards: Allen & Unwin, 1996.

———. *Reports from a Wild Country: Ethics for Decolonisation.* Sydney: University of New South Wales Press, 2004.

———. "Sacred Site, Ancestral Clearing, and Environmental Ethics." In *Emplaced Myth: Space, Narrative and Knowledge in Aboriginal Australia and Papua New Guinea*, edited by Alan Rumsey and James Weiner, 99–119. Honolulu: University of Hawaii Press.

———. "Women and Land Claims." Land, Rights, Laws: Issues of Native Title 1, Issues Paper No. 6. Canberra: AIATSIS, 1995.

Rose, Deborah, et al. *Country of the Heart: An Indigenous Australian Homeland.* Canberra: Aboriginal Studies, 2002.

Rowell, Meredith. "Women and Land Claims in the Northern Territory." In *Aborigines, Land and Land Rights*, edited by Nicholas Peterson and Marcia Langton, 256–67. Canberra: Australian Institute of Aboriginal Studies, 1983.

Sakenfeld, K. D. "Ezekiel 18:25–32." *Interpretation* 32/3 (1978) 295–300.

Saunders, Stanley. "'Learning Christ': Eschatology and Spiritual Formation in New Testament Christianity." *Interpretation* 56/2 (2002) 154–67.

Schneemelcher, Wilhelm, and R. McL Wilson, eds. *Gospels and Related Writings.* New Testament Apocrypha 1. London: James Clarke, 1991.

Schreiter, Robert. *The Ministry of Reconciliation: Spirituality and Strategies.* Maryknoll, NY: Orbis, 1998.

Sharp, Nonie. "Malo's Law in Court: The Religious Background to the Mabo Case." In *Religious Business: Essays on Australian Aboriginal Spirituality*, edited by Max Charlesworth, 176–202. Cambridge: Cambridge University Press, 1998.

———. *No Ordinary Judgement.* Canberra: Aboriginal Studies, 1996.

Shriver, Donald W., Jr. *An Ethic for Enemies: Forgiveness in Politics.* New York: Oxford University Press, 1995.

Spindler, Sid. "A Program for Practical Reconciliation." *Dissent*, Spring 2004, 55–57.

Stagg, Frank. "The Text." In *Interpreting 2 Corinthians 5:14–21: An Exercise in Hermeneutics*, edited by Jack P. Lewis, 23–28. Lewiston, NY: Edwin Mellen, 1989.

Stanner, W. E. H. "The Yirrkala Land Case: Dress-Rehearsal." In *White Man Got No Dreaming: Essays 1938–1973*, by W. E. H. Stanner, 320–39. Canberra: Australian National University Press, 1979.

Stuhlmacher, Peter. "The Gospel of Reconciliation in Christ: Basic Features and Issues of a Biblical Theology of the New Testament." *Horizons in Biblical Theology* 1 (1979) 161–90.

Sutton, Peter. *Native Title in Australia: An Ethnographic Perspective.* Cambridge: Cambridge University Press, 2003.

Sutton, Peter, and Bruce Rigsby. "People with 'Politicks': Management of Land and Personnel on Australia's Cape York Peninsula." In *Resource Managers: North American and Australian Hunter-Gatherers*, edited by Nancy M. Williams and Eugene S. Hunn, 155–71. Boulder, CO: Westview, 1982.

Tavuchis, Nicholas. *Mea Culpa: A Sociology of Apology and Reconciliation.* Stanford, CA: Stanford University Press, 1991.

Tehan, Maureen. "Co-Existence of Interests in Land: A Dominant Feature of the Common Law." *Land, Rights, Laws: Issues of Native Title*, January 1997.

———. "A Hope Disillusioned, An Opportunity Lost? Reflections on Common Law Native Title and Ten Years of the Native Title Act." *Melbourne University Law Review* 27/2 (2003) 523–71.

———. "The Shadow of the Law and the British Columbia Treaty Process: '[Can] the Unthinkable Become Common Place?'" In *Honour Among Nations?: Treaties and Agreements with Indigenous People*, edited by Marcia Langton et al., 147–62. Melbourne: Melbourne University Press, 2004.

Thiselton, Anthony. *1 Corinthians: A Shorter Exegetical and Pastoral Commentary.* Grand Rapids: Eerdmans, 2006.

———. *The First Epistle to the Corinthians.* Grand Rapids: Eerdmans, 2000.

Thrall, Margaret E. *A Critical and Exegetical Commentary on the Second Epistle to the Corinthians.* 2 vols. Edinburgh: T. & T. Clark, 2004, 2000.

Tickner, Robert. *Taking a Stand: Land Rights to Reconciliation.* Sydney: Allen & Unwin, 2001.

Trudgen, Richard. *Why Warriors Lie Down and Die: Towards an Understanding of Why Aboriginal People of Arnhem Land Face the Greatest Crisis in Health and Education since European Contact.* Aboriginal Resources and Development Services Inc., 2000.

Turner, David T. "Paul and the Ministry of Reconciliation in 2 Corinthians 5:11—6:2." *Criswell Theological Review* 4/1 (1989) 77–95.

Tutu, Desmond. *No Future Without Forgiveness.* London: Rider, 1999.

Tyler, Anne. *Saint Maybe*. London: Vintage, 1992.
Van Deusen Hunsinger, Deborah. "Forgiving Abusive Parents: Psychological and Theological Considerations." In *Forgiveness and Truth*, edited by Alistair McFadyen and Marcel Sarot, 71–98. Edinburgh: T. & T. Clark, 2001.
Veth, Peter. "'Abandonment' or Maintenance of Country? A Critical Examination of Mobility Patterns and Implications for Native Title." Land, Rights, Laws: Issues of Native Title 2, Issues Paper No. 22. Canberra: AIATSIS, April 2003. https://aiatsis.gov.au/sites/default/files/products/issues_paper/veth-ntip-v2n22-abandonment-or-maintenance-of-country_0.pdf.
Volf, Miroslav. *Exclusion and Embrace: A Theological Exploration of Identity, Otherness, and Reconciliation*. Nashville: Abingdon, 1996.
———. "Forgiveness, Reconciliation, and Justice: A Christian Contribution to a More Peaceful Social Environment." In *Forgiveness and Reconciliation: Religion, Public Policy, and Conflict Transformation*, edited by Raymond G. Helmick and Rodney L. Peterson, 27–49. Philadelphia: Templeton Foundation, 2001.
Vorländer, H., and C. Brown. "Reconciliation." *The New International Dictionary of New Testament Theology*, edited by C. Brown, 3:145–76. Exeter: Paternoster, 1978.
Walsh, Fiona, and Paul Mitchell, eds. *Planning for Country: Cross-Cultural Approaches to Decision-Making on Aboriginal Lands*. Alice Springs: Jukurrpa, 2002.
Weber, Theodore R. "Guilt: Yours, Ours, and Theirs." *Worldview* 18 (1975) 15–22.
Weinfeld, Moshe. *Deuteronomy and the Deuteronomic School*. New York: Oxford University Press, 1971.
———. "'Justice and Righteousness'—משפט וצדקה—The Expression and Its Meaning." In *Justice and Righteousness: Biblical Themes and Their Influence*, edites by H. G. Reventlow and Y. Hoffman, 228–46. Sheffield: Sheffield Academic, 1992.
Welborn, L. L. "A Conciliatory Principle in 1 Corinthians 4:6." In *Politics and Rhetoric in the Corinthian Epistles*, by L. L. Welborn, 43–75. Macon, GA: Mercer University Press, 1997.
———. "Discord in Corinth: First Corinthians 1–4 and Ancient Politics." In *Politics and Rhetoric in the Corinthian Epistles*, by L. L. Welborn, 1–42. Macon, GA: Mercer University Press, 1997.
———. *Politics and Rhetoric in the Corinthian Epistles*. Macon, GA: Mercer University Press, 1997.
Westerman, Claus. *Creation*. London: SPCK, 1974.
Whitlam, Gough. "Speech at the Gurindji Land Ceremony." August 16, 1975. PM Transcripts—Transcripts from the Prime Ministers of Australia, Australian Government, Department of the Prime Minister and Cabinet. https://pmtranscripts.pmc.gov.au/release/transcript-3849.
Williams, David J. *Paul's Metaphors: Their Context and Character*. Peabody, MA: Hendrickson, 1999.
Williams, Nancy M. "A Boundary Is to Cross: Observations on Yolngu Boundaries and Permission." In *Resource Managers: North American and Australian Hunter-Gatherers*, edited by Nancy M. Williams and Eugene S. Hunn, 155–71. Boulder, CO: Westview, 1982.
———. *The Yolngu and Their Land: A System of Land Tenure and the Fight for Its Recognition*. Stanford, CA: Stanford University Press, 1986.

———. "Yolngu Concepts of Land Ownership." In *Aborigines, Land and Land Ownership*, edited by Nicolas Peterson and Marcia Langton, 94–109. Canberra: Australian Institute of Aboriginal Studies, 1983.

Williams, Rhiân. *Native Title Mediation Practice: The Commonalities, the Challenges, the Contradictions. A Survey of Native Title Mediators*. Indigenous Facilitation and Mediation Project, Report No. 3. Canberra: AIATSIS, 2004.

Williams, Rowan. *Resurrection: Interpreting the Easter Gospel*. London: Darton, Longman & Todd, 1982.

Willis, Peter. "Riders in the Chariot: Aboriginal Conversion to Christianity at Kununurra." In *Aboriginal Australians and Christian Missions: Ethnographic and Historical Studies*, edited by Tony Swain and Deborah Rose, 308–20. Bedford Park: Australian Association for the Study of Religions, 1988.

Wink, Walter. *Naming the Powers: The Language of Power in the New Testament*. Philadelphia: Fortress, 1984.

———. *Unmasking the Powers: The Invisible Powers that Determine Human Existence*. Philadelphia: Fortress, 1986.

———. *When the Powers Fall: Reconciliation in the Healing of the Nations*. Minneapolis: Fortress, 1998

Witherington, Ben. *Conflict and Community in Corinth: A Socio-Rhetorical Commentary on 1 and 2 Corinthians*. Grand Rapids: Eerdmans, 1995.

Young, Doug, et al. "Into the Fray Again: Native Title and the Racial Discrimination Act." In *The Wik Case: Issues and Implications*, edited by Graham Hiley, 57–62. Sydney: Butterworths, 1997.

Yunupingu, Galarrwuy. "Foreword." In *A Rightful Place: A Roadmap to Recognition*, edited by Shireen Morris, vii–x. Carlton: Black, 2017.

———. "From the Bark Petition to Native Title." In *Our Land Is Our Life: Land Rights—Past, Present and Future*, edited by Galarrwuy Yunupingu, 1–17. St. Lucia: University of Queensland Press, 1997.

———. "Rom Watangu: The Law of the Land." *The Monthly*, July 2016. https://www.themonthly.com.au/issue/2016/july/1467295200/galarrwuy-yunupingu/rom-watangu.

———. "Tradition, Truth and Tomorrow." *The Monthly*, December 2008. https://www.themonthly.com.au/issue/2008/december/1268179150/galarrwuy-yunupingu/tradition-truth-tomorrow.

Zimmerli, Walther. *Ezekiel: A Commentary on the Book of the Prophet Ezekiel, Chapters 1–24*. Translated by Ronald E. Clements, edited by Frank Moore Cross and Klaus Baltzer. Hermeneia. Philadelphia: Fortress, 1979.

www.ingramcontent.com/pod-product-compliance
Lightning Source LLC
Chambersburg PA
CBHW070311230426
43663CB00011B/2088